Jalton — Glen Powell — Allen & Farra — Lewis C. Batty — Geo. E. Barry — Homer W. Barry

Cant — A.F. Braga — Rex Brisbois — Alvin Brown — Cecil E. Bryant — Buster Burnette

Carter — L. Caverhill — Norman Caverhill — Roland Chapman — Martin Clark — L. J. Colvin

ardorff — Byars Deardorff — Edgar Deardorff — Mildred Deardorff — Martin W. Derr — Eugene Domas

lbreath — Wm. W. Gardner — Fred Gassner — George L. Gibbs — Elmer Godsey — Al Goodman

Holmes — Bill Hyde — C. B. Patterson — Virgil Piquet — John Porter — Geo. W. Ray & Sons

thworth — Sproul & Sproul — R. E. Sproul — E. T. Stanbro — Dalton Stewart — Chas. Trowbridge & Son

Johnson — Max Justice — Bonham Keerins — Robt. Kimberling — Dennis King — Frank R. King

call / Mascall / y Mascall — R.H. McAlpine — F. B Mc. Girr — Art Morgan — Mosgrave & Bleakman — Joe Officer & Sons

Gold and Cattle Country

Gold and Cattle Country

By

HERMAN OLIVER

Edited by

E. R. JACKMAN

Binfords & Mort Publishers

Portland, Oregon

Gold and Cattle Country

Printed in the United States of America
Second Edition—Second Printing 1967

In Memory of
My father and mother

JOSEPH CAYTON OLIVER
and
MARY ELIZABETH OLIVER

who, with other courageous pioneers,
settled Grant County, Oregon.

CONTENTS

GOLD AND CATTLE COUNTRY

PART ONE—THE OLIVER RANCH

1. A Ranch Is Born - - - - - - - 1
2. Gold Settled the John Day Country - - - 17
3. The County Grows Up - - - - - - 40
4. A Boy in Grant County - - - - - - 64
5. Readin' and Writin' - - - - - - - 71
6. Stage Coach and Jerk Line - - - - - 83
7. Putting a Ranch Together - - - - - 97
8. Life on a Ranch - - - - - - - - 104
9. What Makes a Ranch Tick - - - - - 109

PART TWO—CATTLE COUNTRY

10. Horses - - - - - - - - - - 126
11. Wild Horses - - - - - - - - 141
12. Other Life, Tame and Wild - - - - 156
13. What Goes on in Cattle Country - - - 162
14. Cow Country—Fact and Fancy - - - - 175
15. A Whistle Comes to Grant County - - - 188
16. From Horseback to Jet - - - - - - 203

PART THREE—PUBLIC SERVICE

17. The Bank of Grant County - - - - - - 211

18. New Financing for Oregon Agriculture - - - 224

19. Years in Public Service - - - - - - - 233

20. The National Farm Program - - - - - 241

21. The Nation Needs the Livestock - - - - 257

PART FOUR—RECOGNITIONS OF PUBLIC SERVICE

22. Gifts, Awards and Rewards - - - - - - 267

23. Letters - - - - - - - - - - - 274

Conclusion - - - - - - - - - - 304

Index - - - - - - - - - - - 306

INTRODUCTION

The day's orders from the boss to this book:

Get out there, book, and act like a cowboy bringing 'em in from the mountains in the fall. Look behind rocks, in the deep draws, in the thickets, and especially around the far water holes and find:

> *Readers with faces tanned by wind and weather, not by stuff out of a bottle or a can;*

> *Readers with pairs of legs bowed from years in the saddle;*

> *Readers with hands permanently roughened and curled from working with lariats;*

> *Readers with eyes that squint from looking at the sun, but have good humor lines running back from the corners;*

> *Readers with levis shrunk down to a tight fit;*

> *Tolerant men who don't envy anyone on earth and don't want anything free.*

If, book, you can round up men like that, you'll be worth your salt, and we'll keep you on for a spell.

HERMAN OLIVER

HISTORY OF THE BRAND, A2,

FOR EIGHTY-FOUR YEARS

by Herman Oliver

A brand is a record of ownership, the same as a deed to a house, or a license on a car, but it is more than that. Time lends to it something akin to a coat of arms, so that the owner hesitates to use it on a poor, slab-sided animal. He wants it to indicate superiority—an animal he can be proud of. Cattlemen who pride themselves on raising high-quality cows develop what comes to be known as a "reputation brand," and its mere presence will often add $10 or $20 to the market value of a steer and up to $30 to the price of a breeding animal.

Brands in Oregon are recorded by the State Department of Agriculture at Salem. There are many special laws dealing with them and the department enforces these laws, prosecuting those who try to re-work or obliterate brands, or steal branded animals.

Our brand was A2 on the left hip of cattle, on the left stifle of horses. The original owner was my father, Joseph Cayton Oliver, and his wife, Mary Elizabeth. It was first recorded in 1878. In 1895, the Olivers gave 60 head of heifer calves to their six children, with the A2 brand on the right hip.

In 1906 a partnership was formed between the senior Olivers and the three boys, Herman, George, and Frank. The other three children had left. George died that same year. In 1925, after the two original owners had died, the brand passed to Frank and me. We operated the place as equal partners. In 1937 ownership of the brand was expanded to our wives and children, and five years later, Joe's wife, Arlene, joined the partnership.

In 1949 the partnership was dissolved. A price of $5000 was put on the brand and Eliza and I took it as our personal property. We still own it, though for a time our daughter Anna and her husband, Sam Keerins, had a part interest.

Sentimental folk are constantly suggesting other ways for marking animals, such as ear tags or tattoo marks. Many other methods have been tried. They work reasonably well on farms, but are useless on the range, where a brand must be read, as the animal runs by, or as a rider's horse gallops by the branded animal.

Most range livestock men can not only distinguish their own brands at a glance, but they also learn the brands of all others for perhaps a hundred miles around. If they see a strayed or stolen animal, they send word at once to the rightful owner.

The Oliver sheep brand was the letter J stamped on the left shoulder of the ewes and on the rump of wethers. The ear mark was a swallow fork in each ear of the ewes and a swallow fork in the right ear and a crop in the left ear of wethers. In the early history of the range-sheep industry, there was no such thing as leg of lamb or lamb chops. It was a leg of mutton or mutton chops. The lamb crop was carried to mutton stage—usually two- to three-year-olds. To sort for sex, they were run through a dodge chute where the gate tender sorted by marks and brands. This mark and brand was also used for claiming ownership in case bands of sheep became mixed, which often happened on the range.

The ewes were lambed out on the open range and were then brought into a corral, and it was a common practice to mark and brand from 1,000 to 1,200 head of lambs a day. To determine the percentage of sex, as the tails were removed, the male tails went into one pile and the female into another. At the end of the marking operation each pile of tails was counted and a record made of the same. And here ends the "tale" of the Oliver brand.

The boss himself—75-year-old Herman Oliver. ➤

A favorite horse, Mickey, and a right good outfit.

Joseph Cayton Oliver, founder of the famous Oliver ranch, was born in Portugal, on the Azores Islands. He came to the United States as a stowaway on a sailing ship. He arrived in Canyon City with 75 cents.
His wife Elizabeth was a German immigrant girl, just over 5 feet tall, but strong, with great spirit.

The Oliver headquarters ranch, near John Day.

PART ONE

THE OLIVER RANCH

CHAPTER 1

A RANCH IS BORN

A boy grows up unheeding. His father and mother are there just as the seasons are, and the land, the creeks, the meadow larks, and the sagebrush. He takes all of them for granted. But when his parents are gone, he wishes a thousand times that he knew more about them. A problem arises and the answer won't come. There are so many alternatives. Troubled, worried, he thinks, "What is right? What would my father have done?" and suddenly the answer is clear because he knows with certainty how his father would have acted.

Perhaps his father lacked education, certainly he lived in a less complicated age, but he lived by some simple standards that are as easy to apply now as then, and with a rush, it comes to him how little he knows about his father, as compared to what he might have known, had he just realized.

In talking of my own father and mother, I am concerned with all of the things I don't know. Why did they leave their homelands and come to America? What was their childhood like? Were they more adventurous than others? Was it hard to leave home?

My father, Joseph Cayton Oliver, was born in the Azores Islands, Portugal, March 16, 1850. He never saw his father, who, a sailor, was lost at sea. His ship just sailed away and was never heard of again. When 16 father came to the United States as a stowaway, con-

cealed in a barrel on a sailing ship. His ship called at
the Isthmus of Panama, and he and another Portuguese
boy, John Silvers, walked across the Isthmus and somehow made their way to San Francisco. Father knew no
English, but reached Portland somehow.

This was in 1866. Gold had recently been discovered
in eastern Oregon and in various places in Idaho. Portland was called "Stumptown" by other Oregon settlers,
but gold in the interior gave it sudden life and importance. It was really only a suburb of Canyon City, because
it was just a stopping place for a flood of gold seekers. By
1862, when gold was found, the Willamette Valley was
fairly well settled and many of our miners came from the
Valley, often called Columbia Valley then.

Ships by the dozens arrived at Portland with gold-
hungry men of all nations. There was a huge mass
stampede to the gold mines and somehow father was
swept along to The Dalles with the feverish mob. From
there he took a 200-mile stroll to Canyon City to seek
his fortune. His pockets assayed 75 cents and he could
now speak a few words of English.

He was 17, strong, and ambitious. He wanted to
work, to work hard, 12 hours a day or more. Like many
Portuguese of those days he loved adventure. Here in
this big free land he wouldn't always be poor. How could
you stay poor if you worked hard, proved you were honest, always did more than you were paid to do, and
saved your money?

My father worked mainly in the mines at Canyon
City until 1878, 12 years in all. He made friends easily
and his good humor and easy smile soon made him welcome everywhere. The mine work was a little haphazard;
water gave out, there was a cave-in, or the flume broke,
but whenever the work stopped, he didn't. He hiked into
the hills at dawn and cut cordwood from the free timber.
He sold it for $2.50 a cord, all the time looking around
at the soil, visiting the few farmers around, eyeing their
crops, and occasionally working for them.

He wanted to farm, he had some money saved up, but he decided to go at it slowly. He got a job at $20 a month with a family named Gregg who were renting what was known as the "China Ranch," a mile below John Day, on the north side of the river. A group of Chinese had title to the place, but rented it to white men, in order to give their own time to mining.

Now let's talk about mother, because she was Mrs. Gregg, whom father married after August Gregg died. While still a young girl in Germany, she became an orphan. The family had adventurous blood, as witnessed by two older sisters and a brother who had gone to San Francisco when that city was only a village out on the edge of nowhere. At the age of 13 she followed them around the Horn and worked at cooking, house maid, or whatever an honest, sturdy German girl could do. She was only five feet tall, but tremendously strong and could put in hours that would shame a present day union worker. She worked for a Jewish family who were kind and good to her and when they moved to Portland, she came with them, where she married August Gregg. The gold rush swept them to Canyon City, too. In those days large numbers of men left Portland daily, bound for the interior by boat, horse, mule, or on foot, all attracted by the gold, free for the taking. Gregg worked in the mines and later rented the China Ranch. The Greggs had three children, all born at Canyon City, two boys and a girl.

So father worked for them, clearing land, milking cows, tending garden, making fence, chopping wood— whatever the season demanded. August Gregg one day choked on a chicken bone and died before anyone real- ized what was happening. Father stayed on, worked the farm, and eventually he and my mother, Mrs. Gregg, were married.

Life as renters did not appeal to either of them. Both had the old country passion to own land. In Europe the land owners were the aristocrats, the nobility. Others looked up to them. Much of the pull that America had for Europeans was due to the rumor that in America anyone could own land. There is a sort of mystical or ingrained feeling in many Europeans that land owner- ship is the only real security. A business can fail; money can become worthless; only the land is permanent.

Father had managed to get hold of a few cows and mother had some, both lots totaling 16. They were more or less Shorthorn, or Durham, a beef breed, but with better milking qualities than Texas or Mexican cattle available locally. The folks had started a milk route on the China Ranch, but wanted to enlarge it.

They found a ranch up the river from John Day owned by a miner friend of father's, Bill Clark, who had homesteaded it. There was a shack, 160 acres, prac- tically no cleared land. Bill was a miner and didn't really want to be tied to a farm, so he sold the place to father for $2,000. Terms were nothing down and the balance in equal payments for ten years. On this farm my two brothers and I were born.

This ability of father's to inspire trust and confidence was due in part to his personality, but due more to a creed that he followed all his life. If he made a promise he stuck with it, fair or foul. If he borrowed five dol- lars or five thousand and said he would pay it back June 1, he paid it back on that day, no matter what sacrifice. So, among the miners and storekeepers the news spread that the word of Joe Oliver was good. He was almost passionate about this and drilled it into his children thoroughly. That is why he was able to buy a farm on a promise.

Father and his bride moved to their own place early in 1880, full of hope and plans, and had an immediate set-back. Of their 16 milk cows, eight died, poisoned by hemlock, known for centuries as a poisonous weed, but unknown to father. Perhaps it didn't grow in the Azores.

But they borrowed money, got more cows, and en- larged their dairy. Father delivered milk for 37 years, arriving at John Day at 7:00 o'clock in the morning every day, rain or shine, 365 days a year. The miners

and housewives could set their watches by him. During
the 37 years he missed delivery twice. One spring day a
sudden thaw raised the John Day river and washed away
the bridge, leaving a raging flood between the house and
the cows on the other side. It was too wild to swim and
there was no quick way around. The Canyon City and
John Day housewives had no milk that day. The other
milkless day was due to an accident to the milk wagon,
resulting in loss of all of the milk.

Father's delivery cart was a two-horse hack or spring
wagon with a crate built in the rear end, holding 9 to
12 three-gallon cans. The price schedule was:

Pint daily	$1.50 per month
Quart daily	2.00 per month
One and a half quarts daily	3.00 per month
One half gallon daily	3.50 per month

Prices now are roughly four times as high.

Both father and mother were good gardeners with
a passion for making things grow, so their big garden
flourished wonderfully in the virgin soil. Each summer
day they took orders from their milk customers and
the next morning delivered strictly fresh vegetables. In
the winter they sold storable products, as carrots, onions,
squash and potatoes.

Most of the early settlers along the river set out large
orchards, and in no time there were more apples than
could be eaten or sold. My folks got a cider mill and
squeezed out barrels and barrels of cider. Then, if the
barrels were treated with what was called "vinegar gut,"
or "vingar plant," it changed to vinegar instead of just
souring and this homemade vinegar was put into quart
jars or even five-gallon kegs and sold to the milk customers. I seem to remember in the cool big cellar about
twenty 50-gallon vinegar barrels. Each barrel had the
year of making painted on it.

Then mother made barrels of the good old German
kraut that she had learned to make in Germany and
many of the dairy customers developed a taste for it.
The German people knew ways of mixing this with sour

cream and baking spare ribs in it. That was only one dish. Cooking with kraut is getting to be a lost art. She also used sour cream with fresh sliced cucumbers, lettuce and cabbage, and with roast mutton, or with beef gravy.

In delivering the milk, father used three-gallon cans, as stated. He carried a quart measure and one of the three-gallon cans to the back porch of each customer and rapped on the porch with the measuring can. People soon learned this noise. Some had a little box or cupboard with the container they wished filled, but others had to come to the door. Some weren't even up at that hour and all father saw of such customers was a bare arm rimmed at the top by a kimona sleeve. At least one customer told him not to rap on the porch, but to come into the kitchen and pour the milk into a dish. In this kitchen, dishes were seldom washed and the milk usually had to go into a dirty dish. One family had four boys. The doctor had ordered, for these boys, milk from an individual cow. So for years father had to keep this cow's milk separate and delivered it in its own container. This family never paid as much as a penny. Father referred to these four boys as his, because he had supported them from babyhood. This wasn't good business but his logic was simple. "How would they get milk otherwise?"

He always poured the milk back and forth several times so that no customer could ever justly complain that the first on the route got all the cream.

He had a well-trained team. One old faithful called "Blue" was on the route 26 years. His mate, who only worked 20 years, was "Frank." This team soon learned the route. When the driver would get out with his three-gallon can and his measuring can, the team would walk to the house of the next customer, turn corners, stop, and start, with never a word of command. The horses watched the milkman walk from house to house, governing their movements by him, thus delivering in half the time required with an untrained team.

At the ranch the milk, as fast as it came from the cows, would be strained and put into one of the three-gallon cans, that would be put into a narrow vat with cold spring water flowing around the cans. No refrigeration in those days. By the time breakfast was over, the milk was nice and cool.

In the winter they "put up" ice from the river, or got it from a pond at Marysville, five miles from the ranch. The local brewery flooded this pond every night during a cold spell so as to assure thick ice. They cut blocks 20 inches square, hauled these by wagon or sled to the ice house at home and buried them in sawdust. Each summer day they chopped out some of the ice and put chunks around the cans with wet burlap over all. The town kids ran along begging for chunks of ice. They were in full glory if father would allow them to drive the team. A group would be waiting at the entrance to John Day and another group at Canyon City. He had to make them take turns driving. One of these town boys was Phil Metschan, later prominent in the state.

The money coming in every day of the year accumulated, and the folks began to buy land. This was the foundation for what was later the well known Oliver Ranch, which at the peak was over 54,000 acres, carrying 4,500 cattle, 7,000 sheep and many horses. It was built solidly upon milk cows and hand tended rows of peas, beans, and carrots. It covered a span of 80 years of history.

The eight-cow dairy grew to 75 cows, with about 40 milked daily. They were mostly beef shorthorns selected from range herds and broken to milk, sometimes with an unwillingness that lasted for months and resulted in many buckets of spilled milk. They were bred to Shorthorn bulls. Milking was all by hand, of course.

One of the first jobs on the Clark homestead was to clear off brush and trees. Big cottonwoods grew all along the river and the meadows were covered by wild thorn-bushes, to be chopped out by hand. The first of this meadow sod that was plowed after clearing was broken by a hired ox team. The soil was full of roots that would break and snap back against the shins of the plowman. The oxen took this work slow and easy and stopped when the plow stuck on a big root. Horses might charge ahead and break something.

There was always land to be cleared. When hobos or men genuinely in search of work came along, saying they would be willing to work for a meal, they could always be put on the end of a grub hoe in the field or an axe in the woodshed.

Gradually the good meadowland was cleared, some of it by contract at $20 an acre. Each new dairy cow required more meadowland for raising hay for winter feed. Many ranches in those days put up little or no hay, depending upon native bunchgrass. This led to disaster in cases of hard winters. It didn't work at all with dairy cows. They had to be kept up, close at hand, and had to have hay.

Gradually father bought more land by buying out discouraged homesteaders, or by furnishing money for someone who could see greener pastures over the mountains. He said, "There are very few persons who have the patience and determination to stay in the same place more than 20 years." Homesteaders, even with good places, got itchy feet in about ten years. They couldn't look ahead and foresee values.

As father bought each place, he started to figure at once how he could improve it by water, or by stopping erosion, or by fencing. He was a soil conservationist 50 years before the term became popular. He loved the soil, would feel it with his hands with satisfaction. He told us repeatedly, "Never be afraid to buy land."

In the early days there were deep snows. Father even delivered milk by sleigh. The deep snow would sometimes go off with a rush when a chinook hit. Then the John Day would change from a narrow, meandering stream to a big wide river, tearing holes in the banks, changing its course and ruining a meadow, and perhaps destroying in a night a season's patient, hard work of land clearing.

Father took out the big bends, straightened the channel, rip-rapped the banks and made each meadow safe. He dried up the wet places. For draining, he dug by hand ditches about two feet deep and 18 inches wide. In the bottom he put five tamarack rails, then refilled the ditches. The water followed along the rails beneath the ground. These drainage ditches, made with little expense, except hand labor, were put in 65 years ago and are still working.

For short drainage he sometimes lined the ditches with stones from the creek, laid up to make a wall on each side, covered the top with flat rocks, and covered with soil. Some of these are still on the place, still effective.

Regularity and promptness were sort of a religion with him, but those traits didn't always appeal to growing boys. The schedule, day-in-day-out, was:

Breakfast   6
Dinner   12
Supper   6

Milking by hand started at 4:00 a.m. and the night milking was after supper at 6:30. This made two eight-hour days the same day. Starting with Monday morning we had put in our 40-hour week by Wednesday noon.

Mother was a good cook and a plentiful cook. There was lots of food on the table. Anyone passing by at mealtime was asked in to eat. In Cleveland's administration, times were really bad and many came walking by, asking for food. No person was ever turned away hungry, whether his plea was legitimate or whether the man was purely a hobo.

By 1895, when I was ten years old, the ranch had grown and then carried over 150 beef cows, and a small band of sheep. Father, trying to instruct and encourage us, gave the six children the beef cattle heifers to be born in that calendar year. There were 60 such heifers, so each of the six had ten nice heifer calves. He supplied feed, and each of us was to do certain work in payment. We used his brand, A2, but on the opposite hip. We ran them with his. He clothed us, gave us spending money, and a grade school education. The understanding was that if any of us left the ranch, we couldn't take the cattle, but must sell them to the remaining children. We children were also to have the heifer calves from those 60 when they reached producing age.

My half-sister, Lizzie, was the first child to marry. Father bought her calves and gave them to the other children. One half-brother, Henry Gregg, wanted to do something else, so he married and left, and his cattle were paid for and divided between the remaining children.

Then tragedy struck; typhoid fever carried away William Gregg, and, within a few days, my older brother, George. Of the original six children, Frank and I were the only ones left on the ranch, I was 21, Frank 18.

So 1906 was a turning point. Two boys died, and I was married to Eliza Laurance of Prairie City. Those events changed the entire ranch set-up, removing George, the logical successor to father as manager, and bringing a new member into the family.

The death of the older Gregg boy, and of George, was an enormous shock to father and mother. Their life plans were disrupted and they became despondent, wanted to sell out and move to some new place where everything in sight would not remind them of the tragedies. Father negotiated with a Lewiston, Idaho, man who came with his wife and his attorney and looked over our place. By this time the Oliver ranch had grown to 8,000 acres. We made a tentative agreement by which we were to take as down payment, an orchard near Lewiston in exchange for the ranch.

After the prospective buyer had left, I could see that this might easily be a sad ending for all of the years of toil that my parents had put in, so the family sat down and discussed the matter until two o'clock in the morning. At the end we all agreed that father should call off the deal. Within less than a year we heard that the Lewiston man had been sent to the penitentiary for defrauding a widow out of the orchard that he was going to give us as a down payment.

This illustrates the way the family worked. Mother was conservative, father liberal and optimistic, mild mannered, slow to anger. The family always took up business matters as a group, somewhat as a board of directors might do. Mother tended to hold back, she scrutinized carefully, was slow to decide, and avoided mistakes. She didn't take all people at face value. Father looked far ahead, usually with optimism, and tended to trust people too much. Frank was more like mother, I was more like father. But in the interplay of these opposite attitudes, there was always at last a meeting of minds, which seemed to work out very well.

In these family councils, it had always been assumed that George would take over management of the place and before his death, father had begun to turn over more and more authority to him. The feeling of priority for the oldest boy ran strong in the European people. Land is scarce there and if it were broken up by subdividing between sons, very quickly there would be no estate worth having. That is why so many fine European young men come here—they are younger sons and there is nothing for them at home.

When typhoid fever removed George and the oldest Gregg boy, the thread of existence was cut for both father and mother. They felt insecure and the future seemed troubled. For several years they traveled. They stayed in San Francisco to visit mother's relatives. They lived in Portland for a time, just to see new faces. Eventually the wound healed and they returned.

The ranch wouldn't have developed the same way without mother. I have mentioned her strength. She loved being out of doors and her instinct to make things grow was as deep as any other one thing in her character. It gave her real satisfaction and joy to plant seeds, watch the little plants come bravely through the soil and into the sunlight. Hoeing the garden, weeding and irrigating it, were not work for her at all. She did these things more as a loving mother might care for her baby. She rejoiced as the plants grew, worried if they did not, and grieved if one died.

She made most of the clothes for us as children. Our underwear was from flour sacks, that also furnished dish-towels, curtains and all kinds of things. Whenever a baby was imminent in the neighborhood, everybody saved flour sacks for diapers. Our thick, heavy boots were made by an old German bootmaker of Canyon City. His name was Antone Hupprich. We wore sox only on special occasions. We put nothing on our feet at all or else wore what were called "foot rags." These were made by splitting a flour sack in two, then wrapping a half sack around the foot and slipping the boot over it. This had to be done just right. It was quite an art. If not wrapped exactly right, it would be uncomfortable and it might ball up and leave part of the foot bare and cold. Mother bought heavy blue denim and made our shirts and trousers. Sometimes it took two or three boys to wear out one shirt. In the winter we wrapped burlap around our boots and tied it on with string. Mother knitted scarves and sweaters. When we rode in a wagon or in a sled in cold weather, she heated rocks in the oven, wrapped them in old flannel or in newspaper, and put them in the bed of the wagon so our feet wouldn't freeze.

Merchants didn't get rich selling to the Oliver family. We didn't buy much except coffee, tea, sugar, salt, and spices. Some families of that day ground their own wheat in a little mill, much like a coffee grinder, but we took our wheat to the local mill, and had it made into flour for 50 cents a sack. We brought home the bran for hog and cow feed. We cured our ham and bacon and made our lard, sausage, and headcheese. We sold some of these things, too. Mother's headcheese and sausage were locally famous. Fruit of all kinds was canned in half-gallon jars—at least 1,000 jars each year. In addition we dried enough fruit to fill ten seamless sacks. Our sheep camps used most of this. Seamless sacks are getting scarce now. They were made of heavy cotton and one could out-last a dozen burlap sacks, which were more loosely woven and made of jute.

Father was not a drinking man, but he always kept a gallon jug of whiskey. After a day in the cold wind, he would take about a tablespoonful of this before supper. When we boys were little, he would tip the jug for us and let us touch our tongues to the whiskey. Mother made cherry and currant wine in 50-gallon barrels. A pitcher of this wine was often on the table, with water glasses to pour it into, and available for hired help and all. We children grew up accustomed to seeing liquor, but none of us became a heavy or habitual drinker.

A story from father's later life may show his character as well as anything:

After I was doing most of the ranch management, I developed a liking for good horses. I got a fine team of driving horses, buckskins with a black line down their backs, and with black manes and tails, giving a splendid two-tone effect. They were perfectly matched, had lots of style, and when I hitched them to a good buggy and trotted down the road, I really felt like somebody. I was proud of them, so asked father one day to go to town with me.

We met a friend of father's, a fellow Portuguese, who was driving a team of worn-out little mustangs with a sorry outfit. Father, thinking to please me, said, "Why don't you get yourself a good team like this?" The man replied soberly, "Joe, I drive what I can afford." Father, realizing his mistake, said miserably, "Let's go, Herman." He was silent for a mile or two, then said, "Turn around, I have to apologize." So we drove back, overtook the man, and father got out and tried to make amends. He was silent and at odds with himself for the rest of the drive, and at the end he told me to fit together a good team, and take them to his old friend as payment for his thoughtless remark.

Even now, chance sayings of his come to me from time to time and help me with some decision. He often said, "For every man opportunity comes knocking once. If he has prepared for it, he can seize it and go on to success. If he isn't prepared, it doesn't make any difference, he will fail anyhow."

He liked people of all kinds and found something to admire in everyone. He greeted each person he met and somehow, though he worked harder than most, he found time to visit. He rarely criticized, pitying wrongdoers instead. If someone defrauded him, he would say sadly, "He can't help it, he was born that way, with a weak spot in his brain." When a hired hand did something obviously wrong, he would comment to the family, "After all, if he knew how to do everything right, he'd be working for himself, not for me."

Probably father's most outstanding business trait was his farsightedness. Most persons assume conditions will always be as they are right then. If times are bad, they'll always be bad, so people sell out at a fraction of the true value. If times are good, they will always be good, and deals are made at prices that prove ruinous, Father looked ahead. For example, he was one of the first to contribute to the Pacific International Livestock Exposition at Portland. He gave $250 to it when it was held in a tent. He predicted it would grow into a big show; would help the livestock business, and make Portland a better livestock market.

I like to think I inherited some of father's ability to keep his eye on the future, some of his persistence and determination, and some of mother's wonderful energy. These things, as an inheritance, are worth far more than land, herds, and flocks.

Mother always kept a flock of geese. They were good to eat and the feathers were necessary. They were plucked from the live geese, a job that I always helped with as a boy, but never learned to like. We put the geese in a wind-proof room so the feathers wouldn't blow about. In case you want to pluck a live goose, here is the way.

Put an old sack over the head of the goose, sit on a box with a burlap sack across your lap. Lay the goose in your lap, upside down. Catch the wing tips and legs in your left hand. Put the head of the goose under your left arm. Remove the soft feathers that you want by a quick jerk against the grain, or opposite from the way that particular feather is growing. Have a bag hanging on the wall close to your right hand and drop the feathers in. Geese are ready to pluck when a feather can be pulled out with no blood showing at the end of the quill.

In the winter time, we slept between two mattresses filled with goose feathers, a fine way to sleep in zero weather. The use for the geese didn't stop at feathers. A fat roast goose was our standard holiday dinner. The goose grease, rendered out, waterproofed our boots and added a year or more to the life of the leather.

When we had the first sign of a chest cold, mother mixed turpentine with the goose grease, rubbed it onto our chests with her strong, practiced fingers, and bound a piece of soft flannel over it. Our chests grew fiery red and itched unbearably. It was easier to get well than not to. This was supposed to "draw out the cold" and I guess it did, because we didn't have many. We hardly dared to. To offset this, mother dissolved rock candy in whiskey, making a highly palatable syrupy drink. We had a table-spoonful or two of this at night if we coughed and it made a throat soothing taste to relieve coughing during the day. It wouldn't surprise me if we coughed on purpose occasionally.

In writing this, I keep thinking of things father said.

"Never use a nickname for an older person, call him Mr., and always treat older people with respect."

"Never put yourself over another, or force your opinion over the other person's. Advance your opinion, but put it on the same basis as the other man's, if it differs."

"We are not born into this world as drones, do something for the hive."

"A man's wife can make or break him, just by her attitude. She can throw more out the back door with a spoon than he can put in the front door with a shovel."

Photograph showing the general area where most of the $26,000,000 was mined. John Day is in the foreground and Canyon City is in the background. Identified by number are: (1) Highway 26E, (2) Marysville Placer Mine, (3) Ike Guker $65,00 gold pocket, (4) Canyon Mountain, (5) John Day race track and fairground, (6) Intersection of Highways 26 and 395, (7) Where gold was first discovered, (8) Little Canyon Mountain, (9) Canyon City, (10) Whiskey Gulch, (11a-11b) Canyon Creek. Here, in the summer of 1862, were more than 5,000 miners. (11b) Mouth of Canyon Creek, (12) Humboldt Placer Mine, (13) Highway 395 South, (14) Airport, (15) Grant County Hospital.

CHAPTER 2

GOLD SETTLED THE JOHN DAY COUNTRY

The covered wagon folks, so vivid in history, missed the John Day Valley. From 1843 to 1862 they streamed past to the north and south, but not through it. It would have made their journey far easier had they followed what is now Highway 26, the John Day highway, rather than the Oregon Trail from the Snake up through Huntington, Baker, the Grande Ronde, Pendleton, and on down to Arlington. Not only easier, but shorter. No Indians lived here, either.

I knew the man well who first found gold here in the spring of '62. He was William C. Aldred. He lived on the John Day in later years. He was a bachelor, and when I was a boy, he liked me and would tell me mining stories by the hour. He was extremely stooped and said it was due to long hours of work in low damp mine tunnels. When every pound of soil and every rock had to be carried out of a tunnel by hand, or by wheelbarrow, the tunnel was made no bigger than it had to be.

His story was that he came to California with the throng in '49 with a bad case of gold fever. He worked in this and that gulch for 13 years, but, like fishing, the gold was always somewhere else. In the spring of 1862 the birds brought news of a wonderful strike at Florence, Idaho. In those California days, a gang of maybe a hundred or more men would be working in some isolated canyon. At night these men would congregate in the local saloon where perhaps a stranger would show up. After a few drinks, he would unguardedly drop the news that he was bound for Oregon, or Idaho, or British Columbia to a place where nuggets lay around like pine cones. One by one the listening men would steal away and by morning that camp would be nearly deserted.

So into Aldred's camp came the whisper of a rumor that Florence, Idaho, was the place. In no time 60 men were on their way. They came up the Oregon Coast to Astoria, thence to Portland and The Dalles by boat. There they took to horseback. Their route was eastward via Antelope, Burnt Ranch, Mitchell, Antone (now a ghost town out of Mitchell) and up the John Day Valley. To avoid anarchy on the trip, they had elected a leader. This first group crossed Canyon Creek June 8, near the present Canyon City. At that time Aldred said there was no sign anywhere that any white man had ever been in this valley before. They were passing through virgin territory.

As the horses splashed through Canyon Creek, Aldred saw some sand and gravel he wanted to investigate. It looked like the places in California where gold had been plentiful, but the band passed on to the east a mile and camped near a place now called Marysville (this was once a town, now only a memory). Their horses needed rest and feed, so they turned the horses loose to graze on the fine bunchgrass. Some men threw themselves on the ground to rest, some looked around, exploring a little, but he, Aldred, took a shovel, his pan, and hurried back down the steep hill to Canyon Creek. He didn't really expect to find anything, so left his gold pan, and waded the waist-deep cold water to the other side. He thought he saw "color" so he took off his woolen drawers, tied the legs at the bottom, put a few shovels of sand and gravel in each leg, and waded back to the pan. He emptied the contents of each leg in a pile, washed the drawers free of sand in the ice cold water, wrung them out, shiveringly put them on, then panned out the little pile of sand. He got $4.50 worth of gold, illustrating one advantage of the old long johns over the present shorts.

He hurried up the hill, arrived out of breath, and told the others that here was their chance—forget Florence. Their guide pointed out that they had started for Idaho, and by gum, if they were going to stop at every little old stream that might have a thimbleful of gold, they'd never get there. Aldred said he guessed so, and went along with the majority, looking back over his shoulder at the sure thing they were passing up.

They camped four miles east at what was later called "The Prairie Diggins" and here too, they found gold, but went on.

At the upper end of the John Day Valley, the river bends to the south to where it runs out of the mountains, so they had to cross it. At that point it seemed deeper and swifter than any place they had seen. The leader rode up and down trying to locate a ford. The other men, noticing the tall cottonwoods, started to make a crude bridge by falling some big trees across the creek. The leader came back, pooh-poohed this idea as too time-consuming and said, "Just jump your horses in. It won't hurt to get a little wet, I'll show you." But his horse didn't want to jump into the swift water of unknown depth, so the rider went far back, put the spurs to the horse and came to the stream at a swift gallop. The horse, at the stream brink, put on all brakes and halted abruptly. The rider sailed like a bird over the horse's head and into the deep water, but caught his long-shanked spurs in the bridle reins. The horse jerked back and pulled the rider against the bank, where he hung, his legs threshing around in the air, his head under the swift water.

Aldred hastily jerked off the bridle, and then, in attempting to help the leader from the water, got pulled into the stream. The drowning man clutched Aldred frantically and pulled him under, but he managed to reach land and saved the other man's life.

They drained the victim, dried him a little, and went on to Auburn, a busy new mining city southwest of Baker. (It's now a ghost town, as is Florence.) There they heard that the Florence strike was petering out, just a pocket, and a man would be crazy to go there. So Aldred persuaded 17 of the 60 men to go back with him to Canyon Creek. When they arrived, they stared in disbelief, open-mouthed. Both sides of the creek were lined by miners happily panning out gold, and all desirable locations seemed to be filed on. Other Florence-bound miners behind them had found nuggets and coarse gold in the creek, had heard about the bird in the hand, so they had promptly forgotten Florence, and had settled down to enjoy the Canyon Creek bonanza that turned out $26,000,000 in gold, most of it on the surface, and easy to come by.

Aldred and party remembered their camping spot near Prairie Diggins. They turned back and located 18 claims. These diggins speedily yielded $180,000, or $10,-000 apiece.

Aldred stayed on and later found a quartz vein that led deep into a hill. He interested enough capital to build a 25-stamp mill that employed 80 men. Around the turn of the century, this vein supplied quartz to the mill for three years. The miners working there bought meat, fresh and cured, and other products from the Oliver Ranch. The Prairie Diggins and adjacent mines later became a part of our ranch.

The big influx of miners in 1862 totaled 5000 men who worked from the mouth of Canyon Creek to a point about three miles up the creek. This made Canyon City larger than Portland for a time. No gold was found south of Canyon Mountain, but from that point on down the creek, gold was in every gulch.

As winter approached, the 5000 miners worried. No one had lived in the John Day Valley before, so the miners had no idea what winters would be like. They knew they had only day to day provisions, and they feared a possible winter catastrophe. So they measured out their supplies, estimated how many men their store of food would winter through, and the others scattered to Portland, The Dalles or California. The agreement, seriously underscored, was that no man staying on would go scouting around the claim of any absent man. Some of those who left never came back, and in later years wrote long, regretful letters to the local paper, telling how they had passed up their one big opportunity.

On the last day of December, 1862, the miners remaining at the diggings, unable to mine much because of frozen ground, could foresee that with the rush of newcomers in the spring, things might get a bit hectic. If the man with the claim next to yours didn't show up, at what date could his claim be jumped? If a gulch above the creek proved unexpectedly rich, how far up the gulch could the original claimant go? All sorts of such things came to mind, so as sensible men, they gathered and made their own laws.

Here are a few of their rules, that henceforth had the force of law:

Article 1: defines the area where the rules apply and names it "John Day Mining District". It roughly embraced all land south of the John Day River up to the summit where waters drain into the Malheur River, and east of the ridge on the west side of Canyon Creek.

Article 2: provides for a recorder who shall keep a record of all claims; call meetings to decide upon disputed points; provides for a big book of claims, to serve as the official record.

Article 3: divides claims into kinds and states the size.

"A Creek Claim shall be 75 feet running with the stream and shall extend from high water mark to high water mark.

"A Bank Claim shall be 75 feet running with the stream and extending back 300 feet from the Creek Claims.

"A Shaft Claim shall be 75 feet front and extending to the center of the hill.

"A Surface Claim shall be 150 feet by 100 feet.

"A Gulch Claim shall be 150 feet running with the gulch and 50 feet in width on each side of the channel."

Article 4: allows each miner two claims, but each must be of a different kind. Thus, a man could locate one Creek Claim and one Gulch Claim, or any other two combinations.

Other articles provided that a claim must be worked within five days of location; that Shaft Claims must be worked at least two days a week; that those absent would be judged to have abandoned their claims if they weren't back by June 15; that work on a ditch or sluice box would be considered as work on the claim; that six months grace could be allowed on claims if absence due to sickness or other factors, with proper procedure outlined; that one man couldn't run tailings onto another man's claim. All of these rules had the force of law, but some were changed as time went on.

Article 19 stated simply, "No Asiatic shall be allowed to mine in this district." That was changed when Chinese came and wanted to work the tailings of the old placer mines.

These items are all taken from one of the first papers published in eastern Oregon, *The City Journal,* of Canyon City. The paper didn't last long. The ex-miner editor made it for only seven issues, "Published occasionally," according to the mast head. In the last issue he philosophically said he was "returning to the pick and shovel for a living." My copy of the *Journal* is dated January 1, 1869.

There were other strikes, one on Dixie Creek, 12 miles to the east, near where Prairie City is now, more around "Prairie Diggins". And the gold continued to pour out. Some of the better financed began to figure on long flumes for placer work. Arrangements for mail and supplies were necessary. Stores, saloons, and livery stables were needed. A grist mill was started at John Day in '65, so flour didn't have to come from the Willamette Valley any longer.

In 1864 the government gave a mail contract to Henry H. Wheeler, who was also hired by Wells Fargo, the express people, to take out gold. He ran a four-horse stage outfit from Canyon City to The Dalles, Oregon. On one of his westbound gold-carrying trips, he was surrounded by Indians. The only passenger was a Wells Fargo agent. Both men jumped down between the horses, hastily cut the leaders loose, mounted them, and hurried away from there. Wheeler was shot through the mouth. Near the Burnt Ranch area to the west they came upon a party of whites who organized a posse. When they got back to the stage, they found everything scattered about. The Indians seemed to know about gold, for it was gone, but $10,000 in greenbacks was just worthless paper to them and was untouched.

Wheeler then continued down to The Dalles for medical care. His face was somewhat disfigured thereafter. Wheeler County was named for him.

The gold all went to The Dalles at first, thence to the mint at San Francisco. Later, after the railroad came to Baker, the gold went there. The Dalles was also the trading center for a wide area. All in-bound goods came to The Dalles by water, then by pack train to the gold camps. There wasn't much outgoing merchandise at first, but soon wool and hides were following that route to Portland.

All transactions were in gold for quite awhile. Every store had gold scales and it was more important for a clerk to be able to estimate impurities than it was for him to have any other education. It was a long trip for the gold to go by pack train to The Dalles, thence by riverboat to Portland, and then by ocean to San Francisco. A merchant never knew for sure how much gold he had until the returns came back from the mint.

Accordingly a demand grew for a mint at The Dalles. Oregon was a state in the Union and her representatives in Congress pressed this demand. Finally a strong granite building was constructed at The Dalles, 50x60 feet, and 35 feet high, costing $105,000. But by the time it was built, the loose gold had been picked up and mining enterprises were pretty much in stronger hands, so the demand for a local mint had petered out. The Dalles mint was never used for that purpose, but it was nice to have it. The local people could say to strangers, "There's our mint."

Land at that time had not been surveyed. The claims were described in some detail, located by rocks, or trees, or the creek.

Most of the miners used water to hasten their work. They ran the water down sluice boxes and threw shovelsful into the boxes, or used a rocker arrangement, or some other device, but water was necessary to wash the soil away.

The very first ditch dug was in the year gold was found, 1862. A flume was necessary and there was no lumber, so hides were used instead, shingled over each other. This was known for years as "the rawhide ditch".

The longest ditch in our county led to a placer operation at Marysville. It was dug in 1864 with picks and shovels. Earning a living with a pick and shovel was no joke then. This ditch led from Indian Creek and was 11 miles long.

Next longest was the John Long ditch, dug and owned by him. It headed on Pine Creek and led right to John Long's claim in a gulch where Canyon City is. Part of the original town was then called "Whiskey Diggins". My father lived with John and worked for him for six years. Mr. Long died after I was a good-sized boy. Father often said John must have plenty of money buried someplace, and after his death there was considerable speculative digging around his cabin. No cache was ever found, so far as anyone knows. It may be there yet.

This ditch of John Long's was bought by my father years later. By that time it had been neglected, requiring flume repair and much removal of soil and rocks. We used one horse and a slip scraper, I remember. One of the flumes led along the side of a cliff for about an eighth of a mile. My brother George, with 16 men, did this repair job.

We bought this old ditch to irrigate our benchland holdings but we paid for it by selling water to some placer miners along the route. We paid $6,000 for the ditch and water. We also bought the Aldred ditch to get water from its source.

This was the Aldred who was the original discoverer of gold and his ditch was one of the first, dug in 1862. It was on Dean Creek and led to the Prairie Diggins that yielded $180,000.

After the first free gold along the creeks was pretty well worked out, placer mining came in. The biggest placer mine was the Humboldt, high on the west side of Canyon Creek. The operations gouged out an enormous slice from the edge of the hill. This placer was operated for years by Ira Sproul and his partners.

Each week, after the clean-up from the sluice boxes, the owners cached the gold and once or twice a month took it to Baker. Sproul and a husky helper, Dutch Hupprich, son of the bootmaker, would leave Canyon City shortly after noon, ride all night, reach Baker about bank opening time and deposit the load of gold. There were no banks in Grant County then. The riders would rest in Baker, then ride back. They always stopped at the Oliver place to water the horses. By the old road this was a trip of about 80 miles, one way. It takes a good horse to go 80 miles without resting. The horse Ira always rode was a grey and carried his tail a little to one side. The other mines shipped by Wells Fargo. I never knew why Ira carried out his own gold.

After the coarse gold had been picked up, the Chinese came in. At John Day we soon had a Chinatown with 600 inhabitants. They had their own stores, restaurants, laundries, and doctors. Two of the doctors stayed on, long after the workers had gone. By that time most of their trade was with white people. Of course, they had no license to practice and the medical association got all haired up about it. The Chinese doctors, one of them blind in his later years, were repeatedly hailed into court with carefully prepared cases. They would demand a jury trial. The jury would listen attentively, examine the marked money and the documents, assess the evidence carefully, file out, and in ten minutes file in again, "Not guilty". No jury of Grant County citizens would find them guilty. The white doctors finally gave up and these two old men practiced until they died, far beyond the three score years and ten. They could treat certain things, but if they felt an operation were needed, or some treatment beyond them, they would say earnestly, "You see white doctor quick."

The blind Doctor Hey told me that in his youth in China, the medical course took seven years. At the end, the examination consisted of standing in front of a curtain with a three-inch hole in it. Through this hole a sick person thrust his bare arm. The student doctor was supposed to diagnose by the pulse, the temperature, and the appearance and feel of the flesh. If he failed, he was sent back to study for seven more years, when the test was repeated. A second failure meant loss of his head. He did not know enough for a doctor, but knew too much to live. I do not know whether this was true or not, because Chinese, as is the case with Indians, love to spoof white men. But that old Chinese doctor had something. The county was full of instances where he had saved arms and legs that white doctors were bent on amputating. He had some mysterious system about his doctoring. It was called, I believe, the Ti-zu system. He diagnosed by the "five angels" method, whatever that is. Some tried to fool him, giving him wrong symptoms. He would lay the patient's arm on a small pillow, feel the flesh and pulse softly, stop the blood by gently pressing a vein, and diagnose the case with impressive, almost uncanny accuracy.

The Chinese laborers who came into the John Day country worked out the tailings and apparently did well collecting fine gold. They worked to bed rock. They had what they called "tailing forks" that were somewhat like manure forks, but longer. All their work was by hand. They would dig a trench down to the bed rock, maybe 25 feet deep, maybe less. A man at the bottom would throw the rocks up to a level above, where a Chinese there would pass them up to the next level. The last man would throw them back, out of the way, thus moving all the rock in the old tailing pile, somewhat as an old fire brigade would pass water pails from hand to hand.

Father knew and grub-staked many Chinese and sold others food. I liked to go with him and watch their slow but effective way of moving rocks. One Chinese worked for us for a long time. For months the old records show, at the end of each month, "Chinaman—$20." Finally they read "Ah Shee—$35." Evidently the acquisition of a name brought him prosperity.

Some white miners remained, prospecting and living their lonely lives. One man, Ike Guker, found a gold pocket, long after the gold rush, and reported he took $50,000 from a space about the size of a small house. He then sold to a company that went deeper and found more gold at lower levels.

Later, during the depression years of the 1930's, many miners haunted the creeks, shoveling into sluice box or rocker, making a dollar or two a day, rather than accept relief funds, which they viewed as charity. There is probably plenty of gold left in Canyon Mountain. It stands to reason that if $26,000,000 worth of gold was taken out mainly on or near the surface, there would be buried veins just as rich. Geologists have speculated that a perpendicular dike, or vein, of rich gold-bearing rock once ran from Antone eastward through Canyon City and on to Prairie City, a distance of 60 miles. As water poured over it, erosion followed, scattering the gold in every gulch below.

Actually, this line of gold runs northeast from Antone to Florence, Idaho. Put a ruler on a map, starting at Antone and running it northeast to Florence, which is south of Grangeville, Idaho. The line will run through Canyon City and Prairie City, close to Auburn, Whitman, Sumpter, Cornucopia, and Copperfield, all in Oregon and all mining centers. It crosses Cuprum in Idaho, and Riggins, and on to Florence, all gold areas, with some copper. Maybe the Snake River ran to the south in prehistoric times, down to Pitt River, California, and perhaps we had a mountain range that ran southwest and northeast, long before the lava flows changed things all around. The hot lava may have melted the gold out of the old granite range and concentrated it in this irregular line on the north side of the range. No harm in supposing.

Placer mining was carried on in eastern Oregon for years after most of the surface miners had quit. One ditch leading to Marysville was 11 miles long. The famous Eldorado ditch in Baker County to the east was 136 miles long, dug by hand, mostly with Chinese labor.

The ditches emptied into what was called a "Penstock". This was merely a wooden tank with a large pipe outlet. This pipe diminished in size as it approached the mine, terminating in a small movable nozzle. The water, under high pressure, came from this nozzle with great force, and when directed against the bank of the placer cut, the soil and rocks flew. The muddy water, with all of the gravel and the fine gold, was directed into a sluice box set at such an angle that the rocks and pebbles were carried away. The heavier gold settled behind baffle plates. The big rocks were rolled away by hand. So, from the top of a high bank the gold tended to settle down ahead of the water, and to keep settling until it hit bedrock. At bedrock it washed into the sluice box.

Rule No. 1 of placer mining is therefore to select a place where it is possible to get to bedrock with plenty of fall below.

The big dredges that came in after the turn of the century also had to follow the rule of dredging where they could go to bedrock. There is no way of knowing how much gold left the county from dredging. The big companies never said, believing that we who lived there wouldn't be hurt if they didn't report such things to us.

The first dredge was a mile below John Day on the main John Day River. It was rather crude, a wooden boat with steel buckets. Gold was then $20.67 an ounce. The dredge owners would drill small holes to bedrock, moving back and forth across a strip of meadow. The core from each hole would be assayed separately and the results put on a plat. The final plat picture would show clearly how the gold deposits meandered across the meadow, following some old river bed. From this plat on paper they knew what land to buy and how to operate the dredge.

As time passed, better dredge designs were made. This encouraged capital to build a more efficient dredge and it dug up the marginal areas along the edge of the old dredge workings. Still later the price was raised in the New Deal days to $35 and new, larger, more efficient dredges appeared that could dig with profit most any meadow that had any gold at all. It looked for a time as though Grant County might not have any meadowland left on the main river. This rise in the price of gold was accomplished by simply reducing the amount of gold in a dollar. All private citizens and banks and others had to turn in any gold they had at the old price. On this neat bit of finagling, the government made almost three billion dollars. The worst feature, though, was that in a time of depression, with cheap labor, the dredge could buy land and dredge at a profit where this was impossible with the old price for gold.

The creek bottom land sold to the dredge for $150 to $500 an acre, depending upon what the test holes showed. Land was not worth that on the market at the time, so naturally the owners sold. This benefited the owner temporarily, but he lost in the long run, as did the county. The meadows are taxed more highly than other land, so if all the meadowland had been dredged, the county's tax base would have been hurt badly. After a beautiful meadow had been dredged, it was turned into a worthless, unsightly, formless pile of rocks. The good soil washed away with the water and went down to the Columbia and on to the sea. The meadows furnished the hay for winter feeding, so some ranchers, their meadowland gone, no longer had a year-around business, and had to sell their grazing land or else go somewhere else to get more hay land.

The gold went to Kentucky where it was buried again. The land was ruined forever. Some whose land was bought moved from the county or spent or invested the money elsewhere. The dredge was usually owned by out-siders, and the profits went to San Francisco or some-place outside of Grant County. So the county lost all around. As a county we ended without the land, without the money, and without the gold. Dredging of good land here has now been stopped by invoking a state law where-by land can be classified as to use. If we classify a meadow as farm land, it can't be used for dredging. During the war dredging was stopped indirectly because the War Board classified it as an unnecessary occupation, so own-ers could buy no repairs nor fuel.

The dredge operator reported that the best prospect on the whole river was a fine alfalfa field on the Oliver place. We refused to sell, but did finally let him have a three-acre strip to allow access to a tailing pile, or wash from a gulch above. Placer mines had been worked two miles above there on the higher benchland and had washed lots of fine gold into the river bottom. I do not know how much of the meadow on our old place has gold beneath it, perhaps 200 acres. I hope no one ever allows it to be dredged and ruined. If dredged, it will take the heart out of the home ranch.

George Barry, a farmer down the river near Mt. Vernon, owned at the time only 40 acres of good meadow. The dredgers wanted it badly, offering $16,000, when he couldn't have sold it for over $4,000 for farming. But he grew potatoes and onions. He told the buyer for the dredge, "I can make a good living from this 40 acres. Tell me how I can make a living from $16,000."

Grant County would now be far better off if the dredging operation had never been invented. Some in-dividuals profited, but the county lost some of its best land forever.

Gold in small amounts still leaves Grant County every year. Occasionally someone finds a big nugget or a rich pocket where some forgotten stream concentrated the gold. There are many stories of lost mines, some in my time. Clint Haight, for years colorful editor of the local paper, the *Blue Mountain Eagle,* tells of some of these.

THE BLUE BUCKET MINE

Every mining country has its stories of lost mines. They are prime fodder for TV; the Sunday supplements embroider them endlessly; old timers talk authoritatively about the mule or the dog that alone knows the secret. "I seen that mule myself that got that nugget stuck in his shoe so bad it lamed him—the left hind foot it was." Deer hunters gather closer to the fire at night and look nervously over their shoulders as the story unfolds about the old man who lived "somewhere on this same mountain," struck it rich and disappeared, never to be seen again. "A night traveler heard a long terrible cry, but no one never found hide nor hair."

But of all the stories, the Blue Bucket mine has been told the most—at least in Oregon, for it is part of our pioneer legacy. There are several versions, because roughly 1000 men, women and children were with the lost wagon train of 1845, and it was not until the 60's and 70's that the Blue Bucket stories really got to going good. After 25 years even the best of buckets begin to gather moss. When the story got around to all of the 900 survivors, each remembered something different.

Some facts are known, though. Here are a few. Fort Boise is where the story starts. Six wagon trains pulled into that frontier post in August, 1845, and paused to repair. Steve Meek, brother of the famous Joe, and Dr. Elijah White, missionary, were both well known in Oregon. Steve Meek, sensing a chance to make an honest dollar, claimed that the Blue Mountain route was "terrible, gentlemen, terrible," but he, Steve Meek, knew a cut-off that would take them *around* the Blue Mountains and save 200 miles.

This was welcome news, if true, so the trail-worn pioneers went to Dr. White with the question, "What about this man Meek? Does he just talk, or does he *know?*" It's too late to tell whether the Reverend White was in for some of the profits or whether he was gullible. At any rate, he gave them solemn assurance that Meek's words were gospel truth and if he said he knew of a better route, he knew of one. He, White, would surely go that way if he were going West instead of East.

So 200 wagons, with about 1000 persons, went with Meek, who was to get $5 a wagon for his services. They were encumbered by 2300 cattle, 800 oxen, and 1000 goats. Certainly some horses, too, but the diary didn't say.

There were three diaries, but the writers had no notion that their writings would be scanned feverishly for a hundred years for clues, so not one gives much help. The party left the Oregon Trail August 24, 1845, and spent 45 days of torture and death—hopelessly lost and, at one time, close to despair.

They went up the Malheur River; one account says they took the North Fork, one the South Fork. Shortly they struck a sea of boulders and many wagons shook to pieces. Horses and oxen lay down and refused to move when their hoofs were worn down and each step left a bloody mark.

Turning southward to get out of the boulders, the party struck alkali water. There a plan was nearly carried out to hang Meek to the upright end of a wagon tongue, but, in spite of thirst, fatigue, and despair, a few were left to point out that such a scheme might give some satisfaction, but it wouldn't provide water, which was needed more than revenge. Meek hid out and eventually hurried on ahead, reached The Dalles, and returned with a recue party and food.

In the meantime, a scouting party found water, probably not far from the present G. I. Ranch, but anyhow, at the head of Crooked River. Go down that river, even now, and try to imagine taking over 100 wagons down it, with no road! The terrible jolting, the suspense, the cold

Episcopal church at right was built in 1876 and is still in constant use. These young men were Portuguese. In those days many younger sons came to the United States and often gravitated to places owned by fellow countrymen. Thus, in Oregon Irish immigrants worked for Lake County Irish sheep owners, young men from Germany learned the business from a Washington County German dairyman, and Finns went to Astoria.

This building in John Day was the headquarters of the 600 Chinese in the John Day Valley. It is still standing (1961) and was built about 1866. The firm, KAM-WAH-CHUNG, carried authentic Chinese merchandise including food, medicines, fine silk and china, firecrackers, and opium.

The burro was the prospector's transportation and often his only friend.

Elk Creek placer mine, 1899. Owned by Gail Dewitt, Sloan, and Haskell. In addition to the powerful streams of water, this placer had a steam operated derrick for handling the larger rocks.

The small, but rich, Great Northern mine, discovered by Ike Guker (see page 27) standing in the center. $65,000 was taken out of this little hole. Guker let visitors pick up nuggets and keep them. Man on far right is Frank McBean, stage driver to Winnemucca, Nevada.

The gold dredges could dig up gold from bed-rock beneath a meadow, but they left behind them piles of worthless rock. The soil washed away in the process.

What the gold dredges leave behind them. This was once a beautiful meadow, as were thousands of other acres of such tailing piles in Grant and Baker counties in Oregon. On the Oliver ranch is located one of the richest sites for dredging. Oliver Brothers would not sell.

Gold dredge at work. It dug its floating pond as it advanced, working back and forth across the beautiful mountain meadows, ruining them forever.

by night, heat by day, began to take their toll and each day of the latter part of September brought deaths, mostly recorded namelessly and hopelessly in the diaries as "September 24. Heare we beried 6 persons" with similar entries every day.

It is no wonder that the writers did not describe the route so that it could be followed. They assumed that no one would *ever, ever* want to follow it.

But somewhere along this route, before this death march began, someone picked up pieces of a funny soft rock and saved them. When the lost train reached Crooked River, the stones were used as sinkers to catch some of the numerous fish that lay near the bottoms of the pools. Many of the pretty rocks were still on hand when the party reached the Willamette Valley. Four years later, some of the young men of that train followed the stampede to California. They returned with gold about 1852 and, with growing excitement, found it was the same as the rocks picked up by the lost wagon train and carelessly tossed into a blue bucket.

Soon party after party was organized to hunt for the dry creek bed where the nuggets—the story had it—were lying thick. The Indians by this time were aroused and resentful, drove off the searchers, and stole their horses. Some of the would-be miners were killed. By the time the Indians were on reservations, memories were dulled. To this day the stream bed has never been located, despite dozens of large and small search parties. It is probably somewhere near the place on the map where Baker, Malheur, Grant, and Harney come close together. Even now, someone occasionally finds a rotting wagon wheel, or gleans a clue from an old letter, and starts a wave of new interest in the Blue Bucket mine.

It was agreed by all that the nuggets of pure gold were picked up in a dry creek bed. Perhaps there is another channel now, the dry bed has grown over with sage, and there is no sign of an old creek bed there.

Only two things are sure: There *was* gold in large nuggets, and, number two, it has never been found. One version is that Daniel Herron picked up the gold while looking for some strayed stock. If this should be true, the gold *might* be miles from the route taken by the wagons.

Here are some of the stories told by Clint Haight in the *Blue Mountain Eagle*:

THE McKROLA FIND

In 1910 Charlie McKrola was walking from Canyon City along the old stage route to Bear Valley, where he had a ranch job. About three miles out he found a big chunk of *very* high grade ore, about as big as one's head. He broke off some pieces and rolled the main chunk into the creek. A big piece of gold like that had to come from some nearby vein or ledge, but no such place has been found.

McCORKLE SAT ON GOLD

Charlie McCorkle was from Colorado and was a gold hunter by nature, instinct, and natural desire. He bought the old Elkhorn Hotel in Canyon City in 1915, but prospecting suited him far better than listening to complaints of fussy and infrequent hotel guests. He located and sold a chrome mine. *But he was after gold.* Early in March he forked a horse and lit out for Miller Mountain, south of Canyon City.

The snow was going off, the landscape dappled by patches of it all around. He sat down on a big quartz boulder to eat lunch. More by instinct than design, he broke off several pieces of the dirt-covered boulder and pocketed them. Days later he got them out, washed them and found rich, gold-filled ore. He was not able to retrace his trail and could not locate the spot nor the boulder.

HOWELL LOST HIS CHANCE

Jack Howell was prospecting for chrome in 1918. He was a prospector from all over—wherever ore was to be found, in whatever country. As he walked he always loaded up his pockets with rocks. In February snow was everywhere except along the serpentine rims above Canyon Creek. One day, on his return, he found he had picked up some unbelievably rich quartz—but where? He searched and searched—never found the exact ledge again.

DAN O'SHEA WAS A SHEEPHERDER

Dan knew nothing about mining, but he came off from Canyon Mountain one day with $3,300 in gold. On Miller Mountain he found an odd piece of gold about double the size of his thumb. He could never find the place again, and left the country.

JOHN LONG NAMED A GULCH

John was a placer miner and he worked Long Gulch, right above Canyon City. From the known richness of this gulch, the other miners figured he had about $100,-000 in gold hidden around somewhere. He died suddenly. His gold has not been found, except that $500 in $20-gold pieces was found scattered around in his old barn. Probably a fortune is there somewhere.

A LOGGER LOST A MINE

In 1930 the Hines Lumber people were at work on their big sawmill at Burns. A highway crew was busy building the Canyon City-Burns route, and traffic was temporarily detoured to the west, toward Izee. The millwright for the new Hines mill spent the night at Canyon City, apparently looking for new sources of moonshine, or some persons interested in poker, or something. Anyhow, what with one thing and another, apparently he didn't go to bed. On his drive back, he got to some point on Miller Mountain, when he got out of his car to rest. Before lying down, he tossed some pretty rocks into his car.

Several weeks later he cleaned out his car, and a passerby looked at the rocks, then exclaimed—"Man, that's gold!" It was. The millwright couldn't remember where he had picked up the rocks.

THE PIUTES KNEW ABOUT LEAD

In the early days the Piute Indians came to Canyon City every fall to trade, for this was the nearest big town at the time. They rode their ponies to the east, out past Marysville, into the mountains, out toward Indian Creek somewhere. In a couple of weeks they came back with their ponies loaded down with lead. They traded it all for whatever delighted them and the whites made their bullets from it. Here is the odd thing—no trace of lead has ever been found in the county. The Indians didn't say where they got it. They were pretty well killed off or dispersed in the Bannock Indian War of 1878, and no one knows where they got that nearly pure lead.

There are many others: Indian Alec who talked of where the Indians got gold for ornaments, out near Dixie Creek somewhere; the prospector in 1930 who found raw silver, but vanished, leaving a cabin full of assaying equipment; J. A. Laycock, rancher and county judge, who found and lost a copper mine.

But there is one thing for sure. In a county churned by volcanoes; where mountains have suddenly been thrust up; the course of streams changed dozens of times; where $26,000,000 of free gold has been picked up; there *must* be some buried veins or dikes *not* carried downhill by streams.

If gold ever becomes worth a lot more than now; or if population expands until all resources of the nation must be used, then I expect this county will be systematically cored, much as the dredge operators drilled test holes, or cores, in a pattern.

The one thing I *don't* want to see, though, is any more dredging of good land. This county can't stand that. How much is an acre of good farm land worth? Right now maybe $300, because it will pay interest on that. But what is it worth to the nation? Or to the county? Or State? We hope we have a permanent nation here. Suppose it lasts 1000 years—then, if we take $40 worth of hay each year from a good meadow for 1000 years, is that acre worth $40,000 to the nation?

It's hard to say. The point is that the nation has a far greater thing at stake than the individual has. I think the nation, if it has to, should prohibit such things as dredging of good land.

SIX HORSES DIED

There is one more story worth telling, and it is more of a mystery than anything else told here. A novelist of soaring imagination should be able to make a book from it, replete with outlaws, miners, Indians, treachery, greed, and all the other ingredients that can be mixed to bake a good dramatic cake.

The U. S. Forest Service was created in the time of Theodore Roosevelt. It was handed a big chunk of America as large as Texas, but all covered by trees. No inventory had been made and no one knew what was out there in those millions of acres, mostly mountains.

In Crook County, Oregon, east and north of the town of Prineville, a man climbed up toward the summit of the new Ochoco National Forest, just looking around in the virgin stand of beautiful yellow pine. These ponderosa pine forests at that time were open and park-like. Through the trees the man saw an odd log with six scallops in it, rather regularly spaced, as though someone might have notched it purposely.

He found a halter chain tied around the tree at each notch, together with a skeleton of a horse, and all the metal parts of a saddle, bridle, and halter. Evidently six horses, each fully equipped, had been tied to the log and all had died of thirst and starvation. Before death, each had frantically chewed the portion of the log in front of him, making a V-shaped depression.

Thoroughly mystified, the man reported his find. There was a flurry of excitement in Prineville, and much consulting with old timers. Finally one remembered that in 1863, at the very height of the Canyon City mining, six masked men had ridden into Whiskey Gulch, as it was then called, had arrived on Saturday evening just as the miners were finishing cleaning out their sluice boxes, and had ridden off with a fortune in gold. They had been fast efficient workers. They got clear away.

But if the six dead horses had belonged to these men, the mystery just starts. It is possible, even probable, that they had provided fresh horses at a rendezvous in the hills. After the robbery, they doubtless scattered to avoid leaving a well marked trail, and might easily have picked out this place to gather. It was 100 miles from any settlement, and completely hidden.

But they would *not* have had a change of horses all saddled and bridled. The mere gathering of extra equipment would have attracted attention. And in no case would they voluntarily have left six horses saddled and tied. A man may be mean, unscrupulous, and cruel, but he just doesn't do that. It is a monstrous, unnatural thing and you couldn't find six men who would do it. Besides, there wouldn't be any sense in it.

The only reasonable theory is that they tied their horses, intending to come back, and they left to divide the gold or to secrete it. But in that case, what became of them? In 1863 that part of eastern Oregon was completely uninhabited, even by Indians. There were a few travelers on known trails. No one walked. The arrival of six men on foot at The Dalles, over 100 miles to the north, would have been noted. Besides, gold in the quantity they got would have been bulky and hard to carry very far on foot. Each man would have had to carry perhaps 40 pounds. Each supposition can be met with a strong "Yes, but—" except that they got to fighting over the division and killed each other. Yes—but no skeletons of men were ever found.

Of course, Prineville citizens have imagination, too, so for several years the soil all around there was thoroughly dug up. No gold.

This doesn't exactly fit in with the lost mine or buried treasure stories, but if some story writer wants it —here is a start. I even have a suggested title, "Six Horses Died." It sort of stabs sharply at your interest.

Antone and Charles Kimball, two miners who stayed around long after the gold diggins had petered out. Every gold mining area in the West had such characters. Some, in their old age, still looking for the "mother lode," became a little queer and did not relish company.

CHAPTER 3

THE COUNTY GROWS UP

Gold was exciting because the prospect of sudden riches always stirs up the blood, but its effect is short lived. It's sort of like the temporary prosperity around one of the big dams, when 5000 men move in, work for a few years, then leave, with empty houses and unpaid bonds behind them.

The Civil War days coincided exactly with the gold days in this state. There was a big population in the Willamette and Rogue River Valleys, but few lived east of the mountains. When the statehood issue was debated in Congress before 1859, some senators held that Oregon's eastern boundary should be the Cascade Mountains because no one would ever live east of that barrier.

Gold changed that and put people in Grant, Baker, Malheur and adjacent counties. Almost at once others came to raise food for the miners.

These people mostly came in the late 60's and early 70's. Most of them came from the Willamette Valley and many were sons of the early covered wagon folks. The wagons rolled to western Oregon by thousands and thousands from 1843 on. Sons of the pioneers of '43 were perhaps 25 years old by 1870. They looked around the Willamette Valley, saw much of the good land taken, thought they had little chance there, so lit out for the big open free country to the east. From 1870 to about 1890 there was a constant stream of valley people into all of the eastern Oregon counties. Many brought live-stock with them.

Of the few old timers here, Jack Vaughan and James Officer came from Molalla; I believe the Hydes, McGills, and Harrisons, all at Izee, came from Harrisburg; Bill Hanley was from Medford; Robert Damon from Jacksonville; George Carson from Medford; the famous Joaquin Miller came from Eugene; Billy Stewart was from Yamhill, all from western Oregon.

A large group of settlers came here direct from Scotland. Most of them were sheepmen and the Scotch bur was usually mixed with the noisy ba-a-a of the lambs. Some of these transplanted wearers of the kilt were: Kenneth MacRae, Jimmie Cant, the Senior Murrays, Tommy Munroe, the McClellans, Arthur Begg, the Senior Massons, Johnny Kirk, the Finlaysons, Mrs. B. C. Trowbridge—these are a few.

Another group came from England. The Smith Brothers, Campbell Martin, Jim Small and the Hall Brothers were some. The Smiths caused lots of comment. They came from a wealthy family, used flat English saddles and were "veddy" British. They referred to cowboys as "cow servants."

Some from Germany or of German parentage were the Herburgers, Ringsmeiers, Kuhls, the Hupprich family, the Sels family, Phil Metschan, senior, John Schmidt, William Tureman.

Wearers of the green included: Johnnie Nealan, J. J. O'Dair, the Daly family, Paddy Finlay, J. J. Cozart, and the Lucas folks.

Some early settlers were covered wagon folks on their way to the Willamette Valley. They liked what they saw along the John Day and stopped.

Others were from all over. Jack Craddock was from Arkansas; G. I. Hazeltine came from the mines of California as did Allen Porter; the Dunlaps were from Texas; Charlie Brown was a true Westerner, born in the rip-roaring mining town of Silver City, Idaho.

A few, as my father and others, came to mine and stayed to farm.

One early settler, Joaquin Miller, deserves special mention. Around the start of the Civil War, he was editing a paper at Eugene, after some stirring years in northern California. There, among other things, he joined a tribe of Indians, married an Indian girl, associated with all kinds of characters, and worked as express messenger. He felt wild and free and his writings as editor outraged the peaceful folks around Eugene. It isn't known that he was especially sympathetic with the South, but he was "agin" authority of all kinds, so felt the South had a right to secede if it wanted to. Federal court orders closed his Eugene paper for sedition.

In the meantime he had left his Indian bride and married a poetess who published her poems in his "Democratic Register." She was Minnie Myrtle Dyer of Curry County. After the Federal court forcibly severed him from the editor's chair in 1862, he followed the horde of miners to Canyon City.

Here he was in his element again. He was the first elected county judge of Grant County. He had little formal schooling, but his head was bursting with wild, poetic ideas of sun, waves, love, mountains, streams, man, and nature. It was all pretty chaotic. He could be seen all up and down Canyon Creek, sometimes drunk, sometimes sober, but always with a notebook. He was apparently quite drunk with life. He was known at Canyon City as Cincinnatus Heine Miller. He stayed there four years. His equally poetic wife left him—he seems to have been so immersed in poetry that the woodbox was always empty, and he brought home unfinished sonnets instead of bread.

In 1868 he appeared at the printing office of George Himes (then Carter & Himes) in Portland, with the craziest manuscript ever offered to any publisher. The grammar and spelling were impossible, the meter absent or worse. But here and there a gem of expression flashed out, so the kindly Mr. Himes worked with the author for days and days. At intervals, Miller would shout, "Full many a flower is born to blush unseen and waste its sweetness on the desert air." Then he would slap his own chest and yell, "That's me."

This first volume of poems, written in Canyon City, was called Specimens, and Himes put out 500 copies. The *Oregonian* condemned it, digging deep for its most blistering editorial adjectives. It is doubtful if Joaquin read the *Oregonian*. Why waste time reading what other, lesser men, wrote when eagles were screaming in his brain?

Soon he was back again at Himes's office with another book of poems under the title *Joaquin, et al*. This volume was more civilized, and sold and sold, running through several editions. And the name "Cincinnatus" died suddenly, replaced by "Joaquin," which it has been ever since.

Right at this time, in California, Joaquin Murietta, part Indian, part Spanish outlaw, was making a name that was used to scare little children into good behavior. This outlaw was a wild, ringtailed snorter, and he howled every night.

Miller's new book included a poem that was partly a defence of this man—a sort of poetic apology for murder, robbery, rape, and stealing candy from children. It sold because the populace was shocked that anyone would *dare* to stand up for such a person. Anyhow, it put Joaquin Miller on his way. He was *made*.

He adopted Western garb, much as Buffalo Bill did; he invaded Europe where the "wild West" idea took hold early, and he sang and sang of wild freedom, wild love, wild winds, wild and hopeless ambitions; and he was Grant County's gift to literature.

It is a little hard now to see why he caused all the furore, especially in England and France, and why people bought his books by the thousands. The English called him "The Byron of Oregon."

Anyhow, his cabin is preserved in Canyon City, and at one of the big "62" celebrations in that town, his daughter, Juanita, whose poems carry much of her father's style, came to Canyon City to preside over part of the celebration. She later gathered some notoriety of her own by marrying, in a mystic ceremony, the "man in the moon."

The miners in Canyon City didn't know quite what to make of Cincinnatus. He might be a sort of genius, but certainly he was kind of a show-off, sort of like the self-styled doctor at the medicine show. But then, all the bigwigs in England said he was pretty hot stuff, a child of nature, full of sunlight and mountain air. The miners thought he was probably full of mountain dew. But anyhow, he was famous, so they were all for him—and maybe, after all, he was really a great man, but this stuff about going off and living with the Indians—I dunno, makes a feller wonder, and whadaya s'pose he meant when he said—here it is right here—when he said—and listen to this:

"Life knows no dead so beautiful as is the white, cold, coffin'd past?" Is that, sure nuff, good poetry?

Well, they still don't know. But they kind of suspected, along toward the last, that he wasn't so good as he used to be, and as the New England farmer said, maybe he never was.

But along with the furore about Joaquin Miller, the cattle, sheep, and horse population grew amazingly in the late 60's and early 70's. The horses just ran wild and one would see a grand stallion ten years old without a sign of a brand. Horses could live out all winter, paw away the snow and do all right. Cattle and sheep had to be tended.

Jack Craddock of Silvies Valley, was one of the several Oregonians who got his start by gathering up herds of horses and trailing them east for sale. Eastern Oregon horses came to have a fine reputation at Kansas City.

In 1903, when I was 18, our family, along with the Trowbridges, the Hardys and a few others, gathered 700 wild horses in the John Day Valley, herded them to Ontario and sold them to the John Clay Commission Company of Omaha. We got $7.00 for yearlings, $14 for the grown stock, sucking colts thrown in free.

Some of the first settlers in the valley were obsessed with the idea that Oregon was a fruit country. The nation's magazines at that time were booming the Oregon apple and there were hundreds of yarns about getting rich from fruit growing. D. B. Rhinehart set out a 40-acre orchard two miles east of Canyon City. B. C. Trowbridge put out a sizeable orchard across the river from John Day. Charles Belshaw grew prunes in a big orchard seven miles west of Mt. Vernon. He developed the famous Belshaw prune, well known on the New York market.

These early orchards played an important role before good roads and autos erased distance. Ranchers from Harney County, almost to the Nevada line, came here regularly to buy fruit. Sometimes the whole family would come along as a sort of picnic; would camp out and can the year's supply.

These people arrived at apple time with wagon boxes partitioned, each section with a 6-inch layer of straw. They would then pick Belleflowers, Northern Spies, Newtown Pippins, Maiden's Blush, and other apples, putting each variety in a separate section. Some made several trips to get both early and late varieties. Others brought sacks, but with the roads of that day, the sacked apples arrived at the home ranch, maybe a hundred miles away, rather bruised. The partitioned wagon boxes, with a straw cushion, worked better.

Harney County also made a market for young pigs. We always kept some sows. I remember that Billy Miller of Harney once came to the ranch with the first triple-decked wagon I had seen and hauled away 80 weaner pigs.

These early day folks nearly all had an eye for race horses. There were a half dozen race tracks in the county, and any level lane or pasture would do for an impromptu race most any day. As boys, we would race for money, marbles or chalk. Or just for fun. The expression "at the drop of a hat" grew up that way, for that was often the signal to start a race.

The Trowbridge family were all race horse folks. They were breeders of truly good race horses that sold all over the West. Old timers remember the favorite horse of Henry Trowbridge, named Cal Kern. This famous horse always gave his backers heart failure. He seemed totally uninterested in the proceedings. The high-spirited competition would dance around, turn, make false starts, throw their heads, and could scarcely control their fierce drive to be off. Cal Kern would look over the scenery, strictly unconcerned.

At the start of the race, those who had bet on him would despair, because he didn't even seem to be trying, yet at the end, he always came in first, wondering what all the excitement was about. He was smart and just put out enough to win. Joe Officer of Izee broke Cal to ride when both Joe and Cal were colts.

B. C. Trowbridge produced two other racers that were widely recognized, a big brown named "Dutch" and a gray called "Gray Dick".

J. J. Cozart was a noted breeder of trotting horses. He was an early day packer. Before the coming of roads, the only way to get supplies to the John Day country was by pack horse. Cozart brought to the miners the first pack string of supplies from The Dalles. Miners had to have tools, including picks, shovels, axes, pipe, nails. These all came in on Cozart's pack animals along with dishes, kettles, groceries, clothing, books, and whatever a busy mining camp needed, including musical instruments. Later, of course, others got into the packing business. But Cozart stayed on after wagon freight outfits took over and developed a good trotting horse breeding plant.

The freight outfits usually had six- to ten-horse teams. First they freighted between Canyon City and The Dalles. After a railroad was built to Shaniko, that was the turn-around place. Still later, they took the shorter but steeper road to Baker.

We had some Indian trouble during 1878 in the Bannock War, just before my time. Some Idaho and Harney County Indians came through the Murderer's Creek country and traveled north to the Columbia, hoping to get the Umatillas and Nez Perce Indians to join them in plans to rid the country of white settlers.

They killed two nephews of Uncle Jim Small, as he was called. He was the first sheepman of the county, an Englishman, and the boys were herding for him. He owned what is now called the Bragga place, halfway between John Day and Dayville.

The Indians killed a man named Aldrich and mutilated his body. They came upon a herd of cattle belonging to Billy Stewart, father of Wayne Stewart. As he watched, hidden in the rimrocks, the big band took out on his cattle herds all of their pent-up anger and grievances against the whites. They killed the animals by torture.

When I was little, the Indians, then peaceable, came through here in bands, making regular trips from Warm Springs and Celilo. Whole families came, hunting and gathering wool. The squaws picked wool from barbed wire fences, sagebrush and dead sheep. They picked huckleberries, gathered deer hides, and traded or sold their buckskin goods. There were 50 or 60 Indians in a group and each Indian had three to five horses. Their annual trip was always a time of interest to boys my age.

The Canyon City gold camp was not particularly wild and woolly, and by my time wasn't that way at all. There were a few early day murders, but frontier justice took care of the situation so fast that the worst type of callous killers found it best to avoid this county. Charlie Brown at the Grant County Museum at Canyon City displays the skulls of the first two criminals hung in the county.

Barry Wey was the first. He and his partner owned a pack string and the partner was given $60,000 in gold dust (some said $80,000) to take to The Dalles for shipment to San Francisco. Wey arrived at The Dalles without the partner, saying he had bought out the other man. This was usual enough, because people in gold country picked up and moved for little or no reason.

But a little later, a Canyon City-bound group noticed a peculiar Juniper tree and found a man's body sprouting from it. This was the defunct partner.

When these folks arrived at Canyon City, Wey got wind of their story, and suddenly remembered urgent business in Idaho. The sheriff followed on horseback, always a few hours behind, what with stopping to ask his whereabouts. But Wey stopped in Oro Fino because it was, in those days, about 200 miles north of nowhere and farther yet south, east or west. Mr. Wey didn't understand just how his friends felt, so he thought he'd gone far enough. The sheriff found him easily, tied up his hands, and returned him to Canyon City at a stiff trot. There the miners were so glad to see him that they took him away from the sheriff and proposed to hang him right then.

This seemed fair enough to everyone except Wey and Ike Hare. The latter was eloquent and imbued by a sense of law and order. He quelled the mob spirit by sheer force of oratory. Orderly procedures prevailed when he wound up his oration, "We will give him a fair and impartial trial. We know him to be guilty, and we'll hang him anyway."

This plan was promptly carried out in every detail. The trial was said to have been a model of fairness and impartiality, since everyone knew the outcome. The miners were saved the sense of guilt that always follows a lynching. Wey, just before he died, said, "Boys, I don't want to die with my boots on. Can I take them off?" This seemed all right to everyone and Wey removed them. Afterwards, they were put on top of his grave, there being no flowers; and there they remained for many years until weather and rodents destroyed them. The stolen money was never found.

The second man hung was William Kane, who was more of a cold-killer type and the camp felt a lot better after he was removed. He didn't even have the temptation of $60,000 as a prize if he pulled it off. He just got mad at an employer for paying him off in paper money.

The miners sympathized with him in that. It was only within the last 50 years that greenbacks became as acceptable as silver and gold in such towns as Helena, Montana, and Reno, Nevada. In the gold mining days, a piece of faded green paper didn't look like money to any miner.

But in that early day the miners didn't approve of such a drastic way of expressing disapproval. Kane could have been more diplomatic and gentlemanly—he might, for example, have just thrown the greenbacks into the employer's face and demanded hard money. So they found him guilty, too, and conveniently located the gallows at the cemetery. They hauled him up the hill in a buckboard, with ankles and arms chained. The population streamed along behind, while Kane played solitaire with absorption. As the team slowed on the hill, some of the younger persons in the crowd began to pass the wagon. Kane looked up and called to them, "Boys! Boys, there's no hurry. They can't do a thing 'til I get there." They said he won his solitaire game.

In any new country there are fights and even deaths over such things as fences, water, property lines, and trespassing livestock. In the towns there are bad feelings over card games and swindlers. These things, sometimes leading to fair fights in which one of the contestants goes to the undertakers, are well understood and taken for granted. The ripples they caused were not large enough to disturb the surface of society. They were much like the famous order of the duelist, "Pistols for two and breakfast for one."

But cold murder, not accompanied by anger or quarrel, was more repulsive then than today. Now the lawyer can make all kinds of excuses and put off the final act in the drama for months or years. Finally girls begin to cry over the murderer and young punks parade with signs.

In 1888, in my time, there were two prisoners in the county jail; Buccaro Jim, an Indian charged with killing J. M. Bright of Harney Valley, and Patrick McGinnis, who was caught with another man's horse under him.

One evening Robert Lockwood, deputy sheriff, who fed the prisoners, did not come home. By midnight his family still had no word, so they called some neighbors to help look around. They found the cells deserted, the doors open, and the body of the popular deputy with a bullet through it.

McGinnis was found hiding on a farm and Buccaro Jim was found with some Indian friends. This McGinnis seemed to be without remorse. At any rate, he got hold of some poison somehow, which he spirited into the Indian's tea. If the Indian were dead, presumably McGinnis could have claimed that Buccaro Jim was responsible for the whole thing. But the Indian didn't drink the tea and this second attempted murder did nothing to calm down the general revulsion. Accordingly, after a little legal hocus pocus, McGinnis was hanged.

In recent years there have been a few murder trials— usually over water or fences or trespass, often ending in "Not Guilty" if the fight were fair. Self-defense is still a good plea in the West. A short time ago a man was killed by a neighbor in a fair gun duel. The result of the trial, "Not guilty," was a foregone conclusion. The killed man had, for years, insulted his neighbor regularly, calling him a yellow livered bastard, and such. The man's defense was "A man can be pushed only so far." The jury thought so, too.

In 1937 we had a bank robbery. Three young hoodlums, Patrick Bushman, Chester Crum, and Lloyd Barkdoll, tried what they thought was a perfect scheme. It was the old military "diversionary tactics". They set fire to a rather large warehouse, and of course, the people thronged there, neatly removing the witnesses.

The robbers stopped the assistant cashier on his way to the fire, and made him, at gun point, open the bank and ordered him to open the safe. He explained to them the principles of the time lock. So they had to be content with an auxiliary vault, from which they got $3,600. They slugged the cashier, Oscar Hoverson, and locked him in the vault, apparently thinking him dead. But he came to, opened the vault and managed to report the robbery.

I was in town that night at the theatre, across the street from the bank. Someone came into the theatre and reported the fire. Seeing the whole population of the town at the fire, I went to the top of the theatre building to see that no sparks ignited the roof. The robbery must have been going on at that time. I came down, started back to the fire, when someone ran up and told me the bank had been robbed. I ran to the building, found the door open, with a trail of blood leading out. This, of course, was made by Hoverson, who, in a semi-dazed condition, had tottered out and gone into the nearby hotel.

I called the state police and about the time they got there, someone came running in saying there was a big pile of money out in the highway at the turn just west of town. We drove out and found a wrecked car with the money in it. One bag had broken open and coins were scattered around. We tried to hold the crowd back, but money, loose on the highway, was too good to pass up. We recovered all except $420 of the loot.

The robbers, on their way out of town, took the corner too fast and wrecked their car. In the wreck two of the robbers were badly injured. The third stole the car of a passerby who had stopped to help, when he saw the wreck. The uninjured desperado loaded the two injured men into the stolen car, and drove on. They returned through John Day, turned north into the isolated mining country around Galena and eventually found their way back through Long Creek and on to Kimberly, thence to Arlington, where one of them left the car and went to Portland. After a gun battle and escape, the other two were captured in Washington. The third was taken in Portland. Only 18 days after the robbery, they were on their way to the penitentiary, two of them with life sentences.

So it still doesn't pay to commit crime deliberately in Grant County. Wrong-doers would better pick out a city as the scene of their capers. There it is easier to find sentimental sob-sisters to serve on juries, and easier to delay, to involve the trial in politics, to discredit witnesses, and otherwise thwart justice.

We had one other bank robbery in the county, this time the Prairie City bank. The telephone operator, looking idly out of the window, saw a man run out of the bank, jump into a car, head east. She phoned the Pastime, and two unarmed men lit out after him. Here again, lack of knowledge of the country betrayed this lone criminal. East of Prairie City the highway veers to the left, but there was a road that went straight ahead, then to the right and up into uninhabited timber country. You can travel about a hundred miles on that road before you come to any place.

This robber made a mistake and took the right hand road. After traveling about 40 miles he came to another road, apparently decided he was off his beat, and turned right, only to get stuck in the mud. A fisherman picked him up, brought him back to John Day, unsuspectingly, where he stole another car and headed for Idaho on the right road. By this time police were alerted and he was shot by the state police of Utah. All the money was recovered. He turned out to be an ex-convict from Texas, trying to make a comeback by robbing a bank in a sleepy little cow town. It didn't turn out too well for him, either.

This reminds me about the telephone coming to our country. I was just a boy and saw some men near our place stringing wire on tall poles. To my question they said it was the phone wire. This conversation followed:

I—what's it for?

They—To talk over.

I—How can you talk over a wire?

They—It has a hole through it and you yell as loud as you can. The noise goes right on through, clear to Prairie City.

I was, as usual, on a horse, and this seemed a marvel of the age to me. I waited until the men left, then examined the wire carefully. There wasn't any hole. A country boy had been taken in again by a city slicker.

But I started to tell about the telephone operator. Linnie Grant, then Linnie Parrish, was our best operator at Canyon City. An operator in a small frontier town was proud of her job and took it seriously. She didn't just sit there and plug in wires. She acted as the daily newspaper; kept the community informed on everything from world news to local sports; warned of fires; told of sickness; and gave real service to the patrons. If you called, say Pete Olson, she wouldn't just ring, then say, "Their phone doesn't answer." She'd say, "The whole family is over at Mulcare's butchering today and they don't have a phone." Or maybe, "He was coming to town today. Just a minute, I'll go out in the street and find him."

There is no such friendly, useful service available in the city today.

THE NAMES ON THE MAP

It's a shame that so many of the old names get discarded because, as a county gets civilized, it seems the new citizens think the original names not dignified. Perhaps as good an illustration as any is the case of Squaw Butte, in Harney County to the south of Grant, and originally part of Grant County. Because of its shape, it was universally known among the cowboys as Squaw Tit Butte. When government surveyors mapped the county, they were directed to use local names as far as possible.

The man in charge of the crew had to make his reports from the field and his spelling was not the best. He reported the local name, but suggested the name be changed to Squaw Butte. He misspelled Butte, so his superior wrote back that from that distance it was hard to see the necessity for naming it for any part of the squaw's anatomy, but he would bow to the decision of the field man.

Whiskey Gulch or Whiskey Flat was renamed Canyon City, descriptive enough, but certainly less colorful. Western Oregon, perhaps due to the mild and friendly climate that attracted home loving people, abounds in gentle names, such as Amity, Glad Tidings, Freedom, Forest Grove, Goshen, Fernhill, Fairview, Enchanted Prairie, and the like.

There is more of a tendency in eastern Oregon, due to the long distances between settlers, to name creeks and hills for some man who lived there. Often he was the only settler, so we have Fields Creek, Armstrong Creek, Austin, Beech Creek, Caverhill, Cummings Creek, and many more.

The mining days in Grant County were responsible for Bluebucket Creek, named for the lost mine; Chrome Ridge, for the metal; Galena, an ore containing lead; Granite, for rocks of that kind, older than the later lava that overran the country; Greenhorn Peak, for a particularly green miner out to make his fortune in a business he knew nothing about; Redboy, for a mine of the same name.

The town of Izee was named for the brand, IZ, of an early resident named Bonham. Johnny Kirk Spring, so designated on highway markers and maps, commemorates an eccentric old timer who could spin the most marvelous yarns with the air of truth but with none whatever.

Then there is Chicken Hill. This is far up in the mining country above Granite. An early day freighter upset near the summit. He had several crates of chickens on top of the load. The crates were flimsy and smashed up, whereupon the chickens took to the brush. For some months after, a prospector, thinking he was in country never visited by whites before, would be startled by the sight of a rooster or a big old Plymouth Rock hen.

There are two gulches with odd names, Chickenhouse Gulch and Doghouse Gulch. Both were named for early day shanties that passed for residences. Waterspout Gulch has an obvious name; what is called a "cloudburst" over much of America, is known as a waterspout in our country.

Flagtail Mountain was early named for the abundance of mule deer, with their prominent white flags; Sheep Rock came from mountain sheep that were seen there when white men first came; Fox, a town and a valley, was for an actual fox, or so a hunter claimed, although foxes never were common here.

Battle Creek was so called because two opposing bands of Indians fought each other there. Widows Creek was named for a frontier lady who lived nearby. Her name was Mrs. S. E. Heim.

We had a post office at one time named Range, and another named Yeoville.

But of all the names in the county, I like Murderers Creek the best. Indians killed eight prospectors there. It is tributary to the South Fork of the John Day. It could just as well have been named "Battle Creek" or "Indian Creek" or even "Murder Creek," but it seems a stroke of genius to throw in the extra syllable, to roll around on your tongue.

GRANT COUNTY LAKES

The county is not thought of as a lake county, and most outsiders do not regard it as a fishing county, though we have 800 miles of fishing streams. Our lakes have individual interest.

Magone Lake (pronounced Magoon') —nestles among the trees at an elevation of 5,051 feet. It contains 48.5 acres and is 150 feet deep. It was formed by an earth slide only 150 years ago. The water is clear and from a boat one can look down and see the tall trees still standing in stately quiet at the bottom of the lake.

The lake was named for Major Magone, an imposing six footer whom I remember clearly. When I was eight years old he came to the ranch. He had a fine beard that came to his waist. He was in search of small trout and located them on the ranch in a big spring 20 feet deep and eight feet across. Several of these springs ran together and formed a small creek that ran into the John Day in a continuous year-round flow of cold water. Fish from the John Day came up the little cold water creek, found the big springs to their liking, and apparently spawned there, because the springs were alive with minnows.

The Major had a long pole with a can fastened to the end. With this he dipped out water and minnows and poured them into two five gallon oil cans with the top cut out, and a bale fastened on each. He filled each nearly to the top, then carried them six miles to the lake. He made several trips, straight over the rugged hills and rocks. This was work of the hardest kind, carrying 80 pounds through mountains, up hills, over rocks and logs. But in this act he stocked a lake barren of fish before. So, for his effort, the lake was named for him.

But maybe he didn't regard it as unusual, because in 1892 he casually walked 2000 miles to Chicago to see the World's Fair, averaging over 30 miles a day. He was over 70 years old at the time. Anyhow, I sat on the bank, admired his marvelous grey beard, and was interested in his devotion to fishing.

He was a well known Oregon pioneer, a captain of a wagon train in 1847, and an army officer in the Indian war brought on by the Whitman massacre. But he gained fame by his fiery and effective campaign to keep Oregon on the Union side just before the Civil War.

Strawberry Lake. This is one of the many beautiful mountain lakes in Oregon. As is the case with the better known Wallowa Lake, it fits cozily into a depression scooped out by a hard working glacier. This was way back when glaciers were rampant in Oregon and when the ice shoved the Columbia out of its bed and forced it to form Grand Coulee.

The lake is 6,300 feet high and covers 42 acres. Some of the largest rainbow trout available are taken from this lake every year. There is no access road to it, but many hundreds of campers and fishermen climb the truly steep path every year. It is high up near the top of Strawberry Mountain which towers over it to the south with a miniature glacier resting uneasily near the top, at about 9,000 feet. At least there used to be a small glacier there back when it snowed in the winter.

When the glacier came down and dug the lake bed, as with a giant spoon, it didn't bother to carry away all of the displaced rock and debris. As the ice melted, this material was piled up and formed a wide and deep dam on the mountain side. So Strawberry Lake has no visible outlet, although one can hear the water working its way down hill, below the jumbled rock surface. It emerges far down as Strawberry Creek.

Slide Lake and Little Slide Lake are also on the north slope of the mountain, as is Strawberry. They are reached only by mountain trails. Most visitors come in from the more popular Strawberry. The two Slide lakes are shallower and much smaller than their neighbor. They are about 1,000 feet higher though than Strawberry and the hike between them is not for those whose arteries are hardening by the minute.

In some ways *High Lake,* on the south side of Strawberry, is even more interesting. It is in a depression 7,500 feet in elevation, which is probably the remains of an old crater. The circular rim, high above the lake, has an opening on the southeast side, and Lake Creek burbles merrily out of it, on its way southward to the North Fork of the Malheur River, which flows into the Snake River near Ontario.

It is a shallow lake, full of Eastern Brook trout in such numbers that the State Game Commission allows a catch of 60 fish per day. This limit changes from year to year, but in 1960 that was the figure.

High Lake is a gem of the purest ray, only 10 acres in size. The mountains form an almost perpendicular back drop of sheer rock precipices in different colors. The old crater is well watered; is green with moss and water cress; gay with wild flowers; and birds, deer, and elk are fond of the place. Those who love isolation and unspoiled beauty should journey in from Seneca. The deer always seem surprised to see you and gaze at you curiously, as they might have looked at Lewis and Clark.

THE COMING OF THE SHEEP

Cattle came to the John Day Country first, but it wasn't long until flocks of sheep came ba-a-ing in, especially after Basques, Irish, and Scotch found the country. One man from Ireland for example, would get established with a band of sheep. He would then send back to the "ould country" for two or three "boys". These would be his herders for about five years, paid only enough for overalls and tobacco, because they were apprentices learning a trade. In time the owner gave each an interest in a band of sheep, so it would not be long until there were some new sheep owners in the county.

In those early days, a man paid no attention to rangeland. He homesteaded on some water course where it could be spread out to make a hay meadow. Why pay taxes on rangeland when it was all free?

As a result, the Irish and Basques especially, found that they could get hold of a band of sheep and by close knowledge of the country could trail them north in the summer, south in the winter, and thus could be big operators without owning an acre of land. These folks tended to be careless of the rights of others. How could they help it, if a big flock, several miles long, got under the fence and ate up the entire grain field of a struggling homesteader?

To add to the dismay, eastern commission companies were not long in finding this vast sea of sheep. Their men would meet the Irish and Basques, and with the smooth buyer it took only a quart or two of low grade whiskey to make a deal. The purchasers threw these flocks together into herds of 10,000 and trailed them clear to Omaha before the rails came, later to Utah, then to Idaho, and finally to Huntington, as the rails marched West. The herders would probably never pass that way

again, and carefully tended flower beds, young well loved
trees, and fields of hay were all left waste behind the
sheep. This could break a homesteader, forcing him into
the employ of cattlemen, his independence destroyed.
The fact that he would have failed anyhow didn't make
him feel better. He didn't know that yet.

A man named Pat Healy was one of these itinerant
sheepmen. He was Irish as they come, talking with a
sharp seriousness. In 1934, about at the end of the age
of itinerants, Pat was hired by Bob Thompson and
Harold Cohn of Heppner to take 3000 sheep to Pendleton. They were to pasture off some wheat, excess under
the new Agricultural Adjustment Act. The farmer gave
it to them because he wasn't allowed to sell it and was
about to disk it down. The sheep disappeared into this
tall wheat that would have made 50 bushels. I said to
the herder, "Pat, did you ever have your sheep in feed as
good as this?" He answered, "Ounly in the moonlight."
A whole story of an era is wrapped up there.

A sheepman in Wheeler County had four nearly
grown boys, all large enough to work. As lambing time
came, with its heavy labor demands, he asked his boys
if they couldn't arrange to be at home during lambing
and three of them always said they would, but they never
were. The other always said he wouldn't help with the
— — — — sheep at all. He didn't. One year the father
asked if he couldn't count on some help next month for
the lambing and the three said, "Sure! We'll be around."
The fourth said, "No, dad, I won't." The father said,
"Thank you, my son, thank you. You are the only one
I can depend on."

The cattlemen were beginning to get some idea of
conserving grass, so they attempted to reserve certain big
ranges for later use. When they tried it, invariably they
would find from one to a dozen sheep outfits on the
range, all the grass gone.

So feeling built up against the sheep owners. We had
both cattle and sheep on the Oliver ranch and never had
any trouble, though a few cattlemen looked at us for

awhile as though we were half-breeds—neither black nor white. We carefully instructed our herders to be careful of the rights of others and we quickly got rid of any who seemed arrogant.

But the time came when in desperation some of the cattlemen banded together, marked out cattle range and sheep range and warned all sheepmen out of cattle areas. They marked out driveways and warned herders to keep their sheep within those imaginary lines.

In our Bear Valley range a herder with sheep belonging to Parman of Condon, had been warned out of a certain glade and he paid no attention. One day, as he was trailing along behind the sheep, some unknown riders first shot his dog beside him. The herder was walking, leading a pack horse. On top of the pack was his galvanized bucket. They shot at that, riddling it. They were apparently good shots, because he didn't see anyone. He jumped behind a big pine tree. There was more shooting and at every shot a ewe would fall and die. When the shooting was all over, he came out and looked at the tree. On both sides the bark was in ribbons from bullets. They had pinned him down effectively.

A sheepman had a range adjoining ours. Father and I went to check our own sheep and had to go past the other's range. The sheep were all scattered, there were many killed, and there was no sign of a herder. We rode 40 miles to the owner's place to notify him. Two days later the herder showed up. He said he had been baking bread in a heavy iron Dutch oven. He leaned over with a wooden pot hook to lift off the pot cover. Just as he lifted it a bullet struck it and broke it into bits. He left.

There were many such incidents. They were not perpetrated by the responsible people, but by persons embittered, or by those who would just naturally operate outside the law. In Oregon thousands of sheep were slaughtered, a few men on each side were killed or maimed, and the legislature passed a law making it a special kind of felony to kill another man's sheep.

Two things stopped it; first the creation of the U. S. Forest Service, with resultant allocation of range, and second, the creation of the Bureau of Land Management to handle the public domain.

Charlie Burgess was a sheepman of Fossil, in Wheeler County to the west. He was something of a character. He came from Maine, stuttered noticeably, and had a soft voice, as though speaking confidentially. He had more education than most and his stammer, his manners, and his soft voice set him apart.

The cattlemen had a gunman hired to patrol the sheep driveway and direct the herders. Charlie was driving a flock through Bear Valley and he had just made camp. He had a fire going and I happened along just as the gunman rode up. Charlie, in his gentlemanly, cultured voice said, "Get off, you sh-sh-sh-sheep sh-sh-shooting s-s-s-son of a b-b-b— and I'll b-bake you some bread." This mixture of truculence and hospitality so confused the man that he got off and ate and never gave Charlie any trouble, then or later.

Charlie ranged most of his sheep in the isolated, steep, terribly rough breaks of the John Day southwest of Fossil 15 or 20 miles. No one went in there. But he had a neighbor who owned land there and another man noted Charlie's sheep on the neighbor's land. He found Charlie and said, "That's a hell of a note to run your sheep on his range when you know he's out of the county. You ought to be ashamed to return his friendship that way." Charlie replied softly, "It's n-not his f-f-f-friendship we're ahfter—it's his g-g-g-grahs."

The best herders seemed to be those who drew little or no money until the end of the year. They commanded higher wages than any other hired help, so had considerable money coming. These men then went to town, had a glorious fling. They were rich for awhile. They returned ready for another long year of following the sheep. I could never figure whether they thought it "easy come, easy go," or whether they needed the feeling of free spenders to bolster their egos.

I tried to talk one good intelligent herder into saving his money. The herder said, "If you followed a band of sheep all day every day for six months, looking at their hind ends, you'd be driven to drink, too."

Actually, a herder had to be more stable than other people. You entrusted to him property worth $10,000 to $20,000 and maybe didn't see him for months. If he were flighty, got drunk, or just walked off, you could lose that investment in no time to bears, coyotes, and bobcats. Very few employees can cause you such a loss if they are irresponsible.

I have found most herders honest, hard working, no respecters of hours, and they come to have an ingrained feeling of responsibility for the sheep. A loss reflects upon them personally, and a full count of heavy lambs gives them warm satisfaction worth more than money. Some of our herders stayed with us as long as they could travel. They grew old in the service and we took care of them as long as they lived. One man became disabled after working for 20 years and we took care of him for six years until he died. We had our own social security long before the government thought of it.

The sheep have now mostly disappeared from the range. As they have gone, deer and elk have replaced them. Every range country I know of is carrying less domestic livestock than at the turn of the century, but far more big game.

Deer were scarce in this country when I was a boy. Now a man can't do much riding on any of our ranges without seeing them by the dozens and in some places by the hundreds. This is nice for the sportsmen, but many ranchers are, in effect, paying from $1,000 to $10,-000 out of their pockets to support the deer and elk. That is, without the game animals they would be selling that much more meat. A time may come when the economy of the nation won't permit such lavishness. The pinch from the game isn't on the summer range—it's on the privately owned winter range. Most of our summer ranges would carry two or three times as many deer and elk, but in the winter they come down to the fenced fields, all private property. They can really hurt. I wonder how many of our sportsmen would be willing to put out thousands of dollars to pay for winter feed for game, as many ranchers do, by supplying three months pasture for hundreds of animals? Ranchers pay taxes, interest on mortgages, and keep up the fences on this land. The worst effect of the game on these ranges is that the deer and elk eat the grass into the ground in the early spring. In dry seasons it never recovers, thus ruining that particular range, maybe forever.

There are no better sportsmen than most of the livestock men. They love to have the game animals around and most of them are fine hunters, but an over-abundance of game presents problems and affects a man's financial position.

In another chapter I am suggesting a way for ranchers to get some income from the game.

Main Street, John Day, in 1911. Typical scene of the so-called horse-and-buggy days.

CHAPTER 4

A BOY IN GRANT COUNTY

It's a wonder that any children grow up. When I was little we didn't have modern perils, such as dishwashers, to scald us, autos to run over us, lawn mowers to maim us, but other things lay in wait to hurt, maim or kill us. Probably more things than now, because we were more active. Horses could toss a boy into the rocks or kick him in the face; cows could run their horns right through him; wagons could roll over him; sickles of mowers could chop his legs off; he could fall into cylinders of old style threshing machines. There were perils all around to worry mothers, much to the disgust of the boys. "Oh, ma! Don't be silly!" was heard then as often as now.

When I was two, I started down to the cellar where my oldest half brother Will was sorting apples. I fell and broke my left arm at the elbow. Doctors of the day often had poor equipment for diagnosis and were not specialists on everything. At any rate, the broken bones were not set right and that arm was always shorter than the other, and crooked. It bothered me a little all my life and still does. The arm tired easily and went to sleep if kept in one position. When I was 72 my left hand started to shrink and became numb. A Grant County boy, a skillful specialist, Doctor Roderick Begg, said the nerve was out of place—that the crooked arm had resulted in lifting the nerve out of its regular groove. He made a long incision following the nerve, moved the nerve over about two inches, and the arm is nearly normal again. So a fall as a baby took 70 years to cure.

Father had an exercise lot with some two-year old Galloway heifers with little calves. He was trying to make milk cows out of them. My dog and I started through the lot, just to save our valuable time as compared to going

In his later years, Joaquin Miller dramatized himself, as did Buffalo Bill, with Western trappings. While at John Day, as county judge, he looked like everyone else.

Canyon City band in 1880. Bill Kent, driver. At left famous old Episcopal church, built in 1876 and still in use.

More elaborate than most, this homestead log house was built in Silvies Valley. Picture about 1900. Left to right, Wallace Sheppard, Andy Pierce, John Hopper and one unknown.

David W. Jenkins, an early settler, built this fort to house Mt. Vernon, a prized black stallion, a locally famous trotting horse. The fort was for protection against Indians and thieves. In the Indian War of 1878, neighbors crowded into the stout little fortress, along with the horse. The town of Mt. Vernon, and the adjacent peak were both named for the horse.
Building still stands as shown.

Sheep came into Grant County with Scotch, Irish, Portuguese, and Spanish owners.
These are early day sheepmen.

Early day sheepherders, packed and ready to travel with the band to the mountains.

Freighting to the mines in Baker County. In more level terrain a 12-horse team could pull three or four wagons.

An authentic photo of the 20-mule team made famous by the Pacific Coast Borax Company. Shown is Mr. Nelson, later a farmer of Baker County. Driven by a single "jerk line" to the lead team. The 20-mule teams of the borax company started by hauling borax from southern Grant County (now part of Harney) to Winnemucca, Nevada.

around. From prehistoric days, when every cow had to fight off the wild wolves in the forests of Germany, our present day cows have inherited a deep ingrained instinct to keep dogs away from calves.

These young bovine mothers headed for the dog with the old instincts all aroused. The dog wanted no such fight, so he started for the fence. And I went that way, too, as fast as my bare feet could tick off the rods. The cows weren't after me especially, but I was between them and the dog. They overtook us right at the fence. The dog made it through but I didn't. I went down and I think every dog-hating young cow walked on me. Father saw the ruckus, came running, and grabbed me from under the forest of hoofs. I have since heard of others who were badly scared from such accidents. Father said I was pretty wet.

Another time my dog got me into cow trouble. I was walking through a bunch of horned Durham cows. My dog saw me from a distance, decided he wanted to be with me and ran right through the cows. One cow wouldn't have it that way, so started headlong for the dog. He saw her coming, headed for me as the nearest protection. As she was right on him, he didn't stop, but ran right by, brushing my leg. She was mad and wasn't particular what she attacked, so hit me, one horn going on each side of my body. It was a tight fit, and scratched me on both sides. An attentive hired hand rescued me.

My brother George, like George Washington, was a professional rock thrower. There was lots of raw material around our place, and I think every tree, fence post and bird was well stoned, even the cows, when father wasn't watching. George could throw far and with accuracy. I looked up to him as the best rock thrower I knew. He naturally pitched for the John Day ball teams. In those days schools had baseball throwing contests and George won with ease.

One day I was looking through a crack in the fence when George threw a rock at a cow in front of me but the animal moved and he missed. The rock passed neatly through the crack, hit me squarely between the eyes, and all interest in the scene stopped suddenly for me. George carried me to the house, 300 yards away. The skin was cut and my blood was flowing freely. He was a badly scared Oliver boy and father and mother didn't help him any by their remarks. His rock throwing tapered off for awhile.

I had a town boy friend named Tony Hupprich who came out to the ranch as often as his folks would let him. One day we were short of legal occupations, so with nothing in mind we gathered up a bucketful of old rusty discarded mowing machine sections. We sharpened them with care until each had a keen cutting edge, though too uneven for use in a mower. We then thought we'd have a contest. We'd throw them at something wooden and see who could stick the greater number into the wood. We chose a stepping block leading to the porch. This block was full of nails we boys had driven into it. Tony got the first throw, the section hit a nail, flew up and stuck in my forehead, near the same place the rock had hit me earlier in the year.

The two scars together made an H, for Herman. It was visible for many years. I told people they could remember my name by my brand.

Incidentally, Tony, a few years later, while working for a sheep man in Bear Valley, was killed by lightning. There were two unusual features of his death. He was carrying a lamb, which was uninjured. The bolt of lightning burned a black streak from the top of his head down his back, down each leg and out the bottoms of his shoes. The skin was broken on his head and feet where the lightning entered and emerged.

My brother George and I went to the hills one day to locate some sheep one of the herders had lost. We didn't find them right away, so went to the sheep camp, rustled up some food and sat down on a rock to discuss what to do next. George had a .32 pistol, the squirrels were running everywhere, so he began shooting at them. I was only 11 and had never shot a pistol. I asked him, nonchalantly as possible, if I could just shoot the damn thing once. He agreed, and in passing and cocking it at the same time, the hammer slipped from his thumb, it fired, and the bullet hit my foot.

I didn't feel much, but looked down and saw a hole in the top of the heavy cowhide boot, with its brass toe plate. George pulled the boot off and the bullet dropped out. It had gone through the boot and my foot, but its force was spent and it couldn't make it through the half-inch sole.

We looked around the camp for a bandage, but could find nothing but a bandana handkerchief and some dish cloths not too clean. We forgot the lost sheep, but tied the boot on the saddle and lit out for home, four miles away. On the way we had to pass over a rocky hill visible from the house half a mile distant. We usually walked at that place, because it was extremely rocky and the horses could pick their way better without the extra weight. This time I was riding but George was walking. Mother always looked for us and she sensed something was wrong when she saw me riding. She called father, and they came to meet us. Father caught a team, hurried me to the doctor, and I still carry the scar. A little thing like shooting through a foot didn't hold back a healthy boy much.

When young I thought a horse was to ride, and I rode wherever I wanted to go, often over badger holes, through the rocks, under tree boughs and through the brush. I suppose I have had hundreds of falls. I have had horses turn complete somersaults with me in the saddle at the start of the turn. I have been thrown from falling horses, have been rubbed off on trees, and have fallen in all kinds of terrain, but always seemed to land rolling, and usually didn't get anything worse than a skinned knee or a sore rib where it was stopped by a boulder.

Once, when 15, riding a real good cow horse, I was running a weaner calf that could go right along with the horse. It was early winter, there was a little snow and the ground was frozen. My stirrups were equipped with tapaderos. You don't see them much now. They cover the toe and hang down 16 inches below the stirrup. My horse's feet suddenly flew sidewise and he landed heavily on his side and slid about 30 feet with me still in the saddle, of course with one leg under the horse. The tapadero caught on a snag and turned my foot around, with the toe pointed backward. George was with me, ran up, whipped out his knife and cut my boot off. My foot turned back, but it hurt like sin, and I couldn't walk on it for awhile. An adult would have had a broken ankle, but young bones are pliable.

When I was six we had a gentle blue pony. One day I went to the hay field with father and the men. I couldn't do much there, so started home, about half a mile. I cut through a pasture and found Prince, the pony, just standing and thinking it over. I petted him and tried to get on, but he was too tall or my legs didn't have enough spring. I couldn't lead him to the rail fence, but I got the bright idea of taking a loose rail, laying one end on his back, and cooning up the rail. This worked well. When on top I kicked the rail loose, nudged the pony and he took me home. Father saw it, stopped the hay crew and they all watched.

Prince was worth more than all the new modern toys put together. We could climb all over him, three or four at a time, and he seemed pleased at all the attention. I first started to ride alone when three years old, but of course it had to be on a horse like Prince.

Later I fancied myself as a bronc buster. I worked at it earnestly and got bucked off a lot—never got hurt badly.

During the Boer War, British agents were here anxious to buy horses. They didn't want big animals, so cayuses 850 to 900 pounds suited them. The semi-wild horses that roamed the country suddenly had a market. The buyers would take them if the horses could be shown with someone on top. George, a man by the name of Thurman, and I did quite a business breaking the wild broncs and selling them. One of us would get our rope on the horse, a second would get hold of his ears and twist them to distract his attention, while the third bridled, saddled, and mounted. I was usually this third man. It was a good three-man operation.

I liked this kind of good clean fun, even if the wild horses didn't think much of it. I would stay on if I could, would run the horse some, and teach him to turn so that we could show him to the British.

My major accidents seemed to be concentrated in my youth, but I continued to have horses fall on me, and such things. In late life, I had one disturbance that might have left me with lilies on my chest. In Bear Valley a bull caught me with my back against a fence and he put his horn through me, just like sticking a hat pin into a cushion. His horn was about 14 inches long, and it tapered from a sharp point down to about three inches in diameter next to his head. The horn went into me just below the stomach, right through all the intestines, but by some good luck it ran between them, and did not puncture any. It broke one rib loose from my backbone. My whole insides could have run out, just like cleaning a deer.

Bear Valley is 40 miles from Prairie City, where the hospital was at the time. With me were Frank Oliver, Sam Keerins, Joe Oliver, and some of the hired men. One of them phoned the hospital and doctor, and I kept my insides inside with my dirty hands.

The bull's horn didn't come out my back, but it went clear in and I guess it would have gone through if I'd been a thin man.

The newspaper report sort of indicated that a person didn't recover after a bull had let so much daylight into him. I was full of splinters of old hay, corral sweepings and the like. Fortunately, the sulfa compounds had just come into use and Doctor Fate and Doctor van der Vlugt thought this would be a dandy time to see if the stuff was any good. They said they used two pounds of it liberally sprinkled over everything in sight. I was on the State Highway Commission at the time, they met once a month and I didn't miss a meeting.

Boys didn't get pampered much when I grew up. When 13 I batched at the Bear Valley camp, looked after 1200 sheep, and 300 head of range cattle. You grew up fast that way. No telephone, no one to ask. Nowadays people hire baby sitters to stay with children that age. I had charge of several thousands of dollars worth of property—and had to do my own cooking. It didn't hurt me. It's easier to make decisions in later life if you are forced to make them early. I feel sorry for boys growing up in town with no chance to learn, no way to develop resourcefulness, and no opportunity to work. In my opinion they are handicapped, as compared to a ranch raised boy.

Haystack in Bear Valley on Oliver ranch in a heavy snowfall year. At left is the pile of snow shoved away with bulldozer from around the stack to allow teams and sleds to get to the stack to haul the hay out to the stock. Dark spot on the right is haystack. Note depth of snow that had to be shoveled off before hay could be moved.

CHAPTER 5
READIN' AND WRITIN'

I went to our country school three months in the fall and three in the spring. Most years there wasn't any winter term; weather was too bad part of the time for the smaller boys and girls to walk several miles. There wasn't any high school around here until about 1904, and then in town grades up to the twelfth were gradually added to the grade school. Hardly anybody though, went that far. There was too much work to be done.

The schoolhouse was a little on the sketchy side; I doubt if it would have passed present minimum architectural standards. It seems there wasn't enough money to buy studding for the walls, so they sensibly let the boards on the walls hold up the roof. It was called "board and batten" construction, with a roof of locally hand-made 20-inch shakes. I notice now that many of the real fine homes are board and batten with shake roofs. It was sort of looked down on at that time. It was what you did when you didn't have enough money to buy studding and shingles. In time it had to be held up by pole braces on the side away from the wind.

The two outhouses were the same construction, except it was hurried a little and the snow blew in worse. This had an educational advantage. In the winter no student lost time from his studies by lingering out there in luxury. One or both outhouses blew over whenever a hard wind came along and this made an adventure for the user on windy days.

There was no woodshed, no stable for the horses, no porch, no dressing room for hanging overcoats and hats. There was a big stove in the back of the room. It took wood two feet long. It warmed the back of the room pretty well, but in cold weather it was chilly up front on the recitation bench. The blackboard was up there, too, and once in a while, if you couldn't do a problem very fast, you had to stop and blow on your fingers so they could grip the chalk.

I mentioned no porch. This was bad in stormy weather. We had no place to take off our overshoes except in the schoolhouse. But all around outside was a mile or two of stiff, black clay called "doby". The early settlers sometimes used it to make adobe chicken houses or other buildings. We didn't use it much to make dwelling houses, as they did in Arizona and the other states settled by the Spanish. We could have, though, because when it hardened it was like cement. When about 50 of us came into the schoolhouse in rainy weather and took off our overshoes, we created a floor inches deep in sticky mud. The teacher or the big boys were supposed to do the janitor work. No money was listed in the budget for janitorial services. But a broom had no effect upon this heavy mud. It just got the broom dirty. We all tramped over it and packed it flat. Then the heat of the stove baked it and by night we had an adobe floor. This wasn't too bad up to a point. All the schoolhouse doors opened in at that time, and it wasn't long until the floor built up until the door wouldn't open. We had to take an axe and chop the mud off the floor. The chopping had to be done a good many times during the year.

The seats were small beyond all reason. A big boy or girl could take a mortal dislike to education, just because it was hard to get into the seat. No telling what intellect was doomed to starvation because the student was squeezed into too small a seat. Because space was saved that way, two seats were made as one—each person had a pardner or seat mate. This seems of not much importance, but it introduced an element that could make or break a teacher.

We will say that Tom Bailey and Bill Brown appeared the first day of school and innocently asked to sit together. If the same size and in the same grade, that would appear to be perfect educational procedure, alphabetically and all. But perhaps that was about the worst thing that could happen outside of a skunk getting in. The combination could wreck the entire term of school.

So the teacher had to use all of his or her knowledge in seating the 50 pupils. Another thing to watch out for was the placement of girls with long hair in front of a boy with a long imagination. It is strictly unbelievable what a boy not interested in academic studies could do with a nice long braid right there in easy reach. Of course, it went into his ink bottle, but that was kid stuff. You could smuggle a bee into school and enmesh it in the hair. You could stealthily, but thoroughly, coat it with honey. You could catch a bottleful of ants and let them climb to freedom by putting a strand or two into the bottle. If there were two girls, and they were studious, you could tie their braids together to see what happened when one arose to go outside. There was no limit. We learned something each day.

The back of one seat was the front of the desk for the seat behind. This gave good chances for profitable entertainment. I hesitate to mention this, even now, but it takes only a moment to remove the eraser of a long pencil, run a good long pin through the rubber, replace the eraser, and have a weapon that can upset a peaceful school room. By hardly leaning over at all, this can be jabbed suddenly up through the rear crack in the seat ahead. If barefooted, the weapon, by gripping it with the toes, can be used while apparently reading a book.

Our recitation bench was 16 feet long and a marvel of simplicity and low cost. No taxpayer could complain. To make it, you needed two boards of that length, 20 inches wide, and another shorter board, same width. In case any present day school board wants to save money and copy it, you make it like this:

Nail the two long boards together at right angles as you would to start a trough. Cut two short lengths from the third board, each about four feet long. Nail these at the ends and you have a fine seat, 20 inches wide, with a nice comfortable back, 20 inches high, with a leg at each end. Now take another, still shorter piece and nail it underneath, for a third leg in the middle, to keep the seat from sagging. If you have a little time left, you can then nail a few blocks underneath, side of the legs, to keep them solid.

I think you can see that if the smaller children wanted to use the back, their short legs stuck out straight in front, allowing everyone to see any holes in their boot soles. If, though, they wanted their feet to hang down, then the back might as well not have been there. But this choice of front or back sitting *did* have a good and useful educational purpose.

Suppose, for example, third grade arithmetic had too many children to be seated normally in 16 feet. Would you, as teacher, tell the school board you needed another recitation bench? No, not if you were smart and wanted to be hired for next year. You alternated the class, one child with his back against the back of the seat with legs sticking out, the next child at the front with legs hanging down. You couldn't get twice as many on the bench that way, but 50 percent more wasn't too crowded.

Our blackboard wasn't the best. There wasn't much the teacher could do about it. It was made by nailing foot-wide boards parallel with the front wall, along the front of the schoolhouse, wall to wall, and painting them black. The only good thing about them was that they weren't shiny. They covered with chalk very soon and it had to be washed with soap to get it off. The eraser was a block of wood covered with sheepskin, wool side out. Washing of the blackboard wasn't practicable, so the children just wrote over it. You couldn't see the writing very far away. I suspect some children with poor eyesight always got poor grades just because they didn't have a chance to learn by watching the blackboard. My personal problem was that every time I put anything on the board, I ran into the crack between the boards.

The school board always contracted with someone, maybe a member of the board, to deliver enough cord wood, four feet long, to last the six months of schooling.

With no shed, this wood was piled at one side of the yard where it wouldn't interfere with play. On warm days most of the boys sat on the woodpile at noon to eat their lunches. Chipmunks made homes in it and they cleaned up the crumbs. There was no nonsense about kindling. Some farsighted teachers looked over the pile, picked out some pitchy pieces, saved them and put them under the schoolhouse for kindling. The girl teachers couldn't very well do that.

The stove, with its two-foot limit, meant that each four-foot piece had to be sawed in the center. When we had a girl teacher, all that was needed was a nice reminder, "Boys, we need some wood." It doesn't sound reasonable, but I can't remember a single time when the older boys didn't hop right out to get the wood in. To reduce the time, we took turns on the saw, so we would make it go like lightning. The wood box was full and extra wood was stacked around it in no time.

For one thing, we just naturally looked up to these young teachers with respect and admiration. They were always neat, were better educated than others in the community, wore becoming clothes, and some were downright pretty. The pretty ones usually didn't last long. They got married to some good looking young rancher or cowboy. It would be interesting to know what percent of eastern Oregon ranches were put on a sound basis when the owner married the school teacher.

If we had a man teacher, though, that was different. We figured that his big pay of $30 a month was ample to pay for wood cutting and carrying, as well as teaching us.

We had one man who taught two terms. He was lazy and would neither cut nor carry. He would break up even the most interesting game of ante-over or run-sheep-run by ordering us to get some wood. We finally rebelled. We figured that $30 was more than any of us had seen all at once; that it would pay for 20 pigs or four heifers;

and that in six months a feller could have enough to start a pretty good little cow herd. So he was getting big pay, let him cut his own wood!

I said he was lazy. Maybe he was stubborn, too, because in all the two terms he was there, he cut no wood. He would carry in the four-foot lengths and stick them in the stove, leaving the door open. As they burned, he would shove them back. At first he tried to stand them up, endways, so they would burn and settle down all by themselves—sort of a self-feeder. This didn't work, there was too much smoke. Even when put in from the front, occasionally, if the wind was wrong, it blew down the stovepipe, created a reverse draft, causing weepy eyes and coughing. The children of Marysville school district thus got some good training for the smog of modern living. Everything helps your education, if you look at it right.

Many came to school on horseback. The district was five miles wide, so some rode three miles. There was no shed. The horses stood by a hitching rack all day, which was pretty tough in wind, rain, or snow. My father wouldn't let us ride. He just simply couldn't think of having an animal stand out all day. Some brought a sack of hay tied behind the saddle, others didn't. Some horses had to do double, or occasionally triple, duty, with a child or two behind the saddle.

There were no thermos jugs or factory-made lunch boxes, at least not at the Marysville school. Lard pails, either half gallon or gallon, were universal. The gallon pails were big enough for two or more children.

In my case, mother made us put up our own lunches. If we were big enough to go to school, we were big enough to get some food into a bucket. Many mornings we had beefsteak for breakfast, which I still like. On those mornings, I would take a nice big piece of steak, wrap it in paper to keep the bucket clean, and that was my sole lunch. No nonsense about a balanced ration.

I always seemed to have a lot to do on the way to school, what with running races, climbing trees to look at bird nests, throwing stones at squirrels, and such important and necessary jobs. The lard bucket was in my way something awful. If I set it down to climb a tree, likely as not I'd run on and have to go back a mile for it. So on mornings when mother made her famous sourdough biscuits, I'd grab two of those, put some jelly inside, wrap them, and stuff one in each pocket. I wasn't bothered with a bucket in that way. This wasn't such a skimpy lunch as you might think, if you've had nothing in your life but the little play biscuits that seem fashionable—one of mother's biscuits "would stick to your ribs" pretty good.

The drinking water, or the infrequent scrub water for the floor, came from a swift-flowing little creek about 300 yards away. The school owned a nice three-gallon bucket with a strong bale. Usually two of the bigger boys went for water. Coming back there was a boy on each side and it was a matter of pride to get back with the water clear to the top. This was usually done in school hours. The boys who arrived with it only half full couldn't go anymore. Especially in the spring when birds were singing and squirrels running, this was a powerful incentive to get back with a full pail. Of course, we all drank from the same dipper. This creek had willows along the bank and they were used by the teacher for educational purposes, too.

Personally, I was barely school caliber. I had keen eyes and saw things all around me outdoors. But the books were all so much trash for me, with one exception. I liked and understood arithmetic and could beat many of the boys several grades ahead of me. I could see that arithmetic was necessary to figure weights of cattle, prices of wool, and tons of hay in a stack. For all the rest of it— I could see no use whatever for learning the date of the Battle of Gettysburg or when to use who or whom. I still don't know. Neither did I care a hoot where Mozambique was. I kept on and passed the eighth grade only because father and mother insisted. Each day I'd break out of school as though it were a prison. I would run and jump and even roll on the ground like a horse that has been kept in the stable too long. I learned far more going to and coming from school than I ever did inside.

This was a personal defect, not the fault of the school. These primitive schools, such as ours, graduated boys and girls who more than held their own if they went to college. For one thing, their schooling may not have been wide, but it was deep if they tried. They learned mostly readin' writin' and 'rithmetic, but they learned it or they didn't pass. You could see big boys, almost old enough to vote, still struggling along with little fourth graders. So, if they ever got past the twelfth grade and into college, they knew the fundamentals and could concentrate. A boy or girl who gets his schoolings in an open room with 50 other children in 49 kinds of devilment, just *has* to learn to concentrate. Nowadays we see plenty of high school graduates who are hopeless in college because they can neither read, write, figure, nor spell. Many just can't concentrate, either. What can such a boy do with a subject like chemistry? And we can't even be very proud of some of the college graduates.

Our early day teachers were seldom college trained, as is required now. Many of the girls got about as far as the tenth grade, then started to teach. Here is the astonishing thing. They were *good* teachers! Some were extraordinary teachers. They would still be good teachers now. Some teachers feel they are forced to spend too much time acting as collection agencies for drives; organizing PTA meetings; arranging for dental schools, drivers lessons, and the like. More of this type of work should be done by parents, leaving more time for the teachers to do instructional work.

This makes me wonder if all of the set educational courses for teachers are necessary or if any of them are.

I don't believe you can learn out of a book how to teach, any more than you can learn from a book how to ride a horse. Unless it is purely by accident, there isn't a teacher at the University of Oregon, or Oregon State College, who could legally teach in an Oregon high school or even a grade school. Einstein himself couldn't legally teach mathematics and President Eisenhower couldn't legally teach history or government in a grade school in Oregon. Neither of them had this maze of required educational courses. If you want a history teacher, for example, it seems to me the school board should look for someone who knows about history. As it is, they are forced to take someone who has enough credits in educational psychology, whatever that is.

Some persons have the qualities needed to be good teachers and others do not, and no amount of schooling is going to help the latter class. Some wonderful teachers would be ridiculous as ranchers, just as many ranchers would catch their foot in the stirrup the first day if they tried to teach. A teacher, if good, has certain qualities not taught in schools. Such qualities can't be taught, they are inherited, or else come from home training.

In fact, education starts at home. College teachers have told me that, by watching a little, they can grade the homes quite accurately, of all the students they meet. The home training is the part that is in the fiber and forms the life and character of the child.

The father who scoffs at the law is amazed when his son breaks it. The shrieking mother, delivering blows right and left, is bewildered when her teenage daughter runs away with the village hot-rod boy. The home, good or bad, determines the life of each of us. The girl or boy raised in a good home where understanding of others is an ingrained thing, is likely to be a good teacher. The child with greedy, stupid, selfish parents is likely to be a poor teacher, no matter how many courses in education are crammed into his or her head with the sole purpose of qualifying for a job.

I suspect some day we will be smart enough to watch our youngsters, assess their characteristics, assay their attitudes and see what they "run to the ton". Maybe then we can know whether they have gold, silver, copper or fool's gold in them. Then maybe we can pick out teachers that can teach, rather than just those that have taken so many credits called "education". I don't believe these courses have much to do with teaching.

The medical profession won't let you operate unless you have been through medical school; the lawyers say you can't take money for legal advice or practice in the courts unless you go to law school or the equivalent; so the professional teacher groups have tried to up-grade their profession in a similar way. They try to make people believe that teaching ability depends upon taking certain courses.

I have regretted my lack of schooling thousands of times. My grammar is slightly worse than awful; my spelling is ghastly; I have lost out on history and literature. I have advised many boys and girls to go to high school and college and have helped some to do so. Every youngster I have helped is making good use of his education and is a good citizen. No one respects schooling more than I do. The person without it is terribly handicapped.

But here is a point that I haven't seen discussed much. There is a big, big gulf between education and schooling. Many of my friends are well educated. Some of them have practically no schooling. I think the distinction is important, but it gets little or no attention.

For any job I can think of, I'd rather have a man who keeps on educating himself, no matter what his schooling is, than a man who is well schooled, but who stops growing when he gets a degree. The latter man is worth less at 40 than at 20 and is almost worthless by 50. The former keeps growing and is worth more each succeeding year.

In my own case, I have little schooling, but I have tried to learn from every person I met. You can learn important things every day of your life. I have learned from the cows, sheep, and horses; from the grass, soil, and birds; and even from the wild animals. I think I have learned some things, outside of my ranching career.

I can usually spot a crook quickly; I generally know whom to trust; I am not often fooled by a glib talker. In the field of economics I know far better than many of our well-schooled congressmen that you can't invent money; it all comes from our own pockets. I know that it is the rankest kind of foolishness to get money from Washington for something we can pay for at home. They take our money and only send back part of it. I know that we can stand some inflation, but not too much and not too fast.

So, although my respect for schooling is boundless, I don't mix it up with education, and I don't *always* look up to the well-schooled man. He can, just possibly, be woefully short on education. He may believe in economic fairies. When he is a politician he may be deliberately prostituting his knowledge for the sake of votes. Such people fool themselves with an odd philosophy. They know they are lying, they know they are guilty of a degrading demagoguery, but they argue to themselves, "My overall effect is good, so I'll lie and I'll fool people because unless I do that, I can't get elected." A man who continues this long enough is eventually unable to tell right from wrong and wanders in a moral quagmire close to crookedness.

I have seen young people graduate from college feeling they were well prepared for life. Actually, their education is just beginning.

No taxpayer in Oregon that I know of regrets spending money for schools—providing it is well spent. But if his own children reach high school age and cannot read clearly; if they cannot, to save their lives, write a clear, logical sentence; if they find it impossible to concentrate; then he wonders. He may find, to his utter dismay, that study and learning are treated with contempt by the students in that school. The real student isn't respected by the others.

You can then be sure that not many from that school can succeed in college. They don't know the fundamentals.

We have all seen football coaches who were smart, up-to-date, and industrious. They had studied the game well and taught their squads a large assortment of tricky, intricate plays. But when the teams played their first games, it developed that in their coachs' zeal for modernity, they had completely forgotten to teach how to block surely and tackle cleanly. Some little old squad from somewhere that knew no fancy plays beat them 50 to 0. In the same way some of our teachers are great on educational psychology, real weak on arithmetic.

In conclusion, I'll state again that my lack of schooling has been a sore and painful thing for me all my life. Perhaps, as some have told me, I feel the lack in me more than my friends and associates do. They can't help but notice my poor grammar, but maybe it doesn't distress them the way it does me. If there is a germ of truth in something I say or write, maybe they are more interested in that than in the poor package the germ is wrapped in. I hope that is the case. I could feel better if I knew for sure.

Chapter 6

STAGE COACH AND JERK LINE

In 1862, when gold was the magnet that drew men irresistably to Canyon Creek, the thousands who came overnight called their bonanza city "Whiskey Flat". It was just south of the present town of Canyon City and the area is still known as Whiskey Gulch. This word "gulch" is used only where miners gather. In other parts of America, a gulch may be called arroyo, canyon, coulee, run, gorge, valley, or gulley. These names describe slightly different shapes of V-shaped depressions, but in a mining country, they are all "gulches".

Swift-running Canyon Creek tumbles down from the mountains to the south. One of these is called Canyon Mountain. There isn't much gold south of this mountain —at least, it hasn't been found. From where the gold was first picked up, it is only about two miles on north along the creek to where it enters the John Day, but in this stretch of narrow, steep-walled canyon, there were 5000 miners at one time. The original name of Canyon City was Canon, with a curly mark over the first n, Spanish style. In this three-mile stretch $20,000,000 of the attractive metal went into the buckskin pokes of the miners, and $6,000,000 more came from other gulches.

Canyon City and John Day are practically one town now, with a combined population of 2075 and probably 500 more in suburbs. John Day, at the lower end of Canyon Creek, was originally "Lower Town," to distinguish it from Canon City, up the creek two miles. It was also called "Tiger Town".

My father, Joe, came by boat to The Dalles, but walked the 200 miles to Canyon City. That was all right for an unattached man, but you couldn't carry a cook stove with you, or iron pipe for placer mining. So some other transport was needed. The first, of course, was horseback. Almost at once came the mule pack-trains.

Here was a little two-mile stretch of narrow canyon with a rushing stream down the bottom and 5000 men working from morning to night along that creek. It was one of the largest towns in Oregon then. They had no supplies and everyone was too busy to go and get any. They were making all the way from $10 a day up to $2000, and they couldn't bother with little things like flour and bacon.

But where there is a market for anything, from a needle to a haystack, some enterprising American is going to try for a profit. So J. J. Cozart arrived with a string of pack mules from The Dalles, laden with such diverse things as wheelbarrows, nails, rope, pickaxes, dynamite, beans, flour, saleratus, soap, lard, bacon, shoes, shovels, and shirts.

The pack strings had their heyday from 1862 to about 1885. They didn't come to Canyon City all that time, because a road was soon built and roads doomed the pack outfits. But all through Grant and Baker Counties there were isolated gulches where wagons couldn't go; and there were hundreds of similar places high up in the mountains of Idaho, Montana, and British Columbia. The sturdy little mule saved the day for thousands of miners way out in the ginsengs. This animal "with no pride of ancestry, nor hope of posterity," should have some statues in his honor. He built our western railroads, he fought in our wars, he carried the ammunition that subdued the Indians, but above all, he threaded his surefooted way along every narrow, rocky trail that led to a mine. He should be beatified as the patron saint of all miners.

A good mule in those days was worth $200, even up to $300, if some miner, the night before, had heard of a new strike in Idaho or British Columbia, and he wanted to be among the first to pick up the big nuggets there where you could fill a wheelbarrow with them in no time. It was a little slow going if you had no mule and you wanted to take your wheelbarrow along.

An experienced packer could handle 20 well-trained mules—about 15 if they weren't accustomed to the plan. These pack outfits came up here originally from Mexico and at first the muleskinners were mostly Mexicans. Even now the rigging carries Spanish names such as alforjus, and aparejo. By the way, nearly all English words starting with "al" originated in Persia and came to us by way of Spain and Mexico. Such words as alcohol, alfalfa, and albacore.

The pack trains usually went in units of 20 mules. If there were two men, there were 40 mules; if one man, 20 mules. But if they went past 40, there was always a cook, who rode a grey bell mare. The mules were turned out at night, but they learned to follow the bell mare and each came and stood side of his outfit in the morning, for packing. The packers became incredibly skillful and swift in packing and throwing the diamond hitch.

This complicated hitch, tied with one rope, forms a large diamond on the top of the pack and was real useful to most of the early stockmen. We used it a great deal when we had sheep and every herder had to learn it. I said it was complicated. It isn't really, but it's hard to learn by just watching. You have to actually tie it or you neglect a certain twist and the whole pack tumbles off before you get off the camp ground.

I knew the first packer to Canyon City quite well, J. J. Cozart. He is mentioned in the horse chapter of this story. He afterward lived south of Prairie City about five miles and devoted his life to raising trotting horses.

Before the stagecoach pushed him aside, our county knew the sight of the pony express rider. Western stories are full of him and he was a dashing figure, all right. But he wasn't economical. If one man can drive a Concord stage with eight passengers and 600 pounds of mail and express, it stands to reason that you can get more done that way than to put him on a single horse that can't carry much more than the man. So the pony express rider, with his $1.00 per letter charge, didn't stay around long, only from 1862 to 1864, in our case.

In 1864 the U. S. Government contracted with H. H. Wheeler to carry the mail between The Dalles and Canyon City. It was pretty tough. The Concord stage climbed up the long rocky slopes of Wasco County to the top of Tygh Ridge, then dropped steeply down to White River. The route followed down this rocky canyon to Sherar's bridge, Todd's bridge at first, where the driver paid a toll, and went south past Burnt Ranch to Mitchell, thence across to the John Day River and on to Canyon City.

This stage driving had the pony express beaten all hollow for adventure and everything else. Not too many people are left who ever rode a four- or six-horse stage. I have, and life isn't the same since. For one thing, the driver was King. He was an important man and he knew it. He was as much in command as a captain on his ship. While you were on his stage, if you were halfway smart, you offered no advice. If stuck in the mud, he decided how to get out, and if he ordered you to grab a hind wheel and help to roll it, you did that, no matter whether you owned a bank or a bedroll.

If a storm came up, the river rose in wild flood, and the bridge was out, he decided whether to try to ford or not. If you felt it too dangerous, you sat still, never mentioning such an unimportant idea. Or if you *had* to get through that day or lose a fortune, and he decided to stay there until the creek went down, you went over the hill and out of hearing if you just had to say something.

The stages usually made around 15 miles before changing horses, give or take five miles. The regular stops where the horses were kept, had to have water and some of them had to have eating and sleeping accommodations for passengers. So the distance between stops was regulated by water and terrain. Some customers would ride right through, but others couldn't stand more than 75 or 80 miles in a coach, traveling over what amounted to no road at all, so they would lay over until the next day. The stops were mostly at farm houses and the food was usually good and always plentiful. There are a number of these old stage stop farm houses still standing around Oregon.

As the placer and quartz mines developed and ranches, such as father's, grew and began to demand things, another form of transportation grew up—freighting. Machinery, stock salt, fencing for farms; pianos, windows, doors, and bricks for the farm houses; pipe, hoists, hand carts, and small rails for the mines—these things didn't work too well on pack horses.

These commercial freighting outfits ranged from six horses and two wagons, up to eight- and twelve-horse teams with three or four wagons—one man to an outfit and the lead wagon trailing the others. The size of wagon was indicated by the axle measurement, usually 3½ to 3¾ inch. The trip to The Dalles and back took three to four weeks, depending upon weather, size of outfit, and cargo.

The six-horse outfits had a lead team, swing, and wheelers. The eight-horse teams were called lead, point, swing, and wheelers. The lead team was usually the lightest, the wheel team the heaviest. The lead horses were alert, smart, quick to learn, and quick to follow a voice command. They were out of reach of the whip, so had to keep their trace chains tight just because they wanted to.

The swing teams weren't so important. On our own place, if we wanted to sell some unbroken horses, we would match up a pair for size and disposition, and give them to a freighter. The way they were hitched into one of these outfits, they couldn't do much except go along with the general idea. Each horse had two ropes. One rope led from the halter to the "stretchers" of the team in front. The other rope led to the hame ring of his mate. If a horse lagged back, the lead team pulled him right up into position. He couldn't charge ahead very well, or he would be pulling more than his share, and his own mate kept him in the team. So by the time the freighter was back to John Day, our team was well broken and we could offer them for sale as such.

For our own ranch use, though, we broke our own horses. We wanted them to know other things than the freighters taught them on the road, including a different vocabulary.

Each freight outfit had a set of bells. The bells were clear and loud and fastened to a flat, horseshoe-shaped piece of steel, which in turn was fastened on the hames of the lead team. There were eight to twelve bells in each set.

The bells had two main purposes. The first was to alert an approaching teamster. Roads were narrow then, almost entirely single track. If two of these big freight teams met on a long hill, there was trouble. One might have to back a great distance and that isn't simple with several wagons. One might even have to unhitch. In cases where the drivers heard the bells of another team, each would stop and walk ahead, look over the terrain and decide just how to proceed. There was seldom any trouble about this, because "rules of the road" grew up, based upon courtesy and good sense, and an unreasonable driver was breeding a scab on his nose. Too bad that modern law doesn't sanction this same method of teaching courtesy among auto drivers.

The second bell purpose was to warn the other horses in the team. The lead team had to move first, so as their traces tightened, their bells rang, alerting the others. A good teamster, about to start, usually called the names of all his horses, naming the lead horses first, and on back to the wheelers.

After calling the names in order, the horses tightened up their tugs, and when he yelled, "All ready, boys— let's go!" the wheels slowly started to turn. The horses learned pretty quickly that a heavy load starts slowly, so they leaned into their collars, putting increasing weight on the doubletrees until they could feel the wheels start to move. They moved cautiously at first, keeping a strong steady pull, and as the wheels rolled faster, the horses moved faster, too, until the normal speed was attained, when they all stepped out. A horse that plunged ahead could easily hurt his shoulder.

The pointers were hitched to the end of the tongue and were helpful to the wheelers when they learned their business. In rounding a sharp turn or in dodging a badger hole or a rock, the driver would tighten their reins a little, and they soon learned what that meant. A sharp hairpin turn with a long team meant some clever work, both of the driver and the team. The lead horses might have to be put clear off the road to keep the rear wagon from running off the road on the other side. If that side happened to be rock cliff, or a steep down-slope, results could be disastrous. Drivers of the long truck and trailer outfits now have the same trouble when they get off the highway onto a single track road.

The old teamster terms crept into our language and are still used. "Jones is a good wheel horse" means he will work on a Chamber of Commerce or lodge commit-tee. "Keep things rolling" is used by a generation that never saw a wagon wheel except in an antique shop. And there are others not nearly so genteel.

The wheel-horses were always the largest and the most dependable pullers. They were the ones a driver depended upon to keep from getting stuck in the mud. They knew how to get down close to the ground so as to deliver more power, and when the driver yelled, "Now, George—Jim, do your stuff!" it was a pleasure to watch a good team pull.

Drivers had to pull out of the road in the spring to get around bad mud holes, but experienced drivers learned that water in the road usually meant a solid foot-ing beneath, whereas a soft oozy surface often meant bot-tomless mud. A teamster who got mired and had to get another man to stop, unhitch, and "double-team" to pull him out, had to set 'em up for all the teamsters on the road at the next "gallon house".

Another sort of teamster was known as "the long line skinner," or jerk-line, as they came to be called. He rode a wheel-horse and guided the long line of horses with a single line fastened to the bit of the lead horse. The driver would shout "gee" or "haw" and give the appropriate jerk.* The jerk-line developed when, for some jobs such as the famous 20-mule team borax hauling, drivers began to expand and string out their teams far past the 4, 6, or 8 horse outfits. In Oregon these long teams were used mainly for wheat hauling in the Columbia Basin, but in a few cases were used for long wool hauls, and in Baker County for hauling supplies to mines.

Most of the freighting in our part of central Oregon was done with six lines, six horses, and two wagons. The long strings of wagons weren't practicable in the mountains, though all right on the desert. I never used more than six horses, but my freighting was mainly short hauls. It was far more satisfying to drive six well-trained horses than to drive a loaded truck. I don't know any finer feeling than to take two loaded wagons around a hard turn, with rocks and chuck holes to be avoided. Truck driving takes some skill, but it's hard to train a truck.

The wagons were mostly Bain, Moline, or Studebaker. I always wondered about the paint, it lasted so well. You'd see an old wagon that had been left out in the sun and storms all its life and the paint was still good enough to read the name. Every store then sold "carriage paint" but I don't believe that was the same as the durable wagon paint.

Each wagon box had, on its front, a "jockey box". The glove box on cars is probably a descendent. The box was sturdy with a cover that lifted straight up, and when closed, the top sloped, so as to run the water off and keep the inside dry. The jockey box held a brush and curry comb, a horse-shoeing outfit, a can of axle grease, some horseshoe nails, and a few extra harness rivets, pieces of stout leather and buckskin for repairing harness. It might hold a pint of whiskey, especially

---

* "Gee" is right, "haw" is left; a jerk meant to turn right, a steady pull, to turn left.

in dusty weather, but little drinking was done during the day. "Do not drink when driving" isn't a new term, by any means. You needed all your faculties on the roads of those days.

The horseshoeing equipment was important. Sometimes a horse in the rear would step on the projecting heel of the shoe of the horse in front, and wrench the shoe off. Or the edge of the shoe would catch on a piece of rock. Or a shoe would get worn out. In any case, these freight horses *must* be kept shod. The roads then just went over the lava rock that is everywhere in eastern Oregon. It was tough going and would wear out a man's shoes in short order. Without a shoe a horse was lame in no time.

The driver had to be an expert horseshoer. He usually carried a piece of iron to use as an anvil, but sometimes he just used the tire of the nearest wagon. Most of the shoes had to be shaped more or less for each horse.

A coal oil lantern was fairly necessary, because camps were made after dark, or horses got to kicking in the night. A bucket was real necessary for watering the horses from some small spring. Without it the whole team had to be unhitched. Lantern and bucket usually hung on the side of the lead wagon. A pole axe was fastened with buckskin or rawhide to the side of the wagon box. Such an axe could be used for chopping wood, cutting out fallen trees, or in the winter, chopping through the ice, while the other end was useful for a hundred things— driving picket pins, pounding bent irons, driving stakes, pounding wagon tires into place. It was a combination axe, hammer, and sledge.

With a three-wagon outfit, there were twelve wheels that, in the summer, had to be greased about every 50 miles. The fine lava dust was pretty bad and was probably the single worst thing about freighting. Each wheel had to be taken off for greasing, and that required a heavy screw jack to lift the wheel free of the ground and take the load weight off. The wrench used to loosen the big square burr that held the wheel on the axle did double duty in holding the doubletrees. It was a ¾-inch piece of iron about a foot long with a U-shaped jaw welded to the top. It was known as the "wagon hammer." This jaw fit on the square burr, and the weight of the driver on the handle would start the burr off. The threads on the axle were always such that to take the burrs off, you had to turn them toward the back, otherwise the forward movement of the wagon might turn the burrs and let the wheel come off. The screw jack had its permanent home on a sort of shelf or projection on the outside of the wagon box, with a strap to fasten it.

The chuck block was a 14-inch long piece of wood split in a wedge-shape so the thick part would be ten inches wide, and the chisel-end would be in front, just back of the rear wheel. The front end had an old horseshoe fastened on it to prevent wear and allow attachment of a chain. The other end of the chain was fastened to the wagon. This dragged the chuck block about six inches behind the wheel, the chisel-edge always in front.

These blocks served as an automatic aid when it seemed best to give the horses a rest on a steep hill. The wagons would roll back a few inches and come to a stop at the blocks. The horses could then let up on the tugs, taking the weight off their shoulders. The driver usually put the brakes on at the same time as the wheels hit the blocks, so there would be no danger of the wheels running back over the blocks. Every automobile driver knows that if he stops on a steep hill, there is a little difficulty in starting. If he takes the brake off too quickly, the car starts backward; if he takes it off too slowly, the car pulls against the brakes for a moment. The chuck blocks got around that. They held the wagons so the brakes could be released, and there was never any trouble of pulling uselessly against the brakes. In this one thing the autos and trucks are inferior to the old wagons.

Most of the wagons had a wagon sheet, just like the covered wagons on the Oregon Trail. This went over the bows and fastened securely on the sides to protect the cargo. In hauling ore, or other weatherproof cargo, the bows were taken off, but the driver usually carried the wagon sheet anyhow. It made a tent of sorts if a man had to stop in stormy weather.

Last of all was the bedroll and grub box. The latter was a little on the skimpy side. The driver's menu was simple and bordered on monotony. His dishes were down to an irreducible minimum. They consisted of a fry pan, a tin coffee pot and maybe a kettle. Some ate nothing but fried food and ate it right out of the fry pan. Others took a couple of tin plates. A knife, fork, spoon, and a tin cup completed the elaborate arrangements. For food there was a good chunk of sow belly, some flour, baking powder, coffee, sugar, salt, potatoes, can of molasses, and some real Mexican beans, or Harney strawberries, as they were called. The driver made fry pan bread, fried the bacon and potatoes, and if he had lots of time, he might make gravy out of the bacon fat and flour. This was pretty good on the bread.

If he had a day or two to spare, due to a sick horse, a strayed team, horses to be shod, a broken axle, or a "spell of weather" that made a creek too high to cross, he had use for the kettle I mentioned, the beans, and the molasses. He'd boil up a kettleful, and after ten days of a single kind of diet, those beans were better than anything you can find nowadays in a restaurant for $7.50. I don't remember of hearing any of these professional freighters mention calories or even balanced diets.

At first the outgoing freight from the John Day was mostly wool. The livestock walked to market, which might be quite a jaunt. Before the railroad, horses, steers, and sheep all walked to the mid-west, or sometimes to Montana or Wyoming. Grant County stock was driven farther and over a tougher country, including mountains, lava rock, and desert, than the Texas cattle.

Grant County cattle drives were mostly around 2000 head, but sheep went in bands up to 6000 or more. Horse herds tended to get out of hand if you had over 1000.

The incoming freight included everything you can think of, including grand pianos and big kitchen ranges.

When the railroad finally reached Baker, and later a branch line was built to Shaniko, the routes changed to those towns. Later, the Sumpter Valley road was built, a narrow gauge line, first to the town of Sumpter, and about 1910 over Dixie Mountain to Prairie City. The south end of the county, Bear and Silvies Valley, still had long hauls, but eventually a logging road was built to Seneca, and it carried out the livestock and wool to Burns, thence to the main U. P. line at Ontario.

With progressively shorter hauls, the old dependable wagons rolled out the freight for 60 years, because trucks didn't take over until improved roads made it possible for them to run, about 1920.

The story of the mails is somewhat the story of the other transport. First pony express, then Concord stage. First to The Dalles, later to Baker. The mail didn't all stop at Canyon City, it went on to Burns. The mail ran south to Burns and onward to McDermitt, Nevada, a "fur piece" of 275 miles. I was well acquainted with one of the first of these carriers, Frank McBean. He rode a horse and led one or more pack horses. He had a camp outfit and stopped wherever night caught up. In time, McDermitt got its mail from another direction, so Burns was the terminal for years.

The stages, of course, were running all this time in every direction. The drivers worked 8 to 10 hours. In the winter, they sometimes used sleighs all the way from Baker to Burns, 150 miles. In other winters they had to change from sleigh to wheels and back to sleighs, making three or more changes on the trip, of course changing luggage, express, mail, and all each time.

The stage moved around the clock, because mail and express was where the money came from. Passengers were secondary, and often stayed overnight at one of the stops, uanble to "take 'er" more than a few hours at a time. The drivers were tough hombres and gloried in it. They sat right out in the wind and storm and wouldn't trade jobs with anyone on earth. In 40 below weather, facing a stiff wind, they resembled a bundle of clothes more than men. Then the hostler at each station would have a hot rock, wrapped in burlap, to put at the driver's feet. The passengers' lot was better—at least they were out of the wind. They also had hot rocks to keep feet from freezing, and usually some robes to cover their legs. The stages rocked frightfully on the rough roads and this constant pitching from side to side was tough on tender ribs and elbows. The motion roughly paralleled a storm at sea. Effect on the stomach was the same. In good weather, many passengers preferred to ride outside, particularly if there was a sea sick sufferer inside.

Drivers were cranks about their horses. A hostler who failed to curry and blanket a hot team was spoken to in fire and brimstone words. Horses and harness went together, so the changing of horses would take less time, and the hostlers were expert at having the new teams ready, getting the tired team off and the new team on— all in a matter of a minute or two. In cases I have seen, the stage would arrive and be off again in about the time the reader will take in reading this paragraph.

The driver prized his whip beyond anything else. Besides, it was bad luck to let anyone else touch or handle it. The whip stock was about 4½ feet long and the lash nine or ten feet. The drivers bragged of their ability to pick a horsefly off a leader without the horse feeling a thing. At the end of the lash was a silk popper that snapped like a firecracker. The drivers beeswaxed the lash at every division and usually kept their whips with them. They were hung on a wall with the heavy end down.

The stage roads were narrow, one way affairs, and the singletrees often scraped the trees at the side. As snow piled up on Dixie Mountain, it packed under the wheels and the sleigh runners, raising the road higher and higher. Next spring a person could tell the depth of the snow by the height on the trees where the single-

trees had barked them. In my time, one winter produced
marks twelve feet off the ground on the trees on Dixie
Mountain.

No one can foresee the future; maybe the next change
in transportation of freight will be to the air. Then I
suppose persons of that day will speak regretfully of the
romantic old truck days and the colorful truck drivers.

Hauling wool into Vale, Oregon, before the railroad came. Three wagons pulled by 10
horses driven by jerk line. The driver, in this case, Charlie Cranmer (standing in front
of team), rode the left wheel horse. Saddle is barely visible over the back of the
"wrango" horse, which followed along loose. At night the team horses were turned out
to feed, but the "wrango" horse was kept tied to be available for rounding up the
teams. Horses were fed oats from nose bags and watered from buckets when on the
road. Photo supplied by Denny Jones, Juntura, who says this is the largest load of wool
hauled into Vale. Each bag weighed 350 lbs. Usually they were loaded with the first
tier lengthwise (not visible), balance across.

In early days the "drummer" often had his own stage outfit with four good horses. He kept local merchants informed about styles, brought in news, was often a gay blade and a free spender. Shown is Jake Jacobsen who headquartered at The Dalles. There was a "drummers table" in every hotel where meals were 50 cents instead of the regular 35.

An old timer left over on an eastern Oregon ranch. These were used up to 1920 in many places. They creaked, groaned, and rattled, but for 60 years they carried both in-bound and out-bound freight in Oregon's interior.

Changing from sleigh to hack on the stage line to Burns.

Stage from "Ma Austin's" place near present town of Bates, enroute to Canyon City. Page 191.

out for whittling, sitting on the top of an old worm fence. y meadow in background, the Blue Mountains beyond.

Herman and Eliza in the garden.

A little cowboy, J. C., son of Joe, getting some pointers from a bigger cowboy. J. C., shown here, is the third generation of Olivers named Joseph Cayton.

Here Herman is teaching Anna the bookkeeping job, done for many years by Eliza. Herman felt that no business could be successful without a set of books that would measure the effect on the business of everything that was done. Even now, a minute's inspection will tell the profit in every year back to 1878. The paper weight is an old ox shoe.

Joe Oliver, nephew of Herman, is one of the leading young cattlemen of Oregon. His big growthy cattle; their fine conformation; and the similarity of his calves in weight and age, delight the eye of a stockman. Shown are some two-year old heifers and calves. Here's one of the typical ranch horses, carrying the A2 brand on the stifle.

CHAPTER 7

PUTTING A RANCH TOGETHER

When George died, leaving father, Frank, and me as
equal partners, we decided upon a policy. Each of us
could write checks, but we agreed to write none except
for business and normal personal expenses. At the end
of the year we figured up how much each had drawn
out. One, of course, had drawn more than either of the
other two. We would then make out two checks, bringing the amount each had drawn up to the same identical
figure. In good years, there would be some left. We decided not to draw on this, but to leave it in the bank
and use it for enlarging and improving the ranch. In
other words, we drew no dividends at all. The ranch was
paying our living expenses, but we drew out no profit,
nor interest on our investments, nor pay for our time.
This method of operation would be put out of joint now
by the income tax laws.

At that time there were these ways of acquiring land:

Homestead	160 acres
Preemption claim	160 acres
Timber culture	160 acres
Desert land claim	320 acres (later 640)
Military road land	$1.25 an acre and up
State school land	The state owned Sections 16 and 36 in every township and offered these for sale from time to time.
Railroad scrip	With approval of the Federal Land office, this might be applied on certain sections.
Isolated tracts	Public domain land, not connected with other Federal land.

Proved up homesteads

Many homesteaders never really intended to farm the land and would sell out as soon as they had title.

Small ranches

This was a steady process, starting in earnest when machinery came in and horses started to go out. It is still going on.

Neither father, mother, Frank, nor I used our homestead rights. We were just too busy to take time out to live on a homestead the necessary time to prove up, but we bought land in all of the other ways listed. The Dalles Military Road was an utter fraud. A little roadway was built. The road building company, for some feeble effort, got every odd-numbered section for three miles each side of the road, and was in a sweat and hurry to get rid of its lands, fearing some effort by the government to repossess. It accordingly sold all of this land and the purchasers re-sold, making repossession harder, since the new buyer could claim that if there had been fraud, he was no party to it.

Building this ranch, piece by piece, required no extra managerial ability, because it was built slowly. There were about 250 miles of fence, and we knew every foot of it. There were many miles of ditch, and we knew every turnout and every weak spot. We knew every gate in every field. A new man could not know all of these things, but with us it took no longer to decide to take 1000 steers out of the Jones pasture and put them in the Brown field, than it would have taken to decide to take out 100. Each new homestead, as we bought it, was fitted at once into the overall scheme and things went on as they did before.

The bulk of our land came from homesteaders or small farmers who did not have enough to make a living. We never evicted any homesteaders and forced them to sell, all Western stories to the contrary notwithstanding.

We helped them by supplying feed when they were short, by lending them machinery and horses, by giving them labor, by lending them money when they had to have it— all kinds of ways.

The shoe was on the other foot, really. In the early days we bought out one homesteader in Bear Valley because his place, surrounded by ours, gave it nuisance value. Immediately every other piece of land there was homesteaded and offered to us as soon as the owners had title. So the larger owners virtually furnished a living to quite a group who homesteaded only to sell.

We started with both sheep and cattle, and I still think this is the best way to operate, if possible. Eventually we gave up the sheep. Our cattle were Durhams, the same thing as Shorthorn. We bought better bulls and developed big, roomy, easy-to-handle cows. They were our pride and joy. You could almost set a table for four on the back of one of those cows.

But there came a time when buyers began to grumble at the size of our steers. They bought them, but they kicked. One day I saw a Prineville man driving a herd of Hereford bulls through Bear Valley on the way to Burns. They were moving slowly and I saw their smoothness and ease of movement. Owners were Gray & Son.

I hurried to find father and we overtook them and bought eight out of the bunch. We were on our way Herefordward. Later we bought a good one from Herb Chandler of Baker. We watched the calf crop and saved out the heifers that were smooth, looked like Herefords, but had size and milking ability. Our herd gradually changed to Herefords, but we never forgot size and milking ability and I have always thought the Shorthorn blood, now just a trickle, had something to do with those things. Our cows were always in great demand. They were bigger than those in any other range herd I knew of.

We went along developing our herd, improving our lands, buying more as we could.

Eventually one of the partners wanted to draw some dividends. As soon as we began to draw them our expansion as a unit stopped. Dividends then became of more concern than ranch growth. From this time on expansion was on an individual basis. Oliver Brothers ranch had reached its peak of 54,000 acres.

The original debt for land acquirement and ranch expansion was eventually retired and the ranch then remained debt-free. Father had some of the old country fear of debt. In the old country, people were put in prison for debt. The European policy had run for hundreds of years, and it ground into people a feeling that owing money was somewhat dishonorable.

In 1937 Frank and I—our parents were gone—with the possibility of some accident in mind, decided to make our wives full partners. That made the place a partnership with four owners. Frank and Margaret, his wife, were agreeable partners. Family partnerships are notoriously hard to maintain because four personalities are harder to mix than two. In this case, all men and women were both partners and friends to the fullest.

Our only child, Anna, grew and developed fast. At seven she started to a country school in the same school district where I went, but in a new modern building. One of her teachers had taught me 23 years before. She went horseback one and a half miles uphill, through the same adobe I tracked into the old school. She had a shed for her pony and the sticky adobe didn't get tracked into the school. There were walks, large porches and cloak rooms. She loved to ride, liked to do all the things on the ranch that are done on horseback. After her marriage to Sam Keerins in 1929, she rode a good deal with him. She was a good hunter and one year won the prize for bringing in the first buck. Her husband was raised on a ranch near Izee, a member of a well-known pioneer family. A relative of his mother's was in the Whitman Massacre.

Frank's son, Joe, married Arlene Gay. So the four partners agreed on another change. We would take in Sam and Anna, Joe and Arlene. We then had eight partners.

Frank and I thought we had the course of our lives mapped out and we felt pretty good. As fast as we wanted to turn authority over to Sam and Joe, they were ready to take it. The two got along real well. We had a great family team.

I was getting into public service more and more. Life had been kind to me and the future looked untroubled. I wanted to interest the two ambitious young men to the greatest extent possible by giving them responsibility. Frank and I could foresee the possibility of accidents, and this was intensified by the deaths of some old friends. We could see that if one of us should die, the legal adjusting might be hard to do, with several families involved.

So the next move was to transfer ownership of portions of the ranch to each of the two boys and their wives. This made four complete units, although operated as a single ranch. About this time Frank moved to Salem. His first wife, Margaret, had died some years back and he had remarried. The cattle and other property were still a partnership.

In 1949 we made a complete division of cattle, horses, machinery, everything, and Frank sold his interest to Joe and Arlene, which gave Joe about half of the original holdings, to which he later added other property.

He is one of the many progressive stockmen of the county, and a leader in county affairs.

He and Arlene have three children: the two girls, Gay and Kay, and a son, J. C., named for his father and his greatgrandfather, Joseph Cayton Oliver. Arlene is well known among livestock people all over Oregon.

Sam, by 1949 was assuming some of the ranch management. He and I began to expand. We were more than compatible and I was glad to see him interested in making a good outfit even better. He was coming forward in the county in a way that made me proud and happy. The livestock association began to lean on him, people were coming to him for advice, and he and Anna were taking a larger and larger part in civic affairs. All of these things stamped them as good citizens.

Then, one rainy evening, Sam was killed on the highway when his car collided with an unlighted logging truck. Our plans were smashed and I was cut adrift, somewhat as my father was when he lost two boys in a week. After months of rearranging and trying this and that, we decided to sell part of the place. A man named Conforth came along and wanted to buy part of our 27,000 acres and part of the cattle to match. This took in the old ranch where I was born, and part of the Bear Valley lands. We quickly reached an agreement and sold 16,000 acres and 900 head of cows, leaving 11,000 acres and 1700 cattle.

So we still had some cattle and a ranch, but no headquarters. Our family combined all the knowledge we had in erecting another set of headquarters buildings and corrals, and we had a well designed layout. We ran this for a few years, then decided to sell out slick and clean. For the first time in my life I was out of the ranching business. I kept one of my good saddle horses and my complete riding outfit, something that I prize highly. This ended our ranch activities and ended my ranching career.

Anna then remarried and moved away. Eliza and I moved into John Day, built as comfortable a home as we knew how, and we live there now, 1961.

Anna has a marvelous personality and a fine, balanced mind. After Sam's death, she became a director in the bank. She was active in that capacity, useful, analytical, and an efficient business woman. Her name is now Anna Wiseman, and she lives near Halfway, in Baker County, Oregon.

To complete the family story, Anna's children are Herman Oliver Keerins and May Jeanette Henning.

Herman Oliver Keerins married Audrey Johnson of Dayville and they have four children, Barbara, David, Mary and Ray. They live in Nampa, Idaho.

May Jeanette married Gerald Hankins, who was killed in Korea. He was a brave soldier and a good man. They had a daughter, Kathie. May Jeanette recently married James Henning. Their home is in John Day.

Frank and Margaret had two children, Joe and Claire. Claire married James Maple, prominent citizen of John Day. They have five children, Joan, James, John, Mary and Thomas.

So the Oliver generations run—the story that began as a livestock ranch that my parents started. It began on an uncleared 160-acre homestead, devoted to dairy cows and vegetables. It grew steadily for 70 years, to a peak of 54,000 acres. In recent years we gradually disposed of half of it. Joe Cayton Oliver, grandson of the original J. C., is carrying forward the other half in splendid fashion.

Eliza Oliver, a lover of children, found time on her busy ranch schedule to mind children of relatives and friends. This baby, now a teen-ager, Nancy Bennett, daughter of Willard and Margaret, lives in Boise, Idaho.

CHAPTER 8

LIFE ON A RANCH

About the turn of the centry, if a young squirt like me had a team and buggy, he had the same social position as a youth now with a snazzy convertible. On the ranch we had a team and buggy used by everyone—like the one-auto family now. My older brother George and I were close to each other, so when our turn came on Sunday or some dance night, the two of us took the team and sometimes we each had a girl.

It was only a one-seated rig, but we considered it no particular hardship for the four of us to ride in that seat. It wasn't against any law, either, as far as we knew.

For a time we went with twin sisters and liked them pretty well. George lost his to a young dude-type Englishman. I lost mine to a curly haired barber who had the most delightful smell. I didn't blame her much because I sure didn't smell half that nice.

I want to tell of the outfit. The horses were perfectly matched buckskins, each with a black stripe down the back. They weighed 1100, were named Buck and Dan, were gentle, but high spirited. They always stepped out just as if they knew I was bursting with pride and they were determined to justify it. The buggy was new, with wheels, tongue and running gear an eyecatching red and the body a shining black. Nice harness with the horses' heads reined up by a strap running from the top of the bridle to the back-band of the harness. This could be lengthened or shortened to suit the action of the team.

There was a new buggy whip in a shiny socket on the front dash. With this team, all one had to do was to shake the whip and they were off, stepping high and far. There was a flowered lap robe and two halters. We kept the horses shining, the manes brushed out, clean and all on one side, the tails clean and straight.

There were no highways, just dirt roads that could and did get frightfully dusty in the drought of summer. Many drivers kept linen dusters handy.

As I mentioned, both George and I lost our girls. On this particular 4th of July, I had another date, but George didn't, so I took the team. But at the last minute my date and I had a falling out, so I went on single-handed; but driving down the main street of Canyon City with my fine team, I attracted more attention than a young fellow today with a gold-colored Cadillac. I couldn't possibly feel too downhearted.

At the dance that evening, I met a charming little girl not quite 15. Her name was Eliza Laurance. She told me what a nice team and buggy I had and I could see at once that she was a very sensible girl with good ideas. It didn't hurt that she had extraordinary good looks and a sweet disposition. I just fell like a ton of brick.

Sometime afterward, I went to a masquerade ball at John Day. My attention was caught by a school girl with a jumping rope who seemed to be having a fine time catching people with her rope. I thought I recognized the masquerading school girl, who lived in Canyon City and had walked the two miles to the dance. She threw her rope over me, drew me close, the music struck up, and we danced. I told her she had roped a mavrick who was roaming around alone, wild and free. I was riding a gentle horse that evening that would carry double. I escorted her home and from then on seeing her home became a habit.

Eliza, too, came from Grant County pioneers; all four of her grandparents came in the '60's. Her father and mother were married in the valley just as mine were. Her maiden name was Laurance and her mother's maiden name was Tureman. She has numerous cousins still living around Prairie City and one brother lives near Los Angeles.

Eliza had made her own way since 13 years of age. Her first job in Canyon City was with "Aunt" Martha Chambers, who with her husband, Jack, ran the popular

Elk Horn Hotel. Eliza worked as a waitress. She also clerked in a local store and was a ranch cook at 17.

During the school months she would work for her board in a private home while she went to school. Usually the family had one or more children for her to look after when not in school.

Phil Metchan, Sr., lived in Canyon City in the early days and later his son, Phil, Jr., returned and worked as cashier of the Grant County Bank. Later the Metchans owned the Imperial Hotel in Portland, also the Roosevelt, and they operated the Mallory Hotel. Eliza worked for Phil, Jr., and his wife and cared for their baby. Phil, Jr., was promient in politics and ran for governor at one time. He was extremely popular with eastern Oregon folks.

But back to our marriage. I can't seem to remember proposing, so I guess it just developed by mutual consent. She did not have to ask anyone, but it was different with me. I had no cash, nor house, nor furniture, nor anything else. I did own some cattle, and of course worked on the ranch. It took days for me to work up courage to tell my folks. One day I was cutting some alder wood to use in the smoke house. I saw the folks coming from the barn. Mother had an apron full of eggs. I gathered my courage with both hands, so sat down on the wood pile, and started to tell them my story as soon as they got close enough to hear.

Their first reaction was, "You are both too young." She was 17 and I was 20 and I could answer that one. Lots of people all around us were even younger when they were married. But their next question was harder. "Where are you going to live?" I sort of mumbled, "I rather thought—uh—well—wouldn't it be all right to move in here with you for awhile until something turns up?"

Eliza had two problems to face that couldn't have been so easy for a girl. The first was to put up with me and learn to accept all my weak points. The second was to learn to live with father and mother. Moving in with parents has broken up many marriages. A bride likes to have her own place. Eliza's success in instantly gaining the confidence of my parents is one of the finest tributes to her I can imagine. They loved her as their own child, and in later life they always looked to her when sick or in trouble. She cared for them in their old age as lovingly and untiringly as though they were her parents. This has meant a great deal to me. With a person less loyal, less understanding, and less sympathetic than Eliza, the entire course of the Oliver life would have been different. It could have been disastrous because from that time on the ranch was built by the combined work of the whole family.

Our first purchase was a bed spring, bed, mattress, dresser, and a big chair with wooden arms, which we bought the day of the wedding. I drove to town for her with a wagon with a 14-foot box drawn by two 1800-pound horses, Jerry and Sam. We bought the furniture together, including a Morris chair big enough for two, covered it with a wagon sheet, and started home. On the way the sky opened and poured rain. She got under the wagon sheet with the new furniture.

Eliza entered into our complicated ranch life with a will and was a success at once in my eyes and the eyes of my parents. We had no time for a honeymoon. A week later she was cooking for a lambing crew that I was running. We lived in a poorly constructed house that was cold and without water or any conveniences. A tough introduction for a bride. She buckarood with me; helped survey land by dragging the chain while I handled the compass; raised orphaned lambs, along with colts, calves, and even little pigs; cooked for 14 to 16 men in haying camps far from home. In these camps there was no running water, no hot water tanks, no refrigeration, nor any sanitary conveniences. These lacks were made up by a surplus of yellow jackets, mosquitoes, and flies, with a big black hornet occasionally. She sometimes made lunch for the large haying crews and took it to the field with a team and buggy. In the spring she helped cook for shearing crews with 25 to 30 men, and also for threshing crews in the fall. There was plenty of cooking the year around, and plenty of other work, too.

A ranch wife has a completely different job from that of a wife of a city banker, say, or a factory owner's helpmate. In those cases, if the lady shows up much around the bank or the factory, she's likely to cause trouble. But on the ranch she is really a 50-50 partner. I do not seem to recall any really successful rancher who did not have a good wife.

She gets up in the morning, takes care of the children and cooks the meals. She gets and answers the mail. She keeps the books, shops, answers the phone, and makes appointments for her husband. She takes messages to husband and hired hands in the fields, that may be 40 miles away. She goes to town for repairs and takes them to the proper place.

She is also the public relations expert for the firm, working on civic activities and on regional and state committees. She labors on school and tax matters. In all of these ways she organizes the day, saves time for everyone, and doubles her husband's efficiency. Without her the days are not long enough. With her, the team does wonders.

Eliza was exactly that kind of a ranch wife.

Eliza Oliver on a wintry day on a shopping tour in John Day.

Chapter 9

WHAT MAKES A RANCH TICK

A ranch is no different from any other kind of factory. It is the management that makes it go. The biggest ranch in the West was put together by Henry Miller of Miller and Lux. It was one of the big businesses in America in its day. But after Henry Miller died, it was dissipated in a few years. The new operators didn't know all the intricate management steps that must fit together like wheels in a watch. We've all seen hardware stores, newspapers, and factories come apart at the seams under bad management.

Father said, "Be out in front, don't ever suck the hind tit." Of course, that was one reason why he was a pioneer instead of staying in a place of little opportunity back in the Azores Islands. A pioneer just naturally *was* out in front. So in running a ranch, we never waited to be the last to try a new idea. There are pioneers in ranch ideas, as well as in settling states.

There isn't any system of ranch management, such as systems of bookkeeping. You can't say, "Now do this and this and this and you will succeed." Management is thousands of little things, all tied together. Grass, hay, cows, water, weather, fences, calves, bulls, steers, markets, breeding, health, corrals—all of these things must fit together like a machine. Any one of them, out of kilter, can cause the owner to lose his shirt. Many ranch shirts have been lost due to sudden, unpredictable weather changes.

But the biggest single item is timing all of the operations and getting ready for them beforehand. The man who doesn't get ready to mow until the day he wants to start haying is pretty likely to have some weather-damaged and over-ripe hay.

When you think of a ranch, you just naturally think first of cattle or sheep, but they aren't so fundamental as feed. The cow and ewe do just one thing—they take forage and put it in shape to sell. They eat every single day, the year around. A professional man I know bought a dairy farm and along in May his foreman came in and reported they would have to buy hay. The new owner, disturbed by the steady stream of expense yelled, "Buy hay! Great Scott, man, we'll have some of our own in a few weeks."

So the first thing to think of is feed—feed for spring, summer, fall and winter—365 days. The next thing is to stock the place only as far as the feed will allow, leaving plenty of leeway. "How many cattle do you have?" isn't nearly such a good question as, "What do your calves weigh?" A stockman short of feed year after year is usually in the insurance or real estate business in a few years. He'll soon be an ex-stockman. Feed production varies with the weather and this is the most troublesome single problem on a ranch. The range varies in production as much as ten times from year to year and hay meadows may yield from nothing up to two tons. If we saw we might be short of hay, I went out and bought more in the summer.

Formerly all young ranchers worried first about a place to grow hay. They didn't worry about range, it was free. Now they can buy hay and ship for hundreds of miles if need be, but they can't buy range. So a smart cattleman now is figuring how to get more feed from the range.

Another trait of father's was to try to make everything better. Drain the meadow, get more grass on the hills, get a better calf crop next year, make the lambs weigh more. He pioneered in all of these things, and I tried to follow his lead.

So we seeded crested wheatgrass; spayed heifers; crossed fine wool sheep with a coarse wool breed to get better mutton lambs; fenced our forest allotments on the Malheur forest; lambed in the late winter; dehorned cattle, long before these things were customary or popular. It was sort of a passion with me to make everything better if I could.

This fencing of forest allotments is worth special mention because it became a national policy. We never took our sheep to the forest until about June 10, but we found 2000 cattle already there and the precious cream of the grass had been skimmed off. Chet Craddock's cattle wandered over the ridge into our Antelope range, so Chet and I finally persuaded the local Forest Service man, Cy Bingham, to let us fence the ridge between.

At another point, Ed Southworth ran his cattle with ours, and, like us, he didn't want to turn out too early, and other cattle took the feed, so we got permission to fence.

This worked so well that we devised a plan to fence all of our allotments individually and cross fence them. Then, finally, we could handle both cattle and grass so as to improve both. Grass on our allotments steadily improved, and from that beginning it has become National Forest policy to fence individual allotments wherever water and terrain allow it. The practice is almost complete on the Malheur forest.

This eliminates arguments about bull quality, about different breeds, reduces trouble between neighbors about work, riding, and other expense, and allows each man to handle the feed in the best way. We fenced our allotment into eight different pastures for the cattle. We ran separately the yearling heifers, the two-year olds, and the mature cows, watched each pasture, and as soon as the feed was a little short, we moved the stock out. We also rotated during the year, skimming over lightly once, then coming back later. This keeps the grass strong and gives a higher total yield, which is impossible without fencing individual allotments.

Such new ideas didn't always work at first. When we tried late winter lambing, winter came back. Some American humorist said, "Winter lingered so long in the lap of spring that it caused much adverse comment." It surely did. The March temperature dropped to 20 below zero and the little lambs just died by the hundreds. Out of the first 1000 we lost 500.

But next year we had sheds fixed up to keep them out of the freezing wind, and we never had heavy losses again. We got on earlier markets, had bigger lambs, and practically no cutbacks. The early lambing paid off at three to five cents a pound more at selling time, and we got many more pounds of lamb from each ewe.

We made headway, too, in upgrading our sheep by weighing each fleece. This was quite a bother at first. Every ewe that didn't shear more than eight pounds was branded and sold without mercy. But our sheep were shearing 13 pounds in a few years instead of eight. Five pounds more of wool on 7000 ewes makes 35,000 pounds.

In that same operation we developed uniform wool that the buyers liked. It required almost no grading, so it wasn't hard to sell. We sacked the black wool separately. We sorted out all tags. Our honest way of packing and uniform wool always brought three to five cents more, so we got our money back and a whole lot more, for the trouble of weighing and looking at each fleece. With 92,000 pounds of wool, three cents more is $2760. No ding balls, rocks, or tags in our wool, and once the buyers found that out, selling was simplified.

In the same way we worked up a reputation for our cattle. During 17 years we sold our steers to only three buyers: Monfort of Greeley, Colorado; Safeway; and Bill Boswells Feed lots, near San Francisco.

We thought that a large cattle herd could not possibly be improved much, unless the individual cattle could be identified. So we figured out a combination of one letter and two numerals that would quickly identify each cow in the herd. It showed the age of each animal, its sire and dam. Here is what this system allowed us to do:

1. The cows producing the most beef, that is the biggest and fastest producing calves, could be spotted.

2. Replacement heifers could be chosen from such cows, thus improving the herd yearly.

3. Conformation weaknesses could be selected out, and all cows lacking width, for example, could be bred to bulls strong in width. The same way with other defects.

4. Cows could be followed through their entire production cycle and records kept, enabling quick culling of inferior animals.

5. A new bull could be quickly proved; either for good or bad points. All that was necessary was to get together his first crop of calves. If they were poorer than their dams, we got rid of him fast. If better, we kept him longer than normal. Many herds have lost a chance to improve by selling a bull too soon, just because the owner didn't know that all of the real good calves were coming from that one good bull.

6. A record of mating was possible. Certain cows and certain bulls give superior calves, whereas another mating might not.

7. Health of the herd was improved, because abnormalities could be caught at once. The branding could also be a permanent record for vaccination or testing records.

This matter of identification for life of every cow in the herd by a shoulder brand is the most useful single tool in any attempt to improve.

Someone may want our identification system. The shoulder brand had a capital letter, A, B, C, etc. The letter indicated the year of birth; for example, all of the B cows may have been born in 1958, the C cows in 1959, the D cows in 1960. State regulations dictate a letter and two numerals, so as to get away from any confusion with ownership brands. That makes it apparent that we had to start with our B cows, for instance, with the number B10 and we could go no higher than B 99, a total of 89 calves. But by changing the position of the B in relation to the numerals, any number of heifers could be branded B, for 1958. The B could occur in front of the numerals or behind them; it could be above or below; it could be written as B or ᗺ One could have 10 or more positions for the B. If we had 10, that allowed for 890 heifer calves in 1958, in the example above. Next year the heifers would all be C, and so on.

Overgrazing is a mis-used term. Its use has certainly done more harm than good. America would be better off if this word had never been invented. Ask any cattleman in the West if he believes in overgrazing and his answer will be an immediate "Hell, no! Of course not, it could ruin a man," or some such retort. All kinds of things are called overgrazing, some of which are just poor management. That is, one man can hurt a range with 100 cattle, whereas another man can have the same set-up and his range may improve. A lot of so-called overgrazing is grazing too early.

Let's say a range on April 1 has enough feed for only 50 cattle. By April 20 it may have enough for 100 cattle, and by May 20 enough for 150. But if 100 are turned in early, then the animals take all the feed there is, trample the soft, muddy ground, damage the grass, and the cows will run foot races for each new spear as it shows up. Two or three years of this may pretty well ruin a range, and people say it is overgrazed. Actually, it has been grazed at the wrong time, because another man might see the range improve with 150 cattle on it, turned in later.

Cows do not care about steep ground, so if only one cow is put in a steep 1000-acre pasture, she may overgraze a little flat near the water. If that little quarter-acre meadow is all you see, you might jump to the conclusion that the pasture is overgrazed. Therefore, improper distribution is sometimes called overgrazing.

I think we could just as well say that much of the overgrazed land is underproducing. For example, here is a section of sagebrush. It supports only ten cows when the rainfall and soil would justify a hundred. Surely it is underproducing, not overgrazed. Get rid of the sage, seed alfalfa and grass, and get it to growing something.

Then it can carry ten times as many livestock with plenty of feed left. It is defeatist thinking to say, "The range is overgrazed—reduce the livestock numbers." Let's say, "The range is underproducing, let's make it produce more, and increase the numbers."

Ranchers are natural conservationists of water, feed and soil. There is no good livestock man who doesn't hope to leave his range better than he found it. Nearly every Grant County man I know of is doing his best in that direction. He is seeding alfalfa where none grew before in order to enrich the soil and let it fill up with roots in order to hold it; he is spreading out the water to put a mat of vegetation over the soil so it won't wash away; he is going to great expense to keep the creek and river channels from eroding; he is fertilizing, so more feed can be grown so cattle won't have to be hurried onto the short grass too soon. These things are going on all around us. They can all be found on the old Oliver ranches. A good range can be kept good forever by a wise and careful rancher, but once badly hurt, and the soil washed away, healing is often impossible. The soil, in that case, has been sold down the river.

Today all ranchers are more conscious of cattle improvement than they were even ten years ago; some are not so conscious of grass improvement. Yet, on ranch after ranch, grass improvement will net far more pounds of meat than any improvement of cattle. For example, if a man's calves weigh 400 pounds at date of sale, it would be pretty silly to try to improve the cattle so as to make the calves weigh ten times as much, or 4000 pounds. But ranchers in Bear Valley are making their ranges yield ten times as much, so it's time to devote more attention to the ranges.

Ranch management, with its thousand problems, is also involved with labor management. But we never seemed to have much trouble with labor. Some men worked for us their entire adult lives. If they quit for a month or two to see some new country, they came back. We always ate with the men and I always used the breakfast table as the place to tell each man what to do. In this way each man knew his job for the day, and he also knew the job of every other man. This helped, because, for example, Bill would finish irrigating at four o'clock. He knew that John was the closest man and that John was repairing fence just a quarter of a mile east. So Bill didn't have to come back to the ranch, maybe ten miles away, just to be told to help John.

Your path through life depends upon the way you get along with people, and on a ranch, the hired help is probably the most important single group. We always thanked a man who asked for a job, either in person or by mail. If by mail his letter was answered at some length.

Every hired man helped put our outfit together, and I always tried to give plenty of credit to good, honest, hard-working men. They liked to work at our place, as evidenced by the way they stayed on. I know they told others, "You work at Oliver places and you work under a system. Learn the system once and you can just about know what your job will be each day."

We had rules, too; the first man in the field with his team was the first man to quit at night. If a man helped in haying one year and came back the next, we gave him the same team and mower.

We always saved jobs for stormy days, so kept all the men busy. Idle men are unhappy and restless and trouble can start.

Another management factor is marketing. It, too, is made up of a hundred things. We showed buyers the best stock first, so they would start with a good impression. We tried to have uniform lots and quality stock to sell. But over and above all that, each buyer is different. Study them and their characteristics. Their motions and their tones of voice can tell you things.

You can't store cattle like you can wheat, and especially you can't store lambs. They are more like peaches. Cattle marketing is geared to feed supplies. Occasionally, if the buyer is unusually eager, it may pay to throw overboard your whole marketing policy. For example, suppose you sell yearlings. They are worth 23 cents. Your calves weigh 450 pounds and someone is determined to have them and finally offers the abnormal price of 33 cents.

450 lbs. @ 33c $148.50
646 lbs. @ 23c $148.58

It takes quite a lot of money to put 200 pounds more weight on those calves, and maybe five months of time with the resultant risk.

The big cost on a cattle ranch in these northern climates is winter.

For 50 years I had one hard and fast marketing rule. I never sold cows with their calves in the spring. "Pairs" as they are known. The pair usually sells for only about the price of the cow alone, or the price of the calf alone in the fall. I can't see anything to be gained by feeding hay to a cow all through the winter, then selling her with her calf. The only possible justification would be a season opening so ding-danged dry that the grass didn't start and you saw you would *have* to sell.

There are so many things tied to good management that it is hard to tell where to stop. I put them on paper once, and the state college published the ideas in Oregon Extension Bulletin 690, "Range Cattle Management." It even won a blue ribbon in national competition.

One reason why our calves sold well was their uniformity. I have told of the way we identified each cow and calf, and culled out ruthlessly all cows with calves that didn't measure up. The expression, "I'll keep this cow and get one more calf," shows a dangerous frame of mind. Nearly every cattleman would be better off if he cast out such a thought as though it were straight from the devil.

We kept our calves gaining right from the start, and confined the calving period to 60 days, thereby achieving uniformity.

Proper care of the bulls, before, after, and during the breeding season is important. Also special breeding pastures with level ground and lots of feed are recommended. The bulls don't belong to the Mazama Club and hardly any of them know how to ski. They aren't going to run races over rocks and precipices. If you put them in a rough pasture, you might just as well put roller skates on their hind feet.

Yearling heifers should be separated and bred in pastures by themselves. Supplemental feeding and protein concentrates may be necessary for those heifer calves saved for replacements. A starved yearling heifer is a poor prospect for a strong calf next year. For that matter, all young growing animals need plenty of protein, just as boys and girls do.

The main business of a cattle ranch is to sell the increase. But there are always some old cows or cull cows to sell. These are usually sold in the spring. More than 50 years ago, for three years straight we sold to Ed Coles of Haines, who was a fine man, a straight shooter, and a good man to do business with. The first year he paid us $16.50 a pair (cow and calf), the next year $18.50, and the third year $23.00.

I asked him what he did with those old cows and he said he fattened them to sell in Portland for the logging trade. So I led myself by the hand off to where I could have a good talk with myself, and said, "Herman, if there is money to be made in fattening these cows, why don't you make it?" I replied, "I think I will." So, for the past 50 years we fattened our own old cows. To do that you need some good pasture so they will put on flesh quickly.

When going out to buy bulls, I never bought without seeing the cow herd. If the whole cow herd was better than ours, I felt pretty safe in buying bulls out of it. But if they were inferior to ours, I thanked the owner for his time and the drink of good bourbon he offered, but found I was late for another appointment and hoped he would come and see me sometime. Practically any pure-bred herd in the business will have a few good looking bulls. They may be freaks or accidents and they are likely to be just as freakish in the kind of calves they bring.

There is one other thing to note. On many low elevation ranges in Oregon, the steers start to lose flesh in the late summer. Yet these steers are often not sold until fall. The feeders who buy them may not have feed available early or they may reserve feeding as a winter job, to be started after all the farm operations are buttoned up for the winter. This situation has several results, all bad. The steers lose weight and in doing so, they lose condition. All of their defects show up glaringly, so the buyer has lots of talking points. The owner has fewer pounds to sell and gets less per pound.

This problem is a tough one. We met it by dividing our pastures and keeping on the best feed the steers to be sold. We could watch them and, before they stopped gaining, we moved them to a fresh pasture. A protein supplement is one way out. The steers aren't going to keep gaining on dry grass alone. It has plenty of energy, but not enough protein. They must have this or they won't grow. Milk, eggs, meat are necessary for growing people. So with cattle the protein is necessary. Cattle will live without much of it, but they will lose flesh. This is why bitterbrush may be important. It is a protein feed. This same situation applies to weaner calves. The cow's milk is a protein feed, and a calf deprived of it needs some substitute.

Just one more management point. You can't manage anything unless you know costs and income. About the only good thing that came of the income tax was that it forced nearly everyone to keep records. In our case, we already had 'em. Father kept super careful records of his milk business, putting down *every* delivery *every* day. As we spread out, I improved father's system. When Eliza came into the family, she took over our ranch records, and made more improvements. She received many compliments on her books from employees of the Bureau of Internal Revenue. We have all the old records from 1878 on. Even now, we can compare costs between years.

In this way, any change in ranch operations can be checked—the effect of changing from three-year olds to two or from yearlings to weaners; the effect on wool weights of our selection process; the effect upon income of buying another piece of land. We used these good records in all kinds of ways and they were helpful.

For a long time at the end of each year we classified and inventoried all the livestock. We measured the hay and grain to determine if we had enough or what surplus could be sold safely. We estimated the next year's sales, both weight and price of cattle, sheep, and wool. We were then in a position to talk to buyers at any time. We didn't have *about* this number or that—it was exactly that number. We laid out the year's fencing and ditching programs. Corrals and gates were inspected, loose poles nailed or broken boards replaced. We set corral posts in concrete and bored holes near the base to be filled with oil to keep them from rotting just above the concrete.

We had 13 buildings on the home place, all exactly square with each other and all in good repair. We thought this helped in giving buyers a good first impression.

I was a good rough carpenter, blacksmith, machine repairman, harness worker. A successful rancher must be a jack-of-all trades.

Before we mechanized, our inventory for ranch equipment ran around $10,000. After mechanizing, it was $100,000. Upkeep, repairs, depreciation, were all far greater. When you start a tractor, dollars begin to pour out the exhaust. When you start a horse, he burns up materials you have grown yourself. When a tractor isn't going, it is standing there depreciating. When a horse isn't going, he is giving forth with a valuable product, manure.

High taxes and mechanized equipment have vastly changed the ratio of net to gross. Formerly we expected to keep at least 50 percent of what we took in. Now if a rancher can keep 10 percent of the gross receipts he is lucky.

Should we encourage young folks to go into the livestock business? I'd say by all means, if they have the qualifications. If they are determined; if they can keep on when the going is tough; if they can avoid spending a dollar this year in order to get ten dollars next year; if they can lay out a course and stick to it with some stubborness; if work doesn't scare them to death; if they like the life and will play it square—then get into the livestock business. It has been good to me and will be good to anyone who is qualified.

Livestock takes land. We have only so much land in this country, and it is getting less each year, due to parks, cities, roads, golf clubs, cemeteries and erosion. But we had 3,000,000 more people in 1959 than in 1958. It takes over two acres of plow land for each adult and four acres of rangeland. But in a few years we won't have that much. Our production per acre is going up, but that can only go so far. Many acres are close to their limit.

It seems to me that the only possible result can be that in 20 years a livestock ranch is going to be worth a lot more than it is now. The consumption of meat is going up, too, and that will favor this business. New ways of refrigeration and cooking will make meat more palatable—that will give us another boost. It won't be too long until nearly all beef will be tender, either by breeding, chemistry, or cooking—and that will be more money in the pockets of the levis.

I am afraid that the crook called inflation has stacked the cards all in his favor. So long as we won't elect a man to Congress unless he has an inflationary program, of course, we are going to have it, good times or bad. The only one sure way to hedge against it is to buy land, so 20 years from now the land owner is pretty likely to be in a preferred class.

All of these things make the livestock business look good. I have enjoyed my life in it. The life has been rich and full. I can't think of any other kind of a life I would have traded it for. I feel a little sorry for those who are chained to their desks in the cities.

So, if this is read by someone with a child who would like the kind of life a stockman leads, I would encourage him to help the child to achieve it. It takes more money now, but nothing is impossible. A boy with the stuff in him can usually get credit from someone—after demonstrating that he is worthy of it.

It's a good life and can be a glorious one.

But life on a stock ranch isn't all honey, high heeled boots, high living, and hot cakes. Some other words beginning with H enter in, such as hail, high water, and hollow belly; or hard times, hard winters, and hardships; or hazards, heat, or just plain Hell.

From the time the calf is conceived until it is ready for market as a yearling, there is a period of 29 months. If sold as a weaner, the period is 17 months. During all of those 29 months there are hazards: He may be born prematurely, or deformed and worthless; he may be dropped into a snowbank and die of exposure; his life may be short due to white muscle, blackleg, pneumonia, or shipping fever; he may be killed by hungry coyotes or bears; poisonous weeds may kill him in a painful lingering death or by ghastly convulsions; a trigger-happy hunter may see him move in the brush and end his life with a bullet; a rustler may load him into a pick-up; he can get mired in a mud hole, or have his leg broken in a fall in the rocks, or over a precipice; a tree may fall on him in a storm.

A weaner calf, when taken from its mother and sold, can be compared to a coupon. The cow and the land to carry her represent an investment of from $500 to $1000. When the calf is sold it is like clipping a coupon from a $500 bond. Whenever a cow has no calf, or the calf is lost, you have no coupon to clip. If this happens to very many of your calves, you must borrow more money or sell part of your cows to pay the taxes and other costs. You are then worth less at the end than at the start of the year, and a few such years may wipe you out.

Brucellosis took an awful toll of our calves before the scientists found a vaccine. It put many people out of business. It took 15 percent of our expected calf crop annually. In addition, the test and slaughter program made it necessary to sell many of our best cows, so it was hard to keep our cow numbers up to par.

One spring we turned 300 three year old steers into a fresh pasture and the next morning found 13 dead from poison hemlock, the same weed that killed the old Greek philosopher, Socrates.

One spring I contracted for 400 steers for fall delivery. Prices dropped sharply all during the summer. We lost over $50 a head, or more than $20,000 on that venture, in addition to the feed we put into them. A cattleman can't escape such losses. He can't outguess the market. If he can ride out a severe loss, if his bank will stay with him, if he doesn't get a combination of such losses with poor health—and a lot of other ifs—then, eventually will come a time when prices suddenly rise, and he will be worth more than he thought he was. This takes doggedness and faith—and the income tax man will let you take the loss, but when you win, he will take the gain. It's sort of like playing poker where the house takes some out of every pot. If you lose, no matter, but if you win, he takes part of the gain.

In the early days we knew nothing about liver flukes. We know now that the fluke lives in a snail and produces an egg deposited on a blade of grass; the sheep eats the grass and the egg hatches; the little fluke by instinct finds the liver and there lives on the blood of the cells. If there are enough flukes the host animal loses weight and may die. Most of them live. Since all of the flukes are in the liver, that is the only part condemned if the animal is sold. These little worm-like insects also occur in other animals, including cattle, deer and elk, but they do more damage to sheep.

One spring we discovered our sheep badly infested. Sometimes the trouble clears up if the sheep can be moved to a fluke-free place. The lamb crop was poor, and the ewes were poor. That fall, father, in desperation, decided to ship them to St. Paul to fatten them. So my brother George took 1800 of them. After feeding them for three months, they were sold for less than the freight and feed costs. Father had to send George money to come home on. We lost many thousands of dollars and ended with neither the money nor the sheep.

When I was 16, father sold 1600 yearling ewes to be delivered in Baker. In August I started with the sheep and with a faithful herder. A man with a team and buckboard and food came behind. We ran into a poisonous weed that killed over 400 head of these fine young ewes.

The following year I had charge of 6000 newly shorn yearling wethers. As we started out, a cold rain set in. The sheep, traveling to keep warm, lost their running mates and were cold and restless. We were traveling through mountains on the way to Baker. In crossing a narrow gully they began to pile up. The helpers and I spotted the trouble, but we could not stop it at once, and we lost 100 sheep in a few minutes. This is one of the most pitiful things I ever experienced. The dying sheep groan, making a sound heard in your dreams for months afterward.

When I got the remainder of the big flock to Baker, I ran into more trouble. An inspector told me scab had been discovered in the area and the railroad was forbidden to accept sheep for shipment unless dipped. The nearest vats were 30 miles away near North Powder. I was only 17, but I had to decide quick. There was no telephone at John Day then. So I drove the sheep to North Powder, bought chemical, mixed it, put the whole 5900 through the vat, single file, and finally got them on the train, headed for a Nebraska corn field to fatten.

Coyotes, and even dogs that are household pets, take delight in killing sheep, especially just before lambing. No sheep owner can be free of this fear for a moment.

One year wool had no local market and father decided to ship to the nation's biggest wool market, Boston. We hauled the huge wagon loads 200 miles to The Dalles, shipped the big sacks, and sat back to await the check. The wool sold for 5 cents a pound. Freight, commissions, insurance, and storage ate up the 5 cents. We just gave away the thousands of pounds of wool that year.

Another year we had just finished shearing and had the wool bags, 6 feet tall, standing on end in a shed near a creek. A big cloudburst somewhere above changed the creek to an angry flood that soaked the entire clip about two feet up from the bottom of each sack. We frantically searched for a warehouse and rented one from the railroad at Prairie City. We hauled the wool there, unbagged it, separated wet from dry fleeces, rebagged the dry, and spread the wet fleeces on the floor, turning them daily. The wool that had been wet took a beating in price.

Eventually foot rot took us out of the sheep business. We could control the flukes and all the other diseases, but foot rot beat us.

So wild cats, coyotes, dogs, cold rains, poison weeds, liver flukes, and the herd instinct of sheep, all combined to give us trouble. Cattle aren't quite so likely to die from either disease or herd disasters, but they are far more likely to be stolen, and fluctuating prices can change a man from rich to poor almost over night.

Yet, in spite of all these things, I still think a livestock man has a better life than anyone else. He is close to nature, his work is fundamentally constructive, and that builds something into him that is strong and good.

PART TWO – CATTLE COUNTRY

CHAPTER 10

HORSES

The horse was waiting in Oregon for white men to appear, but he didn't have to wait long. When Lewis and Clark came in 1805, their lives were probably saved by horse meat—this is certainly true of the members of John Jacob Astor's overland party under Wilson Price Hunt. All the fur traders packed out their year's catch on horses. The horses came up from Arizona and New Mexico by way of old Indian trails that led along the base of the Rocky Mountains. "Big dogs," the grateful Indians called them.

The first horse to get to Oregon was stolen from the Spanish by Indians. Other Indians then stole or traded for him and he gradually worked his way north. No one knows for sure when he got here, but he probably arrived in Oregon about 1750, because that is the time that his pictures began to appear on rocks along the Columbia.

The horse changed the lives of Indians fully as much as autos have changed ours. A horse gave an Indian six feet instead of two, and gave him speed and endurance. The mounted Indian could ride up on game; take his tepee and travel; carry quantities of dried fish and berries or camas back to camp; thus, protecting him from the ever-present fear of hunger. He could trade a horse for a nice squaw. It made him a far more formidable enemy. It is no wonder that the Indians measured their wealth in horses. The white man's scalp was not worth nearly so much as his horse, in the covetous eyes of a horse hungry Indian warrior.

In Klamath, the story is told that in the 30's when money was scarce, an Indian came into the local bank and wanted to borrow $800. The banker asked, "What do you own?" The Indian said, "Me got 60 ponies." Investigation showed this to be true, so he got the money on promise to repay in 90 days. Promptly on the day, the Indian appeared, took a big roll of bills from his pocket, paid off the loan, put the scarcely dented roll back in his pocket and started out. The banker called to him to come back, and said, "You'd better leave all that money here with us. There are plenty of folks who would knock you in the head if they knew you had that much money." The Indian disposed of this argument with, "How many ponies you got?"

The horse was an *important* pioneer. Some of the covered wagons were drawn by oxen. But no wagon train was complete without horses. The scouts, wagon masters, and the hunters all rode horses and many caravans used them instead of oxen. About the only advantage of the oxen was that the Indians didn't want them.

After arrival in Oregon, almost all the work was done by horses. They plowed the land; packed the provisions; with the help of their half brother, the mule, they did most of the freighting; carried the mail; herded the cattle; fought the Indians; and went to town or to the neighbors. Pioneering without horses would have been unthinkable.

The horse was at the mercy of his master, just like a slave. A cruel master gave vent to his cruelty by taking it out on his horse. There was usually no one around to check up on this .A man who constantly beat his horse just because he felt like it was looked down upon, but there was nothing illegal about it. Very seldom did anyone object audibly.

In Wallowa County they tell about the rancher who kept an old bronc just for chores. He was 20 years old and had been gentle for years. The first really cold morning when the ground was frozen, his owner saddled him, Whether it was the cold blanket or the nippy air, the

horse bucked the owner off onto the frozen corral
ground. The man picked up a nearby board and began
to beat the horse. His wife ran to the door and yelled,
"Henry, you quit that! That horse don't know why
you're beating him." The man yelled back, "He ain't
got nothin' on me. I don't know why he bucked me off,
either."

But this was an exception. Ordinarily, no one objected. The horse might have a sore neck or shoulder,
a lame or tender foot, or might be weak from lack of
feed or overwork, and some owners gave little heed, over-
working him without regard to his weakness. Uphill, or
through mud, he might be urged beyond his ability.
Some teamsters, stuck in the mud, mad and frantic,
would blame the horses for their own mistakes.

There were all kinds of riders and drivers; many
loved their horses; used good judgment in never forcing
them; looked after their comfort before their own in
bad weather; and carefully attended to harness, bits, collars, or saddles so that no sore could develop. These folks
usually prided themselves upon having good horses. The
best horses tended to gravitate into the hands of the best
masters, because such persons always had an eye for a
good horse, and were usually the best judges of horses
in the county.

In the early days I have seen riders, cold and stiff
from wind and storm, stop in a saloon to warm themselves a bit. You couldn't blame them much for that. But
they would leave their horses, maybe after a hard ride,
tied to the rail outside. It would be nice and warm inside and the intended stop of ten minutes would stretch
into hours and hours, with no way for the horse to shield
himself from the wind. He was chained to a post, as a
slave or a prisoner might be.

A good riding horse will pick his way, carefully and
slowly, through rocks, brush, and badger holes, but I
have seen riders jerk them around the rocks or holes,
apparently thinking they knew more than the horse. A
horse ridden like this will finally get confused, and

A Bear Valley meadow with some typical big, wide, Oliver cows.

Cows and calves on winter feed. Cows are shoulder branded as described on pages 113-114.

A little group of heifer calves sired by one bull on the ranch. All about the same size and age.
At selling time, Oliver Brothers had large numbers of cattle as nearly alike
as management could get them.

Eighteen month old heifers on the Indian Creek range. There was plenty of grass left on every
range to protect the soil and develop the roots.

Taking A2 cattle to the forest. Ponderosa pine in an open stand such as this, furnishes feed for domestic livestock and for big game. It also delivers more water to Oregon's streams than is the case when thickets occupy the forest land.

im Lydston, buyer for Safeway stores, figuring up the amount of the check for 864 cattle from liver Brothers ranch, just after World War II. It was a good sale, judged by the facial expression.

Range improvement on the ranch. Land on left plowed and seeded to crested wheatgrass. Native range on right, with R. G. Johnson, former county extension agent.

This branding crew handled 60 calves an hour. The crew lined up this way: Two teams of three men each, two branders. No horses were used. Two men did all of the branding, castrating, earmarking, dehorning, and vaccinating. There was always a calf down, one leaving, and one waiting. For handling small calves, this method was faster than roping.

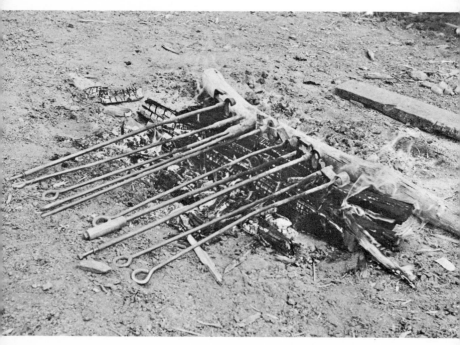

Factories patent, magazines copyright, ranchers brand.
The brand is the public notice of ownership.

should he stumble or break into a rodent hole, he will get whipped for his error.

To get the best use from a riding horse, he should be well fed, but with no surplus fat. At the start of an all day ride, I usually tried to let my horse take it rather easy for a few miles. He may be frisky in the early morning and may want to run, but if a rider pushes him hard at the start, he is likely to get sluggish soon and will stay that way all day. They don't let long distance runners go right out and sprint the first lap, and a horse, if ridden all day, is a sort of long distance athlete.

Colonel Kiester bought horses in Grant County for the U. S. Army at the start of the last war. He knew horses, liked them and was respected by the ranchers. He usually came with his own horse and outfit, a spirited high-stepping horse and a good non-regulation saddle and bridle. Up in the North Fork of the John Day there is some scenic country. The river cuts through the deep lava, surrounded by cliffs and bluffs a thousand feet high. A North Fork rancher had assigned a cowboy to go with the Colonel. The cowboy's outfit was everything the Colonel's wasn't. While Colonel Kiester's horse had his head up, eyes and ears alert, inspecting everything in sight, the horse of this cowboy stood by dejectedly, his head near the ground, not interested in anything at all.

The cowboy apparently began to feel this comparison deeply. The Colonel was immensely alive to the scenery, so when they came to a place where the rim extended a few rods in a narrow peninsula out toward the river so one could see far up and down the colorful canyon, he rode out on the peninsula to look at the wild rugged beauty of the scene.

The cowboy followed dutifully, but when his old nag stumbled, the rider jerked his head up savagely and said, "Watch where you're going, you scenery-lovin' s— — — —."

Every man who has spent years of his life in the saddle knows what it means to ride a good horse, like Colonel Kiesters, as compared to the "plug" of the cowboy's.

We will say you started at dawn, have been in the saddle all day, gathering some cattle out of the timber and are now bringing them down to a meadow that serves as an overnight stop. You are tired, and your horse must be even more so, what with steep climbs, sudden dashes after animals that tried to sneak back, and some tough going among rocks. It is after seven o'clock in the evening. You look back, and to your disgust see one critter a quarter of a mile back that has gotten by you somehow. So you turn your horse and start back. The horse sees the young cow, too, picks up his ears, and is away, determined to get her back as fast as possible. He is a good horse, and his willingness to do what has to be done, suddenly takes the "tired" out of you and you are glad to be alive.

But if you have a poor horse, he doesn't want to turn, he doesn't want to go back, he doesn't care a hoot about doing what must be done; the result is you are even more tired than before, are ill tempered, and you wonder what kind of a damn fool a man is to want to be a cowboy.

I always felt at home on a good horse, sorting cattle, moving and classifying them. Thus engaged, perhaps like other men with golf, I was supremely happy. Nothing disturbed or worried me. I wouldn't trade my job right then for that of governor, senator, corporation president, or anyone. My horse was part of all this. I never could feel right downhearted when on a good horse. How could I? The two of us made a completely satisfying partnership. We turned, started, stopped, hurried, or slowed in perfect unison, each wanting to help the other. At such times political and international troubles were far away.

The man who loves his horse realizes his dependence upon the animal, gets off and walks up steep hills or through rocks; he spreads the blanket carefully on a well brushed back; the saddle is placed gently, and is cinched up only tight enough to prevent slipping. The bridle is adjusted to fit the head and mouth so it is comfortable for the horse. A bridle too tight will pull the bit into the tender corners of the mouth, will cause them to bleed, and will give pain and discomfort to the horse all day. I have seen this happen, even to the extent that flies would be attracted by the sores. A bridle too big leaves the bit hanging too low and will cause the horse to fight it all day long, causing irritation to both horse and rider.

A work animal with a collar too tight or too loose can be compared with a man on a long walk with a badly misfit pair of shoes. Some farmers will have a string of work horses, every horse with stripes and blotches of white on the shoulders, showing perennially misfit collars.

People with horse sense watch all of these things, because a horse well outfitted, well cared for, and driven or ridden sensibly, will always do more work. A horse, irritated all the time by a sore, or poorly ridden or driven, or with improper equipment, shortly has an irritated driver or rider and that is a bad combination for efficient work.

A horse smarter than his handler is unfortunate. In training a colt it helps to know more than the colt, but the essential thing is to have more time than the colt. Horse training takes a patient man with lots of time. Many of the larger outfits in the West formerly had a bronco buster, a cowboy who spent all of his time breaking horses. Some of these men were excellent trainers, others just liked to ride and they would train horses to buck rather than to ride. A horse poorly trained at the start is likely to be poorly trained all his life, just like a child.

Some of my favorite saddle horses at various times had such names as: Prince, Fred, Dusty, Bob, Belley, Target, Two-Bits, Six-Bits, Nubbins, Sunday, Pacer, Browney, Nugget, Bally, Snipe, Buck, Mickey, and Meteorite.

Some horses wear out quickly, due to accidents, or weaknesses in conformation. Common troubles are: ring bone, bog spavin, wire cuts, sweenies, stiff shoulder. This latter is dangerous for the rider if the horse is to be used in rough terrain or among rocks and gopher holes. A sure-footed horse that can catch himself instead of falling, can protect the rider and even save his life.

A ranch horse must be strong enough to carry a 200-pound man all day. Most cowboys aren't that heavy. They tend toward the lean and lanky, bow-legged breed. The old time big cattle layouts with a dozen or more riders, a cook wagon, and a regular cavvy or remuda always changed horses at noon, and if a rider had night duty, he changed again at night. No horse was ridden for two days straight, so each rider had at least four horses assigned to him and more likely six or seven. The word cavvy, meaning the entire string of horses, is a contraction of the Spanish word caballada. The Spanish pronunciation of "b" is so close to our "v" that cowboys couldn't tell the difference. So the Spanish "Vaquero" first became "bucarro" and then, from exaggeration, "buccaroo".

The early day stockman put up very little if any hay, just enough to feed a few days during a severe winter storm. The horses were normally turned out to rustle, which they did right well. So the range, in a few years, was covered by thousands and thousands of horses, many of which just ran wild. The male colts grew up as stallions, the females all had colts, and wild horses flourished everywhere from the Cascades to the Snake River. This was true of course in many other places throughout the west.

In the meantime, a flourishing horse business grew up, long before the railroad. Some adventurous souls found it was exciting and often profitable to round up Oregon horses weighing from 1,000 pounds up, gather them in big herds, trail them east and sell. Wyoming and Montana were pretty well stocked with Oregon horses. Some herds went clear to Kansas City and were sold all over the East, middle West and South.

The Oregon horses made a great name for themselves as hardy, spirited, and with good feet. Ben Holliday, when in the prime of his far-flung stage business, bought many of his horses here. The U. S. cavalry and light artillery looked to Oregon for their choicest mounts. In the Boer War the British bought many thousands of horses, and in the first World War, British, French and American officers could be seen inspecting horses at every eastern Oregon shipping station.

Bill Brown was probably the biggest of the Oregon horse raisers. His horses were everywhere. The assessor of Deschutes County told of seeing Bill on the street one day and had this conversation:

Assessor: Bill, I see my young assistant has you down for 800 horses.
Bill: That's about right.
Assessor: But Bill, you've got more than 800 horses.
Bill: Yes, guess I have, make it 1,800.
Assessor: You have more than 1,800.
Bill: Maybe I have. Let's call is 2,800.

When you figure that assessors in Lake, Harney, Grant, and Crook Counties were also trying to get Bill's horses on their rolls, you can see he had horses.

But, as mentioned, horses raised that way are going to go wild. The wild horses were the downfall of millions of acres of rangeland. Horses have teeth above and below of a size and shape to enable them to eat grass clear to the ground. When hungry, they took crown and roots, killing the plants. Sheep and cattle can't graze that closely. They can weaken the plants so that they may die eventually, but this is a process that takes several years. Horses could and did kill most of the grass on a winter range in one year. I haven't mentioned the Indian horses. They were usually concentrated in a small area, and it wasn't long until that area had no more bunchgrass. The biggest census record of Oregon horses was about the time of World War I when they credited us with 400,000. The low was 40,000. But the figure of 400,000 is far short. Many wild horses refused to answer the census taker's questions, so they were omitted. The true figure for our horse population at its range-ruining height, was probably over 50 percent higher. Numbers have increased lately to 90,000.

The Taylor Grazing Act, low prices for horses after World War I, homesteading, development of horse meat for fox feed, growing need for range for cattle and sheep, the jeep, the gas engine—these things decimated the huge herds. Right now there seems to be a strong demand for riding horses and even work animals. A good horse may easily bring more money than two or more good steers. Some ranchers, tired of the ever-increasing costs for gas and machinery, are turning back to horses for haying and for winter feeding. Joe Oliver says use of horses is cutting his operating costs. The patient, friendly horse may be making a limited comeback.

Just so the terms won't be forgotten, I am putting down a few notes about the rigging for horse and rider. Many of the horses drifted up this way from Mexico, for that country had big horse outfits long before we did. The cowboy really originated in Mexico.

Chaps: This is a contraction of the original Mexican "chapererros," a word too long and too hard to say to stay in our language. The double rr needs a trained tongue to get it just right. The word means literally "leg armor".

Chaps can be defined as a pair of pants without any seat. In the southwest, chaps were mainly leather with no hair. They were as light as it was practicable to make them. They were mainly for protection against thorns and brush. But in Oregon, when I can first remember, they were mainly for warmth and to keep the legs dry; they were usually made of angora skin with the hair left on the front side. They reached clear around the leg. "Chinks" were a leather variation of chaps. They were shorter and didn't reach all the way around. They were mainly for summer use, or use in the brush. They have straps with snaps on them that hook into rings coming from the other side of the leg.

Tapaderos: Another Spanish name. Tapadera is Spanish for a lid, or cover. The tapaderos, or "taps" as they
are almost always called, are a cover for the front of
the stirrup. Their purpose is to keep the feet dry and
warm and in brushy country they keep snags out of the
stirrups. Southwest and Mexican riders can't see why
they aren't used here in Oregon. But Oregon cowboys
usually thought them a little "dressy" and they were
never too popular here. There are two kinds; those with
long pointed tips, hanging down, to suit the taste of the
rider, some as far as two feet; second, the "bulldog" as
they were called here. They tended to turn up in front.
But in Texas they called them the "bull nose". The latter
have much shorter points, often only long enough to get
past the stirrup.

Honda: Spanish again, from their word for the eye
of a needle, hondon. In this state it is pronounced hondu,
accent on the hon. This is the small oval ring through
which the rope slides to close the loop after throwing
the rope. In Oregon it was usually made of rawhide and
was only about $2\frac{1}{2}$ to 3 inches long. Occasionally it was
made of horn. Nowadays a piece of rawhide is stretched
over a metal elongated ring with the edges bent up to
form a groove. Originally the honda was often made of
rope, stiffened so it wouldn't collapse and keep the big
loop from closing. But old timers swear by the rawhide
honda and will use no other.

Saddle: In Oregon single-cinch saddles were mostly
used. A Texas rider would sometimes drift in with a
double rig, or two-cincher. Oregon cowboys of that day
couldn't see any sense to this. This difference of opinion
led to a little difficulty in the bonanza horse days when
Oregon horses, raised on a free range, were selling briskly
to buyers from the Great Plains. A condition of the sale
was that the horses must be ridden in front of the buyer.
If the horse bucked too much, he was cut out. So the
Oregon riders would demonstrate the rideability of each
horse and if he didn't buck, he was accepted. But when
a Great Plains rider put a double cinch saddle on him,

he often performed scandalously. The Wyoming or Oklahoma or Colorado rider would make the prairie ring with his opinion of the low-down skunk who sawed off a bucker as a horse that had been rode. The cowboy philosophy was: "They ain't no horse that's never been rode, and they ain't no rider that's never been throwed."

J. P. Cullen, for years made excellent saddles at John Day, also George Rinehart, Hal Bell, and Tom Pullen. Now Harley Farra is doing a good job. Hamley of Pendleton, of course, sells saddles in all of America, even to some foreign countries such as Texas. There are innumerable types of saddles, each with its advocates.

Riata: From the Mexican la riata. Originally it was a rawhide rope and still is; the hemp rope is usually called a grass rope. Lariat is merely an American way of saying la riata. Lasso is a dude term, and as applied to a rope, isn't a true word. In Spanish it doesn't even mean a rope, but a snare. It can be used correctly to mean "catch" as "lasso the calf".

Harley Farra, saddle maker of John Day, gave me some prices on various ropes:

Riata	$	.80 a foot
Nylon rope		.25 a foot
Hemp rope		.14 a foot
Cotton rope		.10 a foot

He says that Frank Kellar of John Day still makes good rawhide ropes for sale, and that they usually retail for about 75 cents a foot. A 50-foot rope is about $40 now.

Cowboys, often adapting their terms to their profession, used to say of a man who had died, "He has coiled up his riata."

McCarty: Again a corruption of the Spanish mecate, accent on the a, so that it is approximately how a man with a southern accent would pronounce McCarty, omitting the r. It is a horsehair rope, to be used as a rein on a hackamore. It is interesting that the Indians used horsehair ropes long before the white man came and probably soon after the horse arrived. Some of the best McCartys are still made by Indians.

There was a family in Grant County, part Indian,
named George. One of the brothers, Joe, married a red-
haired white woman. They had four girls, some of them
with long red hair like their mother's, others with black.
The hair reached to their knees. One day Joe cut the
hair of all five, made a McCarty of it, real colorful with
mixture of red and black. My brother George bought
it for $25. So far as I know, this was the only McCarty
not made of hair from the manes and tails of horses.

Hackamore: The Spanish have it all their own way
with riding equipment. Spanish for headstall is Ja quima,
pronounced something like Ha keema, and no doubt
some American cowboy couldn't quite make that sound,
so we got hackamore out of it. It is sort of a halter and
bridle combination made of braided rawhide strings. In
Texas it often had a rope bit. It was useful in teaching a
horse to neck rein. Another advantage to it is that it can
be made at home, even of rope if necessary. It has never
been particularly popular in Oregon. Long before the
whites came, the Indians used a somewhat similar device.

Bridles: The bridle proper consisted of headstall, bit,
and reins. The bridle was normally plain but could be
pretty fancy with conchas or silver inlay work. Bits were
usually "half-breed" or full spade. The full spade bits
had a spade-like projection that pulled against the upper
part of the horse's mouth if the reins were pulled. They
could be severe if used by a careless rider. The "half-
breed" was less severe. The snaffle bit was rarely used
except for breaking horses or on a race horse. This had a
link connection in the center instead of a rigid bar with
a ring on each end. There were dozens of special bits,
each with some fancied advantage.

Headstalls were often silver mounted with various designs of silver buttons. Reins were often made of braided
rawhide strings. They were usually fastened together at
the end where the "romal" was attached. "Split reins"
were normally only for breaking horses, where they were
useful because they didn't have to go over the horse's
head and there was no danger of catching a spur in the

reins if the rider were thrown. If a rider was bucked off, the split reins had a big advantage. Even when sailing through the air the rider's instinct was to hang onto something, so he often kept hold of one rein, and then he'd still have his horse. Otherwise, he might be left afoot ten miles from camp. By the time he walked in, his feet would hurt and his pride hurt painfully, too.

The reins terminated in the romal, which was several thicknesses of light leather, braided or riveted into a single strap, up to five feet long, and used as a quirt, or even to reach out and slap a slow moving cow. Some were sewn together, with the edges rounded, others fastened with copper rivets, that, kept shined, gave a highly ornamental effect. This is another variation of a Spanish word for the same thing. Their word is Ramal. Accent is on the last syllable in both languages.

Spurs: All styles were used. Some cowboys spent more money for spurs than for a suit. Spurs can be pretty fancy, with silver inlay work. They had large or small rowels with long or short shanks. There were no standard spurs; good riders rarely used them excessively. They were used to get a quick start, or in riding a bucking bronc, to hold on by your heels, by hooking into the cinch.

Conchas: This is the Spanish word for shells. They are circular ornaments for fastening onto spur straps, belts, saddles, headstalls, breast collars, or even chaps. They are about the only ornament that Oregon working cowboys ever wore. No doubt the original conchas were shells, but now they are usually silver plated or even silver. They can be plain, or can have stamped patterns, sometimes floral, sometimes geometric.

Boots: They were at first plain, strong cowhide, with high heels to keep them from slipping through the stirrups. The two-toned jobs were unknown in my youth. Even now they are mostly used for dress-up.

Hat: This hasn't changed much. It was broad and of good stuff. The Stetson was always preferred. It could be used to dip up water, to wave at a fractious cow, to throw in the air as a joy indicator, or a hundred things. You might see a pretty ragged cowpoke with a good Stetson hat. I always felt dressed up if I had a good hat, clean boots, and new levis. Cowboys are sort of a breed of their own. In any gathering of people, you can usually pick out the working cowmen. Somehow they walk, talk, and act differently, no matter how they dress.

Slicker: This was sort of looked down on, somewhat as an umbrella might be. Most cowboys of my day didn't carry a slicker. Neither did you take a lunch. You were classed as a tenderfoot if you took these things.

Any green hand was fair game, with plenty of embarrassing things about to happen at the most unexpected moments. I saw one cowboy sneak out a couple of pieces of raw beef and tamp them into another man's tapaderos one August. The meat spoiled quickly and the man, to his utter amazement, was plagued by swarms of blow flies all day.

I saw another new hand who was told that the custom of the camp was that all new men had to carry the lunch. So one of the others collected a shoe-box full of horse manure, wrapped it, put it in a sack and gave it to the newcomer. At noon we all managed to be there, had him pick out a nice spot by a creek and unwrap the lunch to pass around. You can imagine what his nickname was for years.

Lum Short was an old time cowman in Klamath County, well known to all the early day folks and to all the Indians. He was riding early one morning near Fort Klamath and noticed an Indian of his acquaintance absorbed in thought leaning against a big yellow pine tree. Late that afternoon he came back that way and the Indian was still there. He rode over and said, "George, what are you thinking about so hard?" The Indian said simply, "All time see black horse with white face, never see white horse with black face." Tell that to a dyed-in-the-wool horseman and after a bit you'll see him off by himself thinking hard.

When I was a small boy, U. S. Cavalry officers and men were still riding over Eastern Oregon, with their picturesque uniforms of blue and their dashing manners. One day 200 mounted soldiers went through the John Day Valley and an officer asked father if they might camp in our meadow. I was all eyes. I can still see them as they lined up their wagons in straight-as-string formation with ropes stretched between them to form a little enclosure for the horses. There was only one rope but the horses wouldn't break under or jump over. They enjoyed the limited freedom though and rolled for a time on the nice clean meadow grass. When the bugle sounded, indicating grain feeding time, all the well-trained horses lined up along the rope fence for their nose bag of oats. I am mentioning this only because it was a sight no one will ever see again in or out of Grant County.

John Devine, left, and Jeff Billingsley, who worked for him and later became state senator. Note the skeleton harness and cart used to get over range land in place of the saddle horse. Devine developed two famous ranches in Grant County near Steens Mountain, now part of Harney—the White Horse Ranch and the Alvord.

Devine was the first settler in what is now Harney County. He raised cattle and race horses. He was known all over the West and was one of the very few "cattle barons" of Oregon. He went broke and Henry Miller, of Miller and Lux, bought his holdings at a bankruptcy sale.

CHAPTER 11

WILD HORSES

No one knows how many wild horses Oregon supported at the peak. Technically, there is no such thing
as a "wild horse" in America. Horses are not native to
either North or South America—the Spaniards brought
them, so a wild horse here was either a tame horse gone
wild, or an untamed descendant.

The horses got to Oregon about sixty years before
Lewis and Clark came. The early explorers found many
horses here, some with Spanish brands. Horses were plentiful among the Snakes, Cayuse, and Nez Perce Indians.
In fact, the Cayuses had so many that Indian ponies of
any kind came to be called "cayuses." There weren't any
west of the Cascade mountains though, indicating the
horses came up along the base of the Rockies, not up the
coast from California.

The Indians, for the most part, didn't castrate their
horses, which multiplied fast. There is evidence that the
Nez Perce tribe, almost alone among the North American Indians, practiced castration of colts to some extent.
The famous Appaloosa horses, with the odd spots on
their rumps, came from the "Palouse" area, where some
branches of the Nez Perce tribe lived. Appaloosa comes
from Palouse.

As long as the Indians ruled eastern Oregon, there
weren't many wild horses, if any. The Indians were slowly
confined on reservations, from about 1850 to 1870. They
staged a last desperate adventure in 1878, the Bannock
War, after Chief Joseph's War the year before. After
that the wild horses came into their own in Oregon, some
of them from the Indian cayuses, but mostly escapees, or
just unbranded horses from white men's herds.

Wild horses have stirred imaginations of poets, artists, naturalists, and writers more than any other wild animal. Somehow, a wild stallion, silhouetted against the sky, head up, nostrils flared, mane and tail flying in the wind, has seemed the very essence of freedom. He is brother to the wild geese, northward flying; to the soaring eagle; to the crouching cougar; to the very wind that blows.

Even before the Indian menace was erased, daring men came into Malheur and Harney Counties and started horse empires. They were followed by others in Lake, Crook, and Deschutes. Their horses were numbered by thousands branded and as many with no sign of a brand. How can anyone know the number of wild horses when not one of these old time horse raisers could tell you within a thousand head how many horses he owned? Two of the largest operators were Bill Brown and John Devine.

The wild horse has left his imprint in names in eastern Oregon. There is the famous Whitehorse Ranch on Whitehorse Creek in Harney County. An Indian, Black Rock Tom, rode a beautiful white horse, gave the whites plenty of trouble and gave the creek its name. There was also a Whitehorse post office in Baker County, named for another animal. The horses congregated on Horse Ridge in Deschutes and on Pony Butte in Jefferson.

Wildhorse Creek in Umatilla is especially interesting. When it first appears in history, it was called Marron Creek. Now in Spanish, Cimarron was originally a runaway slave, which shortened to marron, became in Mexico a domestic animal, gone wild. So the wild mustangs of the border were often called marrons and it is peculiar that the name got this far north.

Wallowa County is full of horse names: Horse Creek; Deadhorse Ridge; Blackhorse Creek, Corral Basin, where Indians corraled horses; Saddle Creek; and Freezeout Saddle.

The most interesting horse name of all is in Lane County, Noti. A white man and an Indian were traveling together. They had only one horse between them, so they followed the "ride and tie" method, each riding half the time. But the white man got in a hurry, and instead of leaving the horse at a frontier settlement, as agreed upon, he rode on. When the walking Indian found no mount, he complained, "Him no tie." The budding town was called "Noti."

There is a Horse Heaven in Jefferson and a Saddle Butte in Harney. Even the more lowly mule left his trail in names. A post office in Harney was called "Mule" and there is a Muleshoe Mountain in Wheeler County.

So, though the wild stallion on the rimrock is pretty nearly past, we still honor him with names. He isn't entirely gone—there are a few remnant bands in isolated places in the Owyhee country. There is a small band in the upper canyons of the Grande Ronde, and there are horses of doubtful ownership running loose in Harney and Lake Counties.

There were many wild horse stories. Tebo was a famous Mexican c h a r a c t e r, an employee of Pete French. He could top any story in a bunkhouse or around a campfire. He would wait until all the others were through, then tell his story in serious, unsmiling style, as though it were gospel.

This time the talk had been running on famous fast horses captured from wild bands. So Tebo told about his palomino, Paly for short. It seemed that this palomino stallion got to be a legend around Steens Mountain. Many cowboys had seen him and tried for weeks to capture him. They tried to wear him down with relay teams; they tried to snare him; they tried to catch him around water holes; they tried to drive him and his band of mares into strong corrals—Paly outsmarted them.

But, he, Tebo, decided to catch Paly. He got a telescope, posted himself on distant points, charted Paly's movements every day of the week and found that every Thursday he passed a big rock, as big as a hotel, at twenty-two minutes after eight in the morning. So Tebo got an 80-foot riata, hid behind the rock, and threw at exactly the right time.

When Paly felt the rope tighten, he turned like a shot and headed north. When he came to the end of the riata, Paly never even hesitated. It parted with a noise like a rifle shot and Paly went north like the wind.

So Tebo, thinking of the faint chance that the riata would get snarled in brush, followed, picking up the trail. About ten miles north he found a Basque sheep herder and asked about a horse with a lariat on him. The herder said, "He passed so close as ten feet and never so fast did I see a horse run. Ze rope, for 70 feet she stretch out straight in ze air behind. Ze horse, she was beautiful, but I pay not so much mind, because of ze rope. For ze rope she was covered from end to end wiz tired horse-flies."

Probably ninety percent of the wild horses of Oregon were in the desert counties of southeastern Oregon, stretching down toward Nevada and extreme southwest Idaho. But we had some bands that ranged in the head-waters of Grub Creek and Beech Creek, north of the John Day. The bands were usually from about seven up to 25, each with its stallion leader, and the others mares. As is the case with the deer now, there was all kinds of summer range, but in winter the snows would force them down into the open grasslands on the ranches. There were far too many for the grass available.

Occasionally a war somewhere in the world would cause a sudden demand for cavalry and artillery horses. The Boer War really was a bonanza for the cowboys, be-cause without much finances or backing, a few men could go out and round up hundreds of these wild horses, break them, and come out of the deal with enough money to buy whiskey and women for months.

Between wars the horses bred and multiplied enorm-ously, except that an occasional hard winter would kill them off by the thousands, as is now the case with deer herds that get too plentiful.

For a long time we didn't pay so much attention to them, but finally came to see that wherever there were wild horses, there wasn't much range anymore. The bunch grass left and was replaced by sagebrush or weeds. They were especially hard on the grass in winter and spring, when they congregated by hundreds on grassy hillsides, pawed away the snow, and dug out the grass— sometimes roots and all. If it happened to be a dry year, the grass on such a range never came back, so then the horses next year would ruin another hill. After this had gone on from 1870 to around 1910, forty years, there wasn't much grass left in entire counties. Anyone can check on this by counting the rings on the big sagebrush plants. Most of them are around seventy to eighty years old, the exact time when the horses were thick.

It was lots of fun, though, to round them up. It took horse sense to do it, together with strength, and good riding horses.

In our country, the mustangs lived in steep areas with big rocky open flats on tops of the ridges or on the south slopes. There might be badger holes, loose shale rock, or steep bare places. Also, there were tree branches that could scrape you off, claw at your face, or even break your neck. When after a band of wild horses, you usually had to take these hazards on the dead run.

We first built a strong corral at some central point, with wide wings extending out to each side from the gate. Then we had to locate our band of maybe 25 or 30. The stallion in charge was the key horse. He was wild and meant to stay that way. He got to be a leader by being swifter, stronger, keener in sight and smell, and by having more endurance than his fellow stallions. If we saw him, we knew he had seen us. Even if we didn't see him, he may have smelled us and hurried his harem away from there by some secret path among the cliffs and over the mountains.

His first act upon seeing or smelling a rider, was to snort or whistle, then he made a few short dashes among his band to alert them and start them on his chosen path of escape. Then the fun started. Our own horses had to be fast, sure of foot, and quick to start. And the riders had to know as much about those hills as the stallion did.

When he started his band we had to guess the pass or trail he intended to follow and someone had to beat him there.

This took judgment, almost art. You had to beat the wild horse to the chosen point, but your horse had to be fresh. If winded, or too tired to dash quickly, the whole thing failed. You just sat there and watched the wild horse run away. Also, in a rocky country, you had to look out, and trust your horse. If he went down among the rocks you might never get up.

I always used a snaffle bit for this work, because you needed a tight rein. A good horse can smell a badger hole and avoid it. But no wild horse chaser in mountainous country got off without some pretty bad spills. He could scarcely keep at it for years without a broken bone or two. These things were all part of the fun for young fellows my age. Danger adds its own excitement.

Riders also had to know what the other fellow had probably done. You had no way of knowing for sure where the other man was, but the trick was to keep the wild band running by turning it toward a fresh rider. He, in turn, would run them top speed for a time and turn them over to another rider who just happened to be at the right place at the right time. It took fine teamwork. In the desert or plains roundups, you could often see the dust clouds and guide on them, but usually in our country you had to guess.

No band can run forever, so if we were lucky or had figured right, eventually the wild horses would be pretty well winded, and in that condition we could gang up and drive them in the direction we wanted them to go. There was only one catch to this. We always wanted the stallion leader, because he was often a splendid animal, and if broken right, he would be a valuable ranch horse. Even if we didn't want him, we could always sell him for more than the mares would bring. And I guess we just wanted him anyhow, because he was so much harder to get. But time after time we would get the mares to the chosen spot but find the cunning stallion had outsmarted us again. For a gathering spot we usually chose an open flat covered with rocks. The horses were easier to hold in such a place.

The first job in trying for a stallion was to maneuver him into open country so that the riders could see each other. The next job was to try to arrange it so that each rider had a chance to rest his horse a little. Many of these stallions could out-last any of our horses and run right away from them at the end. Our only hope was to rest our riding horses some. If we had time we would jerk the saddle off, let the air onto their backs, and smooth the blankets down and shake the twigs out of them. If we didn't have time for that, it helped to get off and loosen the cinch for a few minutes.

Then, with a freshened horse, if the other boys had shunted him back and forth so that he couldn't run his best, maybe when he came your way you could make a quick dash and rope him. I did this once with a nice stallion.

I was sitting on a point, waiting to see where he might turn next. He was a sorrel with a blazed face. He outran a rider trying to turn him and hit for a well-traveled trail that I knew led up and over a brushy knob. Beyond was a flat with no rocks but some badger holes. I had time to reach the flat before he did and I had a good strong horse.

I had my loop ready and as he burst out of the brush, I was at the right place to put the loop around his neck. Fun started then. He dashed this way and that, but I was able to hold him until some other riders came. We threw him, took one of the riatas and made a halter, broke him to lead, and we took him home. I rode him that same evening and he became gentle in time and a real good ranch horse.

After such a success, especially if it is a stallion that you have tried to catch before, and failed, all hands gather about, go over every minute of the hunt, and act just as I suppose a group of tiger hunters in Africa act when they have their tiger. The hunt was good for an hour's talk anytime for months after.

Another thing about these wild horses was that every rancher had horses of his own, and if one of these stallions was in the country, he was always trying to add to his harem, by enticing our mares to become wild. After a man had lost a few hundred dollars worth of horses, and seen his range going downhill in a sickening way, he was ready to go out and help to get rid of the cause of his troubles.

The last big roundup of horses from our range was in 1904. It took thirty days with a crew of twelve men, a cook and cook wagon, and a horse wrangler. Each of us had to have several horses, because this work was tough on them and we wanted fresh mounts every day. We were able to gather 1000 head, and, after cutting out the better animals to keep, we had 700 left, which we drove to Ontario and sold. The twelve riders weren't cowboys out to make something; we were all ranchers who wanted to get rid of the wild horse menace.

In delivering these 700 wild horses we had two adventures. We took them to the head of the John Day river, then over the mountain and east toward Ontario. We were following a narrow road through dense timber with several riders ahead. Usually these wild herds would follow a man on horseback well, after they were away from their own range and into country unfamiliar to them. This time something suddenly stampeded them. They all left at top speed through the timber, brush cracking, colts nickering, riders trying to head them, dust flying in clouds. This was the wildest ride I ever had. A fall might have put one underneath the hooves of a hundred frightened horses. No one could see a thing and most of us didn't know the terrain. No one knew where the other riders were. By circling, we finally did get them back on the trail near the summit, and their herd instinct kept them together. Just by good luck no one was killed or hurt.

It was a hot, dry August. Toward the end of the trail, the horses hadn't had a drop of water for two days. Suddenly they smelled the Snake River two miles to the east and they stampeded again, this time a wild, uncontrollable break to water. When they came to it, they dashed in, oblivious of the fact that the river had a quicksand bottom. Soon horses were sinking and floundering helplessly in all directions. Luckily a farmer lived nearby who had four big work horses and plenty of heavy derrick rope. We pulled out all except one that was too far out for the rope to reach. We gave him to the farmer who saved him later that day.

RANDOM COMMENTS ABOUT HORSES

I have said that eastern Oregon was famous all over America for its horses. Here is an odd thing. The areas most famous for horses all through history have been: Arabia, Morocco, Spain, and the American West (including Mexico). They have but one thing in common —they are all arid. Can it be that rain washes things out of the soil that horses need for stamina, spirit, and bone?

People don't ride stallions much anymore, because there aren't many stallions; but in the countries named, for hundreds of years it was considered unmanly to ride a mare. The old time cowboys never rode mares. They felt just like the Arabs and Spanish did. As for geldings, castration of horses is a comparatively modern practice.

The Indians prized horses more even than scalps. If an Indian had a choice between stopping for a scalp or getting away with a horse or two, he chose the latter every time. They didn't regard horse stealing as a crime, it was an art. The Indian who could steal most skillfully was looked up to by the whole tribe.

Among white settlers, though, a horse thief carried a special bad aroma. I never quite understood the psychology of that. If caught, the judge would stare at him as though the man had killed his mother and would send him to the pen for as long as ten years. Maybe the stolen horse wasn't worth over $10. But the same judge, in sentencing a cattle thief who had preyed on his neighbors for years, stealing steers and cows worth $50 each, would gently deal out a two or three year sentence. Why is "horse thief" a worse name to call a man than "cattle thief"? It has just grown up that way in the West.

The wild horses weren't everywhere. In our country creeks were numerous, as they are in most timbered country, so water wasn't a factor, but in the high desert, there is still good grass in places ten miles from water, indicating that the horses didn't usually feed that far from their watering places. Horses can smell water for incredible distances. Cattle are pretty good at it. Those who drove bands of horses or cattle east from Oregon, tell how, after a waterless day, the horses would prick up their ears, shed their weariness, and go at a brisk trot or gallop to some unlikely looking spot a mile or two away. They would find there a hidden spring, perhaps up on a mountain side, or on the other side of a hill. So far as humans can tell, clean water has no smell, but horses can smell it.

Most ranchers, if they hunt deer or elk at all, would rather hunt horseback, partly because they would rather ride than walk, but mainly because they are more successful. A horse will point out a wild animal to you long before you can see it. If he gets the idea that you are after deer, he will hunt them with his nose, and point them out with his ears. You will see two or three times as many in a day on a good horse as you will on foot.

The wild horses are pretty much creatures of habit, as are most wild animals. They use the same waterholes; have their young at the same spot year after year; winter in the same little draw or valley. If you drive them away from their favorite wintering place, even miles away, they will come back.

Some men never learn to ride. Unless a man can learn to take the jar down near the small of his back, he'll never be much good for long rides. He'll be hard on the horses, too. Some riders try to take it on their feet, some slump and try to transfer it to their shoulders. No way is any good except to sit up straight dividing weight between the stirrup and the tail end of your spine. Once you learn that trick, you can ride all day without getting too tired and without getting sore. You aren't nearly so likely to give the horse a saddle gall, either.

Horses have a strong herd instinct, another reason why they are hard on range. They like to get together in groups, far more than cattle. Cattle tend to spread out pretty well, once they learn a range. There will be one cow with her calf here, another one a quarter of a mile away, and they will cover a range and use all the feed. Horses in large numbers gang up and destroy a range, a piece of it at a time.

I have told of my experiences with wild horses in the steep, mountainous parts of Grant County, with its timbered slopes, frequent creeks and scab-rock ridges. Wild horses also abounded in the so-called desert counties: Lake, Harney, Malheur, and parts of Deschutes and Crook. The balance of this chapter is from information supplied by Reub Long. In the big open country of Central Oregon he spent many years in the pursuit and capture of the horses that ran there wild and free. Says Reub:

"Our country where I have had most of my experience is the open country or the "high desert" of eastern Oregon. This is an interesting area, left over from the volcanic eruptions of millions of years ago, with high mesas, lava rimrocks, sunken areas, hidden little valleys, all covered by sagebrush and rabbitbrush, and a long time between drinks. There are almost no springs or natural water holes and no rivers or creeks, except near the edges where the desert lifts up to the higher elevation pine forests. But at one time this country had thousands and thousands of wild horses—some born in the wild, others tame horses that had gone wild.

"Wild horse gathering was somewhat of a science or art that worked its way north from Mexico, so it, like the gear for saddle horses, gathered some Spanish names. The most successful method was, when I was young, to "parada" them. I don't know the exact meaning of the word. It was used as both a verb and a noun. So it was the operation itself, or a description of it. Old time cattlemen used to use it to describe a bunch of cattle that were to be cut out from the main bunch. I think it means something like to collect, or to bunch, temporarily. In the same way you can "bunch" cattle, but after you get them, you have a "bunch". So you could parada the wild horses, and if successful you had a parada.

"For this method you had to have a herd of your own tame horses, a caballada. Now here is another Spanish word. A Spanish horse is a caballo and a rider is a caballero, and your herd is a caballado. The word got changed more or less, as it worked north, and finally got worked down to cavvy. These tame horses have to be able to run, but must be easy to handle.

"Spring is the best time to parada because the wild horses are either heavy with foal or have little colts with them. Also, the leader stallion has a good-sized bunch at that time.

"You spot your bunch of wild horses, being careful not to be seen. Then, using little valleys or sharp ridges, you work your cavvy as close as possible to the wild herd, but you must be careful to keep them on ground where they can move fast when the time comes. You don't want any high rimrocks or rough lava between them and the horses you are after.

"When you are ready, you send two good men on real good horses around the wild bunch to the other side to start the wild horses into the parada. If impossible to get around them without being seen, you make a 'sheep herder sneak,' that is, you have the men resemble a sheepherder leading his packhorse, slowly, and paying no attention to the herd.

"The riders start the wild horses toward the parada. As they near it, a lookout is watching and ready to start the tame horses running. This takes experience and judgment and perfect timing. If your horses are started too quickly, the wild horses see them too far away and the stallion leader herds his band in another direction. If started too late, the wild bunch goes racing by. If done just right, one running herd meets the other, going the other way, and the wild horses get confused and out of touch with the stallion. Your best men on the best horses are in the lead and they gradually slow down the whole bunch, get them to act as a single herd, and they can then be herded in the direction you want them to go.

"Another variation is to take your parada out into a central location on the open range and then send men out to try to bring horses in. These riders may have to chase the wild horses for miles before they can be herded into the bunch. There's one thing about this business— you may think you have a pretty good horse, but there is no better way to find out than to go riding after wild horses.

"If water holes are far between, trap corrals may be built around the water holes. This takes patience. The horses usually come in at night, and they won't come if you just go out there and build your trap. Build it a little at a time, and after the trap is completed, just stay away from there, so the horses will get accustomed to the whole thing and will go in with confidence. After they are using the water regularly, then someone must hide near the entrance and close the gate with the horses inside.

"These trap corrals are sometimes built in canyons where horses travel up and down, or in passes between rimrocks, or other natural runways. For that type you build wide V-shaped wings out a quarter mile to a half mile, so as to force the horses into the corral. These wings don't need to be solid except near your trap. Binding

twine strung on stakes with a few tin cans tied along it
will turn the horses as good as a real fence, so long as
you aren't crowding them.

"Another method we used to call 'rabbit driving,'
but it takes a large crew and doesn't work well except
in real flat and open country. The boss of the drive picks
out a bunching ground maybe 15 or 20 miles from where
he starts. He sends some men to the bunch ground, then
spreads his crew in a wide semi-circle. Each man must
wait until the last man gets into position.

"The key men are those on the points of the crescent.
They must know the country and be well mounted. They
are the ones that keep the running horses pointed toward the bunch ground. The system works well, provided everyone keeps in line. One rider, too anxious,
who gets out ahead, will turn the horses right back toward the other riders and they will go between the riders,
and the whole thing fails. The secret is to keep the horses
running ahead.

"If the crew is small, only one, two, or three men,
we would do what we called 'coyote' them. You just take
out after the bunch you want and follow them, keeping
on the move every hour of daylight. This usually took
us about three days until they were worn down so they
could be handled. Each rider usually takes some grain
for his horse and a chunk of bread for himself. If he can
come across a sheep camp or an old shack to stay in, he
may have some cover, but mostly you just stay out there
wherever night drops on you. At daylight you pick up
the band again. This works lots better in the winter
when the horses have to break a trail in the snow. This
tires them and at that time they aren't too stout anyhow,
because wintering on the desert isn't too soft a living at
best. The only trouble is that there is quite a difference
between the weak ones and the strong, so the weak keep
dropping out, one at a time, and you've got to decide
whether to bring a few of those in or to keep after the
main band. You can't do both, and it's usually the good
strong members you'd rather have.

"The most used method and the least successful is to take a group of riders and just surround and outride the wild band, running them into a corral. If the country where they are is real rough and brushy that may be the only thing you can do. It takes fast riding and real good judgment all around. Every rider must be well mounted.

"When a man wants a particular wild horse, sometimes he just tries to get close enough and ropes him. That is a last resort, because it can be time-consuming and there are lots of failures. You have to have some sort of advantage to make this work. Either the wild horse has been worn down by other riders, or you catch him where he can't get past you easily, or you have some other advantage. A horse with a man and a saddle on him isn't able to catch up with a wild free horse in an even race.

"A successful wild horse runner has to be able to judge speed and distance and have a sort of instinct for the work. I have seen men who have gathered wild horses all their lives and never really did get the hang of it. You must judge your own speed, your ability to keep that speed, the lay of the country, the kind of ground that you and the wild horses will have to run on. You have to know just how long it will take the horses to reach a certain point and match that time with how long it will take your horse to reach it. They may have the shorter distance to run or you may have. They may have to go over a steep hill or you may have to do that. They may have to run on loose sand, while you have solid ground—and so on.

"After they are bunched and off their own range, they are easier to move than gentle horses—provided nothing spooks them. They soon learn to follow a man on horseback. They usually make no attempt to break away, and they have a very strong herd instinct. If they ever stampede though, it can be bad."

CHAPTER 12

OTHER LIFE, TAME AND WILD

About 1910, Ira G. Boyce, a native of Missouri, went into the hog business west of John Day. All went well until the hogs were ripe for market. The nearest railroad was the narrow gauge from Baker that terminated at Prairie City. He decided to follow the example of the stockmen and trail the hogs out. This decision was based strictly upon cost, not practicability, because there was no wide highway then. The hogs were not at all broken to drive and they could see no sense in it whatever.

The result was a string 25 miles long of the maddest people you ever saw. The hogs dashed through petunia and pansy beds; into chicken houses, through barnyards, and into fields. Once they got into a tall field of grain, one couldn't even see them and they saw no reason to leave. They seemed to know where the river was, and would run through the alfalfa or meadowgrass and hide in the thickets along the river.

It surely was no way to make friends and influence hogs. At last they were all gathered at Prairie City and shipped out. The experiment was not tried again.

In the early 1900's we had lots of hogs on our ranch. A wild clover grew in our Bear Valley meadows and father somehow discovered that it made fine hog feed. So in June we rigged up hog wagons and took the hogs to summer range, just like sheep. In the fall we rounded them up again and hauled them to Prairie City where we rented grain stubble. When that ran out, the hogs were almost ready for slaughter, so from the little pig to the mature animal we put precious little grain into them.

I don't know of anyone now who raises hogs and manages them this way. To finish, we fed cooked barley, and sugarbeets or potatoes.

One season the Mormon crickets came like a bad dream. They are big, about like a small mouse, travel by jumping a foot or two, and an army of them is sort of terrifying. They take a course and go straight ahead. They go over a fence post, a man, or a cow, or a tree, instead of around it. They eat everything green or anything soft enough to eat. It's just too bad if they come to a shirt or gloves or some clothing on a fence. Nothing is left of a hay shock after they pass.

When they come to a stream they jump right in and soon there are enough drowned crickets to make a bridge for the millions behind to cross on. This particular year they made an army three and a half miles wide. They passed right through the meadow where the hogs were and the hogs thought that was all right. The hogs loved them and ate crickets steadily, following them for miles. We couldn't drive the hogs away from such tender, fine tasting food. But with the meadow cleaned of all food, we had to bring the hogs home early.

The next year a swarm of migratory grasshoppers followed about the same course. These were big, soft-bodied hoppers nearly two inches long, as I remember them. They were even fiercer in their appetites. A set of harness or a saddle was just a snack for them. We had to hide these articles away in underground or dirt type cellars or in the house. Hoppers flew from grass to grass, so were on the wing part of the time, whereas the crickets were strictly infantry. To really fill up on the hoppers in short order, the hogs had to wait until sunset, when the insects camped on the ground wherever sundown overtook them.

After sunrise they took to the air again, some instinct directing them straight east. No cow, horse, or man could face them. The swarm shaded the sun, as a black cloud would.

In the early 90's, all up and down the John Day
River, there was a heavy stand of large thorn bushes,
very dense. These were covered by dark berries, which
the hogs liked, and so did all kinds of birds. A neighbor
let a sow and a boar take up residence in the thorn
brush. The pigs multiplied like flies and one person
hadn't a chance to capture them or drive them out. A
few generations, and the thick thorn patch was alive with
wild hogs that came out at night and destroyed grain
fields. Something had to be done.

Father gathered the men of the neighborhood who
took all the full grown, strong, big dogs they could mus-
ter, took guns and plenty of shells and went to work.
The dogs would surround a fierce old hog and bark with
excitement and the men would part the vicious thorns
and hurry to the spot. A shot, well placed, would drop
the savage hog that was trying hard to snap off a dog's
leg. If the dogs found a hog too young to fight, they
would catch and hold the pig.

If these weaner pigs weren't injured, they were taken
alive. If injured, of course they were shot, too. The
weaners taken home were put in with 80 of our domestic
pigs. They were sold to a Harney County man who
hauled them away in a 3-decker wagon. When necessary
he stopped at streams and threw water over them to keep
them alive in the hot weather.

We had another good outlet for hogs—the Chinese.
This was after the main gold rush and John Day had
more Chinese than whites, over 500 of them. They were
all fond of pork—they seemed to prefer it to all other
meat. They often bought our weaners and fattened them
with waste vegetables and garbage.

There is an old Chinese cemetery on the hill at the
edge of John Day. Another group of Chinese on Dixie
Creek headquartered in John Day, where they gathered,
gambled and probably some of them smoked opium. At
least that was the shocked report. Whenever those working on Dixie Creek came to John Day for a holiday, there
would be a big group, maybe 50. They walked single

file, shouted back and forth to each other, and it made quite a racket. It sounded real outlandish and foreign to us boys.

But if one died on Dixie Creek they always hired a livery rig to bring the body to John Day for burial. The dead were treated with great respect and ceremony. Some Chinese would go in front and scatter all along the road pieces of thin paper resembling tissue. These were about 4x6 inches and had many small holes in them, much as though a pencil had been shoved through as often as possible without making the holes join. They told us that the devil had to go back and forth through all of these holes before he could overtake the corpse.

After the gold played out, some Chinese took to ranching or working on ranches. One of the oldest ranches in the valley belonged to Harve Fields. He had a big outfit, both cattle and sheep. For years Fields hired only Chinese—sheep herders, cowboys, cook, everything.

Even the foreman was Chinese. He was called Buckaroo Sam and lived in John Day until his death from old age. He wore a big Western hat and cowboy boots. Everyone liked him.

The Chinese gradually thinned out. I knew very well three of them that stayed until they died. They were Buckaroo Sam, Leon, and Doctor Hey. Leon and Hey built up sizable estates. Leon owned the Chevrolet garage building and agency. Dr. Hey, his friend, was blind in later life, but had a great following. He doctored entirely with herbs, and patients came from as far away as California, Portland, and Idaho. After his death, his nephew, Bob Wah, took up his practice and held it and is still here. Wah's son, Dr. Eddie Wah, is a graduate of the University of Oregon dental school and is a popular and successful dentist in John Day.

As in most Western mining towns, the young boys delighted in tormenting the Chinese. We didn't look at them the way we did at other people. They were strange and foreign. It is somewhat the same way with a new boy in school. Anyhow, when the single file Chinese passed our ranch on holidays on their 15-mile walk from Dixie to John Day, we conceived a sort of devilish sport. We had a dog, Rover, who was well trained to chase cows by catching their tails. The Chinese wore long queues, allowed to hang down on holidays. On work days these were coiled under their funny hats. So my brother George and I would lie in wait when we heard them coming, and sic Rover on them. With the cows in mind, he would grab their queues and swing back and forth. This seemed pure fun for a 10-year old boy. We liked it and so did Rover, but somehow the Chinese didn't take to it much.

We had a lady in John Day, Mrs. Norman, who belonged back in the middle ages, or in Egypt or some place where cats were revered. She had around 150 of them and kept them in an odd barn-like building. The first section of this was small, and as the cats increased, new sections were built on, each higher than the next, until the last was maybe 30 feet high. This alone was enough to attract notice and the town kids made a sing-song rhyme about the old man and woman who built a barn that was a flier, for it started as a little one and each year it got a little higher, or something to that idiotic effect.

Mrs. Norman walked about town every evening, winter and summer, after dark, with a basket of food to see that all cats in town got fed. The cats thought this was great stuff, and 40 or 50 followed her, rubbing on her and giving glad, appreciative noises. She was badly stooped, wore a heavy, long black dress, a shawl over her head, and carried a lantern in one hand, her basket in the other. She always talked to herself and probably to the cats.

She was a milk customer of father's, and maybe due to the cats, she kept no container outside. She asked father to walk into the kitchen and measure out the milk. One morning I was along and was glad to go in with him, because this cat woman excited my curiosity.

Good type young range bull, 18 months old. In buying bulls, Herman always insisted on looking at the entire herd. He shied away from a good animal in a poor herd.

800 head of A2 cows coming through town early in the morning to avoid traffic, yelling children, auto horns, and other distractions. Riders are Joe Oliver, left, and Sam Keerins, right, checking the cattle to keep them from stringing out too far.

Fishing for steelhead in the John Day River. Odd formation of clay, topped by rock in center is one of the many fossil locations.

Fossil and Rock hunters talking it over between Dayville and Kimberly, Grant County.

In the binder days, the bundles were put into little forests of neat stacks, like this. Good stackers were scarce and could get $2 a day when ordinary workers got $1.

This steam engine threshed the grain around Prairie City about 1910. Identifiable are: Ed Martin, on left, with oil can; Ed Anderson with head and shoulders visible in center; C. M. Collier and wife to right of Anderson, and Mrs. Johnson, mother of Mrs. Collier, on extreme right.

Old time haying scene, about 1898, on the Oliver ranch. Herman, age about 14, on the rake; Joe Oliver, founder of the ranch and father of Herman, at far right, with his wife "Lizzie." The three Gregg children are shown here: Lizzie, the left one of the two girls, Henry leaning on pitchfork, Will on the empty wagon on the left. Herman's older brother George is the pitcher near the empty wagon. Near the center is the old milk wagon, with Frank, the white horse. The team-mate, Blue, is not visible. Frank Oliver, Herman's brother, is on the horse behind the buggy, barely visible.

The wild hay was usually put up with a homemade outfit of rope slings on a slide. This made a sloping stack, leading to much spoiled hay, but "what the Hell? It's only worth $5 a ton anyhow." But in hard winters, the price could zoom to $40.

Mr. Norman did not see eye to eye with her about cats—in fact he hated them real bad. Just as we walked into the kitchen, she opened the oven door and out came smoke and smell of roast cat. One had probably crawled in for warmth and the door had been shut in the dark. Anyhow, she blamed her husband instantly and loudly, claiming he had planned it all. But he denied this hotly, although from his remarks I gained the impression that he was a little sorry he hadn't thought of it. I expected a murder right before my eyes, but father didn't seem so worried and we left with the argument still raging.

Mr. Norman was an easy-going little man with a squeaky voice. There was another old timer down at Mt. Vernon, who was also small, with a squeaky voice.

One morning, father, on his regular milk route, came upon these two men fighting furiously. They weren't doing each other much harm, only because they weren't strong enough, but the fire and the will were there. Father separated them, easily held each out of reach of the other, and asked for the basis of the fight. It developed that they had never seen each other before and each accused the other of mimicking him.

Homemade windlass on the D. E. Jones ranch, Juntura. Every sizable cattle ranch in Oregon used such a windlass to hang up an animal for dressing it for home consumption. Larger ranches consumed an average of a steer a week. This windlass is still in use on the Jones ranch.

Chapter 13

WHAT GOES ON IN CATTLE COUNTRY

Black Dan

He was fondly named Daniel La Follett by his parents, but was Black Dan in Canyon City in the gold days. He was dark and handsome, wore a splendid dark mustache that made feminine hearts go pitty-pat, and he earned his daily bread by arts known to professional gamblers.

One day he became careless. The writer of the day didn't say exactly what happened—perhaps each of two men in the same stud hand seemed to have an ace of spades in the hole. Anyhow, what with the adverse comment and all, he got himself shot. Dan didn't seem to act like the stories at that point. He should have called to his poor old mother that he now repented of his life of sin, or at the very least should have made some noble gesture.

He knew he had only a short time to live, so asked those about him, as they crawled out from behind the places they went to when the shooting started, to put him on the table where he could die with more dignity than down on the floor among all the things that might be on a saloon floor in the gold days. He asked that "the women of his acquaintance" be called in. They, presumably by great effort, controlled their tears and made his last moments joyous by singing merry folk songs and giving him whiskey enough to kill the pain. The local reporter said this went on until "the spark of his unprofitable life was quite extinguished."

This is all preliminary. It merely leads up to the interesting things that happened then.

Anticipating the need, a man had been sent to dig Dan's grave. The funeral was expected to be well attended and a proper grave was one of the accessories. The ground was frozen and all of those who have tried digging a grave in frozen ground will recall the jar that the shoulder gets when the pick hits the unyielding sod. It just ain't easy. No hard work is.

But the plot now thickens. Another man was shot, in the interim, or the anteroom, or someplace. Anyhow, a man who flourished in history as Sailor Jack was tabbed to dig a grave for this second defunct citizen. Sailor Jack's character is now unknown, but he seems to have been able to seize upon opportunity.

He took a few ineffective swings at the frozen ground with his pick, stopped to swear and saw the neatly prepared grave made for Dan. He could see that this was his day. He cached his pick, advised haste, as he had to be going, pressed into service some strictly amateur pallbearers, and his late and lamented friend was lowered into the bosom of the earth with appropriate, but slightly hurried words.

It was reported that when the real occupant of the grave arrived with a more ceremonious funeral and the procession found that Dan's grave had been jumped, some words were spoken not in the prayer book of any recognized creed.

But another grave was dug, and with some philosophical remarks from the crowd about the luck of gamblers, Dan went to his reward.

LEARN BY DOING

V. G. Cozad is responsible for this story. J. W. Ashford and J. H. Fell were young doctors in Canyon City who, like the "Doc" in the popular Gunsmoke TV program, got much of their practice from contusions and wounds suffered in frontier personal combats.

Pleas Hankins, pioneer of Silvies Valley, arrived in town in bad shape. His stomach, or something down that way, hurt pretty bad, almost more than he could stand, and he nearly screamed when they touched the spot. This was known as "inflammation of the bowels" and the sufferers from it mostly died.

The young doctors, though, had read that it was now called "inflammation of the appendix." They had not studied about appendectomies in school, since such operations were unknown, but the medical journal had recently described it, with appropriate diagrams.

They were discussing this somewhat tentatively, with sideways looks at Pleas, when Cozad, an innocent bystander, came up with some valuable information. He said, "A murderer committed suicide in the jail last night. I think the cause of his death should be established; maybe he had inflammation of the bowels."

A hint was enough. The two doctors hurried over to the jail, located and inspected the corpse's appendix, decided that he, in fact, had no appendicitis, so, refreshed by the knowledge of just where this organ was and how to get at it, they came back to Pleas Hankins.

They took him to the Ashford home, placed a door on two sawhorses, put Pleas on the door, and proceded with confidence. George Fell, son of Dr. J. H. Fell, and Philip, son of Dr. Ashford, watched through the kitchen window.

Pleas Hankins lived in the county for a long time and left many relatives in Grant and Harney Counties.

The *Blue Mountain Eagle*, centennial edition, published this and several other stories in this chapter.

START OF THE METSCHAN FORTUNE

Phil Metschan Senior opened a butcher shop in Canyon City on or about 1865. He was successful, moved to Portland and started the Imperial Hotel. Later Phil, Jr., took it over and added the Roosevelt and Mallory Hotels. All of these hotels were popular with eastern Oregon folks, but this was particularly true of the Imperial Hotel where Phil would turn away a distinguished guest to make room for some sheepherder or cowboy he knew. Stand long enough in the lobby of the Imperial and you'd see many you knew from eastern Oregon.

But Phil, Sr., was not so prosperous at the start. F. C. Sels, the local brewer of Canyon City, lent him $1500 to start a butcher shop. In those days a merchant had to give credit and it was only a few days until the $1500 was all tied up in accounts. This taught Phil the value of doing business for cash, but the knowledge didn't help right then. He had to buy some livestock or he couldn't very well butcher it.

He had a friend, John Wolfinger, who had a rich claim up the creek a quarter of a mile. Phil went up to see him, found him down in a hole on bedrock. He called up, "What do you want, Phil?" "I need $1700 to buy cattle." Wolfinger said, with no hesitation at all, "Go back to town and tell Sels to pour out $1700 from my sack."

F. C. Sels owned a large safe, used by everyone in town with anything to put in it. Each buckskin sack had the owner's name on it. This was a real simple bank business. No receipts, no records, no bookkeeping, no bank examiners, no checks.

So Metschan reported back to Sels, who on Metschan's word, weighed out $1700 in dust from Wolfinger's sack, and the butcher shop was again in business.

Metschan turned away mere senators or millionaires to give beds to old friends, no matter how humble.

TRANSPORTATION TROUBLES

The *Blue Mountain Eagle* revived this occurrence, maybe of some interest to folks who think that automobiles are more dangerous than older transport. Gus Smith, a bachelor, came here from England with money; not much knowledge of livestock; a beautiful, almost exaggerated English accent; and a gift for being on the scene when something happened. The valley was full of stories about him and his brother.

The Smiths owned a place on Pine Creek, now the Morris Ray ranch, and another on the Middle Fork. This latter is the 101 ranch, or the Felix Johnson place. Gus was riding this day from ranch to ranch, on the old Susanville road. He came upon an overturned wagon—no team nor doubletrees.

He leaned over in the saddle and called, asking if anyone was alive. From underneath came an Hibernian brogue, as rich as Smith's English, "Hell, yes, and I'd be plazed to have ye git me out of here."

Smith found a pole, lifted the wagon bed and peered under. There was Bob Marshall, who didn't seem overly anxious to get out, for he was lying on his back attending to a demijohn of whiskey, which he just barely had room to tip up. He had been there since early morning, and the only real reason he wanted to get out was that the demijohn was nearly empty.

They found the team hung up in a jackpine down the trail, so Smith went on to his ranch and the Irishman, Marshall, seemed to think he had to see a man in a saloon at Canyon.

On another day, E. J. Bayley, cashier at the Grant County Bank in the 90's, was doing a little prospecting and camping on Dixie Creek. About 9:30 in the evening he heard faint cries for help.

He found Gus Smith and his horse at the bottom of a prospect hole, eight feet down. He rescued Smith, who gingerly felt himself all over, then tentatively tried the moveable parts and decided he was not hurt. It took most of the night to get the horse out.

The point of this is, that even now, the old prospect holes offer some hazard. Also, the old mine shafts. Better stay out of them. They have a nasty habit of caving in at the slightest disturbance.

The Bob Marshall who was under the wagon was an ingenious Irishman who positively refused to let poverty stand between him and a drink. The hundreds of Chinese miners had a healthy respect for the law and their main idea was to keep out of court. When Bob found that his name, Marshall, inspired some fear in the minds of the Chinese, he had it made. A marshall, to them, was a policeman, and a person did what the officer said to do.

So when Bob's pockets were flat and his thirst was riding him, he hunted up a Chinese and arrested him for disturbing the peace, or illegal consort, or unlawful possession. Bail was set at whatever the unlucky Oriental had on him at the time. It might be considerable.

Flowers don't bloom forever, no matter how beautiful, and after a year or so, the Chinese decided there was something queer about this whole thing. Marshall never arrested anyone but Chinese, so the good days were over for Bob.

THERE'S ONLY ONE JOHN PORTER

Every Oregon county has some outstanding persons. Someone said that a really good farmer was always outstanding in his field. A man may be outstanding for humor, interesting history, ranch management, statesmanship, or a hundred things. I have been lucky in knowing dozens of these outstanding figures all over Oregon, but Grant County has one man who is surely different from anyone else. He is John Porter of Long Creek.

Most of us have impulses to do things, but we stop, appalled at what people might think; why, they'd think we were crazy! This kind of thinking never enters John's head. All of his life he has done and said what occurred to him at the time as a good thing to do or say.

A cowboy rode right through a big plateglass window and took up a stand on the platform inside, grandly saluting passers-by. When the judge asked him the next day why in the world he had done that, he said, "I haven't the least idea, judge, but I do remember that at the time I thought it was a dandy idea." John has ordered his whole life by just that process, and he has had an interesting time.

He came into the Grant County Bank one hot day in August, leaving a trail of water behind. He was well dressed in coat and vest. The cashier, astonished, said, "John, for heaven's sake, how did you get so wet?" John's explanation was, "It was cool up at Long Creek, but it was so hot down here, I got overheated, just riding. As I crossed the bridge, I saw a nice deep pool in the river, so I waded in up to my neck and stood there 'til I cooled off." Could anything be simpler? What a sensible thing to do! But most of us would be afraid of what people might think.

One of John's stories relates to grass. As he tells it, "A feller told me a sheepman was up on our summer range and had eat out a couple sections of our best grass. So me and the hired man and my brother rode up there pretty hostile and sure enough, here he was with sheep all around him right on our range. The minute we came in sight he began yelling, 'I'm lost! I don't know where the trail is!' But we didn't pay any attention to that, cause that sort of an explanation just comes natural to a sheepman. So we rode up and I guess no white man ever took the abuse we gave him. One of us would use all the corral type words he could think of and when he stopped for breath, the next one would take off.

"He just stood there and took 'er cause he knew he was in the wrong. He was a big, red, hairy sort of feller. But then we made one of these here tactical errors, as the generals say. We figured we'd sort of took care of him, so we branched out and told him what we thought of all sheepmen in general. I guess he thought he didn't have to take that, so he said, "Well, anyway, there ain't none of yuh has ever seen a picture of Jesus Christ in the Bible with a steer in his arms.'

"Mad? I was never so mad in my life. I wanted to say something, but couldn't think of a word to say. I looked to the other boys for help and they couldn't think of anything, so we just rode off. I've been sort of humiliated, I guess you'd call it, ever since. If I ever get money enough, I'm going to pay to have a special issue put out with that picture in 'er."

Somehow he got acquainted with a sculptor in New York, who asked John to come to see him. One night John took the train from Portland to Baker where he had left his car. They got to Baker in the early morning and John was in no mood to wake up. The conductor and porter gave up, mad. When John finally felt ready to greet the dawn with a glad cry he was in Boise. He thought, "I've always wanted to go to New York. I'm part way there, so I'll just go on."

At the big city he hunted up the sculptor friend who was surprised, but real pleased to see him. He took John to some of his hangouts, where John's stories and way of telling them stole the show.

It developed the sculptor was a wealthy man who had as his office a barn-like open room on the top floor of a big building. He gave his auto and chauffeur to John and told the chauffeur to take John wherever he wanted to go. So, as John explained it, "I looked at all that big mass of people, hundreds of thousands and I thought, how do they water all of 'em? So I spent about ten days investigating the water supply. I found out all about it and I can tell you exactly how much water it takes a head a day, how much they use in a year, and where they get it all. I saw all the reservoirs and ponds. I don't suppose more than one or two people know more about New York's water system than I do." This wasn't fooling—he really did know. But how many people would spend ten days in New York that way?

This story has more to it. The sculptor was Frederick Allen Williams, a good-looking, strong sort of man. I met him and liked him and he told me about his return trip. "I decided to return John's visit, so I turned up at his place one hot day in August. He was glad to see me, all right, but he explained he was right in the middle of haying and had no time to visit. He said he had a lot of men around. A man doing nothing would sort of disturb the morale of the crew, so if I wanted to stay, I could go out to the bunkhouse and work along with the men.

"I was real glad to do that, because, though a working sculptor keeps his muscles in good shape by the constant pounding and chipping on hard granite, still the work is all inside. So I worked right along with the other men, putting up some forty-fold wheat hay. We got through in about four days and just as we were finishing a neighbor came over, almost crying.

"He said he couldn't get any help for threshing his barley. He needed four men awful bad and wouldn't John let him have four of his crew? John lined us up and checked off four of us for this sub-contract, including me. I never let out a cheep.

"I worked there and finished the barley job. When he saw I was a green hand the neighbor put me to stacking the straw. Now that was a job I didn't relish a bit. It was hot, and no matter where I stood, the barley beards went down my neck and up my sleeves and my pants legs until by night I was a fiery itching mess.

"The job done, the neighbor said, 'Now I don't know how much John is paying you, but I am paying my men $4.00 a day, so if that's all right with you, here's $12.00 apiece.' Then I finally decided to assert my independence. I drew myself up straight and said, 'Mister! It isn't all right with me. Take your money. There isn't enough money in the whole world to hire me to stack barley straw, because I don't like it.' So I felt better and went back to John's and we had a fine visit. Later he took me to the Pendleton Round-up where we met lots of good people and had a wonderful time."

The point is, who else in Oregon would have hired out a rich and distinguished guest to thresh barley for a neighbor?

FRANK METSCHAN TOLD THE TRUTH

Rod Cozad tells this yarn. When the stage ran from Baker to Burns, they changed horses at the Oliver place, but stopped for the night at the Frank Metschan ranch on Trout Creek. Frank fed the horses and the passengers. Frank was a son of Phil Metschan, Sr. The country all around was settling up with homesteaders and they were a pain in the neck to the big Pacific Livestock Company, who had controlled the grazing all around there for years.

The homesteaders got the springs and creeks, fenced the company cattle out, and when they tired of jackrabbit meat, they butchered and ate the big five-year old steers belonging to the company. The drain got so bad that the company finally turned out 200 yearling heifers and sent word around to the homesteaders to please kill those, not the big steers ready for market.

A salesman stayed at Metschan's place one night, ate steak for dinner and had another for breakfast. He said, "That was the best meat I ever ate, Mr. Metschan. Do you butcher your own beef?" And Frank, being a truthful man, said, "Well, we do our own butchering."

A MEAN MAN

Rod Cozad, son of a pioneer, tells another story. Rod, for years now, has bought land for the State Highway Commission. Most of us don't think about it much, but whenever a highway is changed, even a few feet, the state has to be in the land buying business. Rod makes the deals.

On one trip he was out with a rancher and noticed two parallel fences going over the hill in the distance, only about four feet apart. He thought it might be a livestock lane, but there was no sign of use inside the lane. Puzzled, he asked about it and the man explained that he and his neighbor couldn't agree where the lines were, so each made the other keep up a fence all the way.

At this point the rancher noticed a huge Russian thistle that was still upright. One big round thistle like that has enough seeds to seed down a quarter section, which it does, when it cuts loose and goes rolling over the countryside, shedding seeds at every turn. He carefully loosed it at the ground, gingerly took hold of the root, walked to the fence and threw it over the no man's land into the neighbor's field.

Pleased as a boy scout with his good deed, he said, "Now there's one I'm rid of."

"But," said Rod, "Suppose he comes along this afternoon and throws it back?" The old boy bristled up at once, ready to fight and said, "Yeah! And he's just a mean enough old s— — — — to do a trick like that, too!"

DON'T GET MAD

Chet Craddock of Silvies Valley, was a mighty good operator of a good ranch. Due to his wife's health, he had to leave the place and is now (1961) County Judge of Harney County. His philosophy is always worth listening to. Of a drunk man trying to sing, he said, "He and his tune are just like a drunk driver and the road. The only time he's on it is when he happens to cross it." Of a happy man, "He's purring just like a tomcat in a creamery."

On this occasion a man said, "Now that's something that makes me mad." Chet, always calm, advised, "Oh, don't ever get mad. Trouble with getting mad is you got to get over it all by yourself. Of course, once in a while some accommodating b— will come along and knock it out of you. But you can't depend on that."

BAD LUCK BRINGS OUT THE PLUCK

In modern living there is seldom need for sustained courage. The boy next door with the soft hands and the baby face may never be tested in the kind of life we live now, but in a more isolated country like ours, the old virtues, if they are present, have more of a chance to come to the surface. A California band leader and his wife had a chance in our country to refine the material they were made of and they struck worthwhile metal.

On April 21, 1958, Bruce Davis and wife of Fresno, California, left Klamath Falls in their own plane that Monday afternoon, enroute to Spokane, about 500 miles away. A few hours later the Pendleton radio station picked up a "May Day" with his identification and altitude 15,000 feet. Just the one call, then silence.

Although late in the spring, snow storms played around the mountain tops in all directions, all the way from Spokane to John Day. Search planes took to the air in Washington, Idaho, and Oregon, but storms made high altitude search impossible. Monday passed. Frantic searchers tried all day Tuesday, but storms continued. By Wednesday the searchers were still at it, but pretty discouraged.

On Thursday morning a weary man appeared at Gus Robertson's ranch near Dayville, wearing a short jacket, a child's cowboy hat and a pair of what looked like handmade rubber shoes. He was the missing pilot. Though exhausted, and with two ribs broken, he refused to rest, telling of his wife marooned on Aldrich Mountain to the south.

The story of what happened after they crashed in the mountain with the plane's wings loaded with ice is the important thing. Both were hurt, he with broken ribs, his wife with a broken hip. Davis crawled from his wrecked plane, carried his wife to some trees that broke the force of the freezing wind, took the wings and doors of the plane to make her a shelter, and gave her as much clothing as he could. He put his pants and socks on her, wrapped her in four sweaters, plus his jacket and overcoat.

He then set out through four feet of snow, in a blinding storm, wearing oxfords, shorts, and a light jacket. He walked all night, falling many times in the darkness and storm. Some time the next day he stumbled into an abandoned cabin where he found a handful of rice, a child's cowboy hat, an old coat, and a pair of overshoes, which he could cut down for shoes.

Shoes are the most important thing in the snow, and the shoes saved his life. He also got a little sleep in the cabin, not much. For two nights and two days he pushed himself on. As the time went on, it took him longer to rise each time he fell, but the thought of his crippled wife on the mountain made him drag himself on.

Aldrich Peak is 7000 feet high and it was still winter up there. Directed by Davis, men on horseback rushed to the scene, but snow made it impossible for the horses to travel and the last mile and a half was made on foot. A helicopter came as soon as the spot was located. The searchers found the wrecked plane and the crude shelter, but Mrs. Davis was not there. Then they heard feeble cries and found her at the bottom of the snow field. When she heard the plane circling, she wanted to get out where the plane could see her. But she could not stand and rolled down the steep snow slide. Had the searchers missed her that afternoon, she would have died of exposure.

She was weak and her feet were badly frost-bitten. The helicopter took her to the hospital.

Despite the loss of her left foot, her chin was up, and she called her children at once. Both the Davis folks seemed almost unable to understand why people made such a fuss over them. They were grateful to tears for the way Grant County people looked after them. Love and courage still live in the hearts of Americans, but sometimes it takes a primitive experience to make us see how strong those traits really are.

CHAPTER 14

COW COUNTRY—FACT AND FANCY

Grant County, Oregon, produces high quality beef cattle, known all over the West and clear to the Hawaiian Islands, where some buyers specify beef from here. The county has four other sources of income: minerals, lumber, sportsmen, and tourists. The mineral income is now small, but could blossom into something big at any time. The income from sportsmen's dollars is already large, and gets larger each year. The tourist income is sometimes a combination of fishing and camping, or hunting and camping, but is partly from fossil hunting, because this John Day valley was submerged repeatedly and here are found, permanently preserved in volcanic ash, the bones of all the fantastic animals that roamed this country millions of years ago.

Volcanic eruption would throw a dam across a water course, the panic stricken animals, as they saw the waters rise, would congregate in a milling, frightened group on an island, where they sank into the mud. The waters closed over them; more volcanic dust sifted down; the entire island was then compacted by pressure from below so that the red, or yellow, or green mud was pressed into laminated semi-rock; and now the forces of erosion have cut into the area, exposing these rich pockets of prehistoric lore.

I am no student of such things, but a local resident, Tom Weatherford, Dayville, has a remarkable fossil collection, sought after by museums. He says that some of the animals found in the local beds include:

Peccary
Mastadon
Three Toed horse
Prehistoric antelope

Wild boar
Oreodont
Creadont
Miniature horse
Camel (small)
Rhinoceros
Bear dog

By some tilt of the earth, our county had a different climate then, and this amazing collection of animals, all extinct, apparently had plenty of feed among the tropical vegetation that covered hills where growth is comparatively sparse now.

The John Day fossil beds are known to every geologist in the world, and most of them come here, sooner or later. Every summer finds groups of students from Yale, or University of California, or from some other state, busy climbing around the cliffs, or the many-colored hills of our fossil country. The county seat of the next county to the west, Wheeler, is the town of Fossil. It appears that at some distant period, the earth's axis was different, and our valley was near the equator. At any rate, imbedded with the animal fossils, are innumerable leaves and trunks of tropical trees. Probably nowhere else in the world are fossil beds so rich and varied.

But our main income is from the dependable steer. "Cattle from the John Day" is a sort of trademark of quality that often adds a cent or two to the market value. Here is a queer thing: John Day lent his name to our river, our town, and our highway. He even gave his name to another river, down near Astoria. Almost all of Grant county lies in the John Day drainage basin, with its various forks, the South, Middle, and North Fork, and its numerous tributaries, but the man we are named for—John Day, was never within a hundred miles of our valley.

He was a hunter for the Wilson Price Hunt overland party sent West by John Jacob Astor to found Astoria as the Western anchor for what Astor visioned as a big transcontinental fur empire to rival Hudson's Bay. This overland party found nothing but trouble, and some men, including John Day, were left behind on the Snake River, because they were too weak to go on. Later, he and another man were rested enough to try again, were fed by some friendly Indians, and with restored strength, they pressed on toward the mouth of the Columbia. But near where The Dalles is now, other Indians robbed them of all clothing, and turned them loose to die. They started back toward the friendly Nez Perce tribe, a party from Astoria happened to see them at the mouth of the John Day River near where Arlington is—and that is our somewhat slim connection with early history of white men in Oregon. It wasn't until 1862, just 50 years later, that our county hit the front pages again, with gold discovered.

So this is cattle country. There are right now about 26,000 beef cows in the county. Mainly they winter on the river and its tributaries, where hay is cut. Along in April or May they go out to the open hills adjacent to the hay lands, and about June 1 they work their way uphill to the forested lands, part public, part private forest. They stay in the forest for four months, then start downhill again. They live on the aftermath of the meadows for a month, or on the grass on the home range for a month or two, then go into the feed lots and winter feed grounds near the ranch. Cattle have been doing this in various lands since long before the birth of Christ. They follow the grass. "All flesh is grass" says the prophet Isaiah. Grass is a common theme of all of the old writers, from the Biblical authors on down to Shakespeare. Grass, the seasons, the sea, the mountains, the rivers—these things run like stray threads through the Bible, as they do through the conversations of cattlemen.

City talk has always seemed a little thin and weak to me, maybe artificial is the word. When country people talk of the weather, it isn't because they can't think of anything else to say, or because it's a safe thing to talk about, with no danger of argument. The weather is all-important to us. It determines every move we make. It kills our new-born calves, it keeps the grass below ground, it makes our roads impassable, it determines when we must move our cattle, and it decides whether or not we have enough hay. It decides whether we lend or borrow. We can't make one decision all the year around without taking weather into account.

The kind of ranch life shown in the TV programs, and outlined in the stream of western books, is a marvel to me. I have lived on a representative ranch all my life and never once have I rescued a lovely maiden from a fate worse than death; I haven't ridden full gallop down the hill and through the creek, splashing water to the tree tops on the hot trail of the man who shot my best friend; I haven't burned down the nester's cabin and broken all his nest eggs; I haven't had to make a hard choice between the weak forces of law and the strong forces of evil, knowing that if I chose one way my wife would be against me and if I chose the other I might have to shoot my partner.

It seems strange to me that eight out of ten of the most popular TV programs should be Westerns. I can't help but wonder why that is. Maybe a little verse from the poet, Quincy Kilby, gives the answer:

> "Here in my library I sit,
> Amid rare volumes richly bound,
> A mine of cleverness and wit,
> From authors everywhere renowned.
> Tonight their words seem flat and stale,
> Their weakness fills me with disgust,
> I want that crude, hard-fisted tale,
> Where seven more redskins bit the dust."

Anyhow, in the fiction of the West, there aren't too many plots, only variations. You could list them something like this:

1. The wicked cattle barons gang up on the poor but pure homesteader. By a remarkable coincidence the latter always has a beautiful daughter.

2. The tall, handsome, tough, rider comes into town (usually he's from Texas) and he gets embroiled in a local feud, greatly against his will. He has to see it through, of course.
3. The new marshal is a tall, handsome, tough man, who, alone, subdues the wild elements that infest the countryside. He gets the girl. He fights the villain, fist and skull, and makes him yell, "Uncle."
4. The silent, but tall, tough, handsome stranger comes to town bent on vengeance against the snake in human form who killed (maimed), (imprisoned falsely), (defrauded) his father. The snake, by this time, has used all his snakely arts to snake himself in as sheriff, where he is busy stealing blind all the honest men.

In the first chapter there is nearly always a barroom fight that breaks all the furniture and most of the bottles on the shelves. I have wondered how the saloons of those days stayed in business. Their chief expense must have been chairs, tables, and lamps, all freighted in at great expense, and broken nightly in the fights.

Incidentally, my experience was that they did not have all those bottles on the shelves. The freighters brought in 50-gallon barrels. These freighters were no slouches, either. The long days sitting up on the wagon, eating dust, just about wrecked a man's tonsils. So freighters of my acquaintance knew how to get medicine. I have mentioned the pole axe they carried. They used it and a horseshoe to pound down a barrel hoop about a quarter of an inch. They then drove a nail into the wooden barrel between the staves, pulled it out, and inserted a straw, through which the medicine ran out into their tin cups. They then drove the hoop back into place, sealing up the illegal entry. They could do this as often as necessary, through the long ten days or more it took to drive from The Dalles to Canyon City.

Bank robberies or stage holdups usually figure in somewhere. Sometimes the robberies are pulled off by one of the desperate dry farmers the cattle barons are try-

ing to squeeze out. "I was only after money for seed," the
desperate robber sobs, but his poor wife suspects that he
was trying to get enough in addition to buy their little
girl a dolly. This teaches our little children that it is a
splendid thing to rob a bank if you need the money.

There is almost always a stirring and terrific gallop
for miles and miles, trying to "cut 'em off at the gap."
Often an Indian lurks in the silence and darkness. He
may be a good Indian, bent on warning his one white
friend of the impending attack, or he may be on the trail
of a lonesome scalp. Anyhow, most bona fide westerns
have an Indian, who lurks.

What one thing makes the West? I'd say it's the range.
That's about the only real difference between the East
and West. The range is wide and unplowed. It allowed
the cattle drives, the long gallops without a fence, the
bad men hiding in the badlands and the good men dashing about on well lathered horses.

Now just think a bit of all these things I've mentioned; cattle barons, feuds, marshals cleaning up the
place, crooked sheriffs, stage holdups, galloping cowboys,
Indians, claims jumped right and left, the poor but
honest homesteader robbed of his land— I have never
seen any of these things. Grant County is truly like the
West—a real Western county, but it isn't at all like the
TV West and never was.

We had gold miners, homesteaders, stage coaches,
freighters, cowboys, sheriffs, big cattle layouts such as
Miller and Lux, sheepmen, even bank robberies. I'll tell
you what Grant County is like and what cattlemen are
like. Of course, there isn't any standard or average cattleman. They come light and dark, tall and short, fat and
thin—just like lawyers, except that those who ride horses
may be bowlegged. Instead of tall, dark and handsome,
plenty of them are short, light, fat, and homely as a mud
fence. But they do *tend* to have certain characteristics,
because a person who succeeds in the cattle business has
to have those things.

They tend to stand up under disaster—even to joke about it, and they hate a whiner or cry baby. Thus, in a drought that may wreck them financially, they tell about the new well that the neighbor dug, which turned out wonderful, 1000 gallons to the minute, but the water assayed only 40 per cent moisture. If the blizzard is bad, they tell of the neighbor who went to the front door to see how it was blowing, he yawned just as he got there, and "honest, the wind was so hard it blew the seat of his of his pants right out." A person is reminded of the old Montana cattleman who advised a complaining tenderfoot, "Son, don't never git tired 'til you git to where you can rest, and never git hungry 'til you git to where you can eat." That is fine advice for anyone, banker or bootlegger.

They tend to be reasonably generous with money, but niggardly with information. R. G. Johnson, former county agent here, told of his old uncle: R. G. was riding with the uncle one day, moving several hundred of the uncle's cattle down the road to another range. A stranger stopped them. This conversation followed:

Stranger: "Whose cattle are those?"
Uncle: "Feller up the ridge."
Stranger: "Where you taking them?"
Uncle: "Over the hump."
Stranger: "How many you got here?"
Uncle: "Quite a few."

There is a strong tendency to regard a debt as a sacred obligation. In another chapter I have said that few cattlemen in Grant County during the depression years, took advantage of the bankruptcy laws or crawled out from under their debts in any way. It took them a long time, but they paid in full. There is another reason for this: A cattleman *must* make thousands of decisions. His business requires it all the time. He can't pass responsibility to anyone else—often there isn't anyone else around. So, in making all the decisions he gets into the habit of accepting responsibility for them. He may decide wrong, but it's *his* mistake. Probably that's why poker came to be popular in cattle country. It's the one game where your mistakes are visited upon you alone.

If he doesn't buy hay and should have; if he takes the cows to the hills too soon and a late blizzard kills the calves; if he sells in June and sees the price rise 50 per cent in the fall; or if he turns down a good offer and sees the bottom drop out of the market; if he takes a chance on a fence and his cattle break out and scatter; if he puts off irrigating and the creek stops running—these are his own mistakes and he doesn't try to blame the government, or big business, or the neighbor. He made the error and he will suffer.

Even now, when horses ride in trailers, and a jeep can replace half a dozen horses, the cattle business on any range operation still depends upon horses. They color the conversation. Chet Craddock, describing a man who never reached his capacity, summed it up, "He's afraid of his horse." Jimmie Cant of Dayville, telling how tight he really is, "I gie all my riders only one stir-r-rup."

Reub Long of Fort Rock, when asked what sort of man a certain neighbor was, answered by a parable, just as Abe Lincoln often did. His reply was, "A long time ago when they were killing people over around Wagontire, a man from here worked there all summer. He came back in the fall and I supposed he would have all the dope. So I said, 'What did you find out at Wagontire?' This man had a deep voice and kindly manner." Here Reub dropped his voice to a deep rumble with the kindest tone, as though talking to a child. "He said, 'Reub, when I was a little boy, my papa told me how to git along—out here—on the desert. Always ride a good horse —and breathe—through your nose'."

And Bill Dalton of Klamath Falls suddenly found that, by inheritance from a silent partner, the University of California owned a considerable interest in his ranch. President Sproul wrote asking him to call in if he ever went to San Francisco. Later he took down a trainload of cattle, wearing his boots, Western hat, and all. I happened to see him as he returned and asked him how he got along with the University president.

Bill said, "Oh, fine! I think. He told his office girl to call off all appointments and not let anyone else in, nor to call him on the phone. He and I hit it off like two jaybirds in a tree. I may have caught my foot in the stirrup right at the end, though. He said their animal industry people had some kind of hormones or something to give to bulls to make 'em more potent. He wanted to know if I'd take some to the ranch to try it out under real practical conditions. I told him, 'Sure, send it along. But I won't guarantee that none of it will ever git to the bulls'."

Whenever Bill made a bad deal of any kind, he always said, "I was riding a lame horse."

There aren't any 40-hour weeks on the cattle ranches. Reub Long says, "I always tell a new hand it don't take long to spend a night here; that in the morning he should reach down and feel of his clothes and if they are cold, he's overslept." The stock must be tended to, and if the weather is bad, it's quite likely the working day will be longer.

Almost without exception these people don't criticize much. Maybe a neighbor does something I don't do— maybe I do something he thinks is pretty bad, but we don't criticize. John French, Grant County rancher, was sitting in a car early one morning with friends. It just happened they hadn't been to bed. One of the others said, "We might go over there (pointing) and get my brother out of bed. He *should* be home." John said severely, "Don't say that! Don't *ever* say a thing like that! Maybe from your standpoint he should be home, but maybe from his that's the last place on earth he should be. My dad taught me not to *ever, ever,* say another person should do this or that. I think he does silly things and he thinks I do, but we don't mention it. I never know what he's going to do. It wouldn't surprise me a bit to look along side the road here and see him in the ditch." At this point he rolled down the window, looked long and earnestly front and back, and said, "In fact, I'm kinda surprised I don't see him."

I mentioned the ease with which some of these folks follow the example of Lincoln and tell a story instead of giving a direct answer. Chet Craddock is such a person. Once we were digging a ditch and we came to a good-sized boulder. One man was mechanically inclined and he rigged a complicated pry system. The only trouble was, the boulder was round and wet, and just as it got to the top, it slipped off. After several failures of the ingenius application of the law of levers, another man just stooped over and lifted out the boulder. The mechanic said angrily, "You damn fool! You are strong enough so you don't need a lick of sense."

Chet, standing by, said, "That reminds me of a cow puncher I had once down at the sod house. He had his rope on a horse in the big corral and was trying to work his way up the rope to get a halter on the bronc. The horse would snort, wild-eyed, take a run, and drag the man halfway across the corral. Finally, the puncher wrapped the rope around his waist, caught the horse off balance, and dragged him back a few steps. He said, "You S— — — —, you may be smarter than I am, but I'm just as stout ."

Most of the cattlemen I know don't want something for nothing. They think the constant howl for security is the ruination of the country—the slaves down South are the only big fragment of our population that ever had security. If a man's Union ties him up, hard and fast, and he can't exercise any freedom of decision anymore, that man just naturally isn't a free man any longer. If the government should ever give the orders to farmers, such as under the Brannan plan, the farmers wouldn't be free. Independence is worth more than security right now, just as it was when we fought for it.

Well, that's about what we cattlemen are like. Most of us don't care particularly about some other way of life. We like our own pretty well. We may lie a little—exaggerate is a better word—but we try to get along with what is in sight, and can have as much fun in some old log cabin as we can in the fanciest of night clubs.

I have never lived out of Grant County. I am kind of like my friend Reub Long. When a stranger asked him in a kind of pitying way if he didn't ever long to travel, Reub exclaimed in great surprise, "Travel! Why, I'm already here!"

Our thoughts are pretty much on our cattle. Years ago there were no real roads out at Long Creek and no way to get feed in there. So if a man ran out of hay, his plight was serious. Bob Crowley up there was in that fix. One neighbor, George Rader, had plenty of feed, but he and Bob were not on speaking terms. Crowley went to Allen Porter and suggested that Porter go to Rader and buy hay, then sell to Bob.

Porter said, "Now there is just simply no sense in you and George acting this way, and now's a good time to make up. You go to Rader, throw yourself on his mercy and tell him you are sorry for the trouble. I'll bet you a horse he'll let you have feed."

Rader said heartily, "Sure, I'll sell you feed—and reasonable, 'cause I like your cattle. You take 'em all down and turn 'em into that north field where there's plenty of feed. I like your cattle, like I said, and I can't stand to see 'em starve. But that don't make me like you, and I never will!"

Grant County is about 70 miles each way and its western edge is close to the center of Oregon. The John Day River dominates it. Other rivers, the Malheur on the south, Burnt River to the east, and Crooked River to the west, all have their beginnings in Grant County, but we are pretty stingy with our water and we turn most of it right down our own river, the John Day.

Practically all the gold mining was on the John Day watershed. Elevations run from 9600 feet down to 1800. The Blue Mountains are in the shape of a reverse L, with the lower leg turned the other way. The long leg starts up in Wallowa County, right above the famous Hell's Canyon, runs south through Baker County, then the other leg turns west to form the drainage between the John Day on the north and the Malheur and Crooked Rivers on the south. Starting at Strawberry Mountain, the John Day runs 60 miles west, makes a big elbow to the north and west, then runs about 80 miles northward, making a river 200 miles long from the Alpine heights— over 9000 feet—on down to the Columbia River, where the elevation is only around 200 feet.

All of this power goes to waste except for a few little home layouts. And there are no large storages anywhere on the main river or any of its tributaries. Irrigation of 53,000 acres in the county is mostly by direct stream flow. The only trouble with any dream of dams is that there isn't too much reasonably level land in Grant County that isn't already irrigated. This big unused flow of water to the sea won't go on forever, but it may be some other county that will eventually use it, maybe Gilliam to the north. And Silvies River to the south will probably some day have storage to irrigate Harney County. A portion of Burnt River, eastward, is already stored to irrigate Baker County. Crooked River irrigates Crook County. Here then is an odd situation: In Grant is the headwaters of rivers that run north, south, east, and west, but present and potential irrigation storages are for the counties that border us on all four sides. We start the water downhill, probably they will use it. We can extend our irrigation a little—especially on the bench lands that are now dry.

Our big future developments lie in other directions: Dryland alfalfa and more grass on our open hills; more feeding at home of our truly superior beef calves; use of our lower grades of timber for paper or hardboard; replacement of weedy range plants by useful kinds; and, some day, underground prospecting for minerals. Because of our location, far from any large cities, we may eventually have a measurable income from persons who want to get away from the dust, smog, and turmoil, and rest their bodies and nerves in our hills and woods.

I am not speaking so much of dude ranches, although we have some fine locations for them. I think that sooner or later every Grant County rancher so inclined, can take in from a thousand dollars up to two or three times that amount from city guests who want to get rid of noises and smog and tensions for two or three months. I don't know of a better place to do it than on a cattle ranch where tolerance, pioneer spirit, good humor, and common sense prevail. Some of these people won't want to be entertained by dude ranch antics of fireside singing, amateur rodeos, or organized horseback trips. They will want nothing at all except a place to rest and reflect and get closer to nature than is possible in cities.

Maybe, in time, this source of income will be considered as part of the regular income that goes with ranch ownership. If so, then it just could make it possible for a family to get along on a smaller ranch than is now the case.

I haven't mentioned hunting and fishing, but there is today a tendency for hunting rights on property to have value similar to rights for water, grazing, or mining privileges. That is, a few Grant County people sell hunting privileges to city groups who seem willing to pay quite a sum for the chance to shoot a deer. We may all hate to see the time come when a man can't hunt wherever he wishes, but a ranch that takes in a gross of $15,000 a year from calves, may soon take in $2,000 or $3,000 from hunting rights—which will give another boost to the value of property, and supply another reason why a man shouldn't be afraid to own a cattle ranch. The game is on the ranch for only one reason; feed is there. The rancher pays out plenty of money to produce the feed, even if it is native forage. He should be able to get back some of that money.

CHAPTER 15

A WHISTLE COMES TO GRANT COUNTY

The John Day Valley saw its first white settlers in 1862. For 48 years afterward there was not even a faint echo of a train whistle anywhere within the boundaries of Grant County. A child born there the year of settlement could have lived to nearly senior citizen age without ever having seen a train.

A map of the county shows the present stage and truck lines radiating from the central Canyon City-John Day area. It shows why county residents have always had more than a passing interest in transportation. Everything we buy or sell has to travel on one of the spokes of the wheel. (Map on opposite page.)

There are a few other short stage runs, such as from Long Creek to Kimberly. In our country we still use the word "stage," a hold-over from the horse stage days. This is pretty well true of all the isolated places in the West, especially off the main bus lines.

These local stages are important to us, though not so important as in the old days because most of them do not take passengers now. Our mails all come over them, and some types of freight. We can drive east to Baker and catch a train there for Portland; can go southeast to Ontario and catch a train east to Chicago; can go west to Redmond and take a plane to Portland, or to San Francisco; or can go north to Pendleton and go any direction by either air, rail, or bus. All of this takes time. A few local citizens have planes for hire if we are in a hurry, but at my age I am getting a little nervous about pitching around in a light plane in the air currents over the

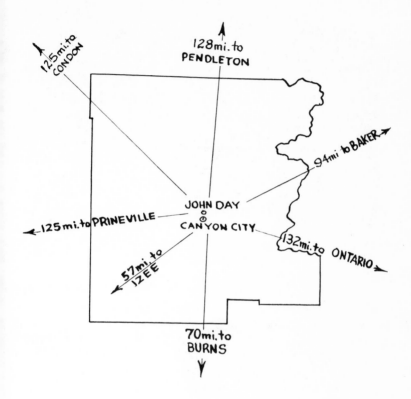

GRANT COUNTY, OREGON

Stage and truck lines radiating from the central Canyon City — John Day area.

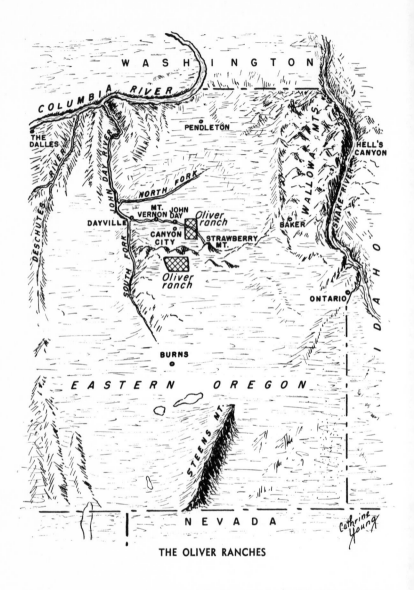

WASHINGTON

COLUMBIA RIVER

THE DALLES

PENDLETON

HELL'S CANYON

NORTH FORK

MT. JOHN
VERNON DAY

DAYVILLE

Oliver
ranch

BAKER

CANYON
CITY

STRAWBERRY
MT.

Oliver
ranch

ONTARIO

BURNS

EASTERN OREGON

STEENS MT.

NEVADA

Cathrine
Young

THE OLIVER RANCHES

The artist's sketch of the location of the Oliver Ranches and the John Day River
in relation to the general topography of eastern Oregon.

mountains in all directions. My bucking horse days are over, and I don't like to reenact them all over again up in the air.

When a railroad began to build our way from Baker in 1889, we were all pretty excited. David Eccles was a Mormon from Utah. He, like so many of that faith, was vigorous, constructive, and full of vision. He was of Scotch descent and was reported to have two wives, each with numerous children. He came into Baker, founded the Oregon Lumber Company, and shortly saw that he needed a railroad to run west in order to funnel logs down to his mill. That was only the beginning.

As the rails crept westward, and as the adjacent timber was cut, he looked at the 200 miles of unbroken virgin pine forest running through Grant County to Prineville. This was and is one of the largest stands of pine in America, so Eccles began to dream of having it for his mills.

Then his dream expanded. He thought of running his railroad west and south and connecting with a northern spur of the Southern Pacific somewhere, maybe Burns, maybe Lakeview, or Bend. That would put him right up among the big boys, Hill, Harriman, Weyerhauser. Why not? That dream didn't materialize, for him. He was a little too early, but he did toot his railroad whistle in Grant County, even though the toot was from a little puddle jumper.

Eccle's road was the Sumpter Valley Railroad, a narrow gauge. It was owned by a corporation separate from the mill, but with interlocking directors. He hired Joseph A. West, well-known engineer, to lay out the road. It ran smack into a high mountain, Dixie, and ran through a rough, rocky terrain most of the way. There were trestles, bridges, and switchbacks. As it headed west from Baker it first went to McEwen.

The next main objective was Sumpter, a mining town in a beautiful mountain valley. At least it was beautiful until a gold dredge ruined it. At the time, though, it was a busy mining center, with free gold in every gulch. Most of the miners were from the south, and as they wrestled around looking for a name for their eldorado, they were jubilant over the fall of Fort Sumpter, some months before. The new town was named Sumpter, over the objections of some northerners. But Sumpter it was, as was the case with Dixie Mountain to the west.

Sumpter thus offered considerable mail and express business, so Joseph West laid out a track to that city.

Building started at once, with two-horse and four-horse teams on Fresno scrapers. I was just a boy then, but I remember the exciting railroad news. Besides, it was a bonanza for the homesteaders that by then were thick all over Baker and Grant County. They could get a dollar a day for each of their horses on the railroad and a dollar a day for each man. During all the years of this railroad's slow march westward, homesteaders worked on the road, and those who were steady and saved their money would frequently buy out neighbors who didn't have this extra source of income.

The rails reached McEwen in 1892. It was a stage stop between Sumpter and Baker. The railroad stopped there for five years to rest and gather more money, then built on to Sumpter. At first there were four trains daily to that mountain mining metropolis. At its height Sumpter had a population of about 6000.

Eccles already had a big mill at Baker, but he built a second mill at Sumpter, where the road paused again to make some money by hauling out logs and lumber.

When I was 16, I visited Sumpter for the first time. I was a boy from way out in the ginsengs and I couldn't have been wider-eyed if I'd been suddenly dropped in New York. I remember a 100-foot long bar in a saloon, with a bartender every six or eight feet all the way.

The room was large and packed with miners, loggers, and friends. There were lots of girls who danced with all who came. There were tables and gambling—all with gold or hard money. In the back of the room were

Stud poker has always been popular in eastern Oregon. Usually you aren't supposed to check a cinch hand, there are no jokers or other wild cards, and there is no "ante." You bet after the second card, with one down, one up, and after each additional card.

There was always plenty to eat on the Oliver ranch—enough on hand to last for weeks, stored in meathouse, cans, barrels, sacks, and root house.

Ponderosa, or yellow, pine is one of Grant County's resources. Students of the human race, in describing the best environment for people, have marked out the climatic conditions where Ponderosa pine also does its best.

Cattle and sheep use millions of acres in the United States that cannot be cropped due to one or several of these things: drought, thin soil, steepness, rocky soil, alkalinity, inaccessibility, tendency to erode.

Homesteaders coming into Harney County. About 1880. Harney was part of Grant County then. Homesteading would have been impossible without horses.

Homesteaders starting for the picnic. About 1910. Isolated areas couldn't have been settled without horses or mules.

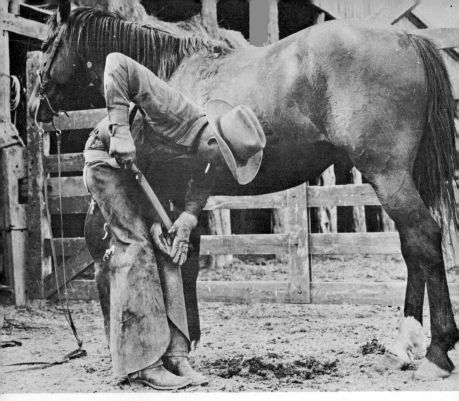

Each cowboy was expected to keep his own horses shod. Each freighter carried horse-shoeing equipment. Rough, rocky lava country was hard on horse shoes.

Ay tank ay go home now!

Ranch horses strung out, single file, to break trail for 1500 sheep marooned in the snow on a high range. The lead rider, choosing the route, is Herman Oliver. A sudden snow is a hazard for either sheep or cattle if very far away from feed. The horseshoe in foreground is the hook on which the mail pouch was hung. --

After the trail had been broken for them, the big band of sheep followed, glad to be out of the mountains and into the security of the home feed yard. (Picture taken in 1913)

Oliver sheep being trailed in from the high country to be shorn.

Herman, as a young man, showing the thick, heavy fleece sold from ewes on the Oliver Ranch. Ranch was combination sheep and cattle for years—after 1940, it has been strictly cattle.

numerous places that looked like box stalls to me, and I noticed that a girl and her dancing partner would retire to one of these box stalls now and then.

This town—as happened to many frontier towns—burned in 1917 and was never rebuilt.

In 1901 the rails went on to Whitney where Eccles built his third sawmill, and a town grew up. This town was deserted in time, but it did not burn and some old buildings are still there.

The next move of the restless narrow gauge was in 1904, on west to Tipton, about a half mile from the Baker-Grant County border. The logs from there were hauled to the Whitney mill, so Tipton was not a real town.

Five miles west of Tipton was the old Austin House, famous for years as a stage stop. Every traveling salesman in Oregon bragged about Ma Austin's cooking.

When I was 17 I was in charge of a band of 6000 yearling wethers, trailing them to Baker for delivery. There were four of us doing the work. The sheep needed salt and we needed some grub. I took a pack horse and went to the Austin house where they ran a small grocery. My folks were real good friends of Mrs. Austin's.

When I came in, Ma insisted that I sit down with the stage passengers and eat one of her famous meals. I had been with the sheep for days, getting full of the dust, and I knew I must smell pretty sheepy, though I couldn't tell. I looked over the 14 guests. They were all well dressed and so clean it hurt. I would have turned and run right then, except that I didn't know how to say no to a woman like Ma Austin, she was so friendly.

I took my seat at the extreme far corner of the table, as far away as I could get, and I suppose I unconsciously had my plate pulled past the edge of the table. Anyhow, I loaded it with some of all the wonderful things on the table. I started to cut a piece of beef, and my heaped-up plate, gravy and all, turned upside down in my lap as it left the table, completely covering me with mashed potato, jam, jelly, and all the rest. I got out as fast as I could, almost blind with mortification and embarrassment.

The way it is with a boy, it wasn't funny to me. I couldn't even bear to think of it for years and years. I thought my life was ruined, and that I would be known forever as the dirty, awkward sheepherder who spilled his food before the fashionable folks. Life stretched out before me in endless gray days of misery and solitude. It was the worst thing that I had ever heard of anybody doing. It hadn't just happened; I did it. Like a peacock looking at his feet, whenever I felt like I might amount to something, I'd suddenly think of the spilled food and enthusiasm or pride would sink into my shoes.

At Austin, Eccles built his fourth mill, a mile west of the Austin House. This mill still runs, though now owned by the Hines Lumber Company. Eccles renamed the place "Bates," to honor a Portland realtor who had helped the company in land and timber buying. The mill built a hotel for their help, and for years the train from Baker to Prairie City stopped there for lunch, after the fashion of the famous Harvey Houses on the Santa Fe. They set an ample table, with better than average food, but all the old timers remembered the good old days of Ma Austin. No commercial hotel could possibly approach her way with food.

Bates, or Austin, is in weather competition yearly with Bear Valley. At both places 30° below zero is not too uncommon and occasionally the mercury heads for the 50° below mark. The snow, though, never seems to get so deep as it did.

In 1909 the tracks hit the trail again, this time to Prairie City. The first run was July 4, 1910. So at last we could hear a train whistle. Just out of town there was a Y in the track, allowing the train to come in backward, because there wasn't any turn-around place. There was lots of publicity. It was the Fourth of July, and in addition, our whole transportation system was about to change. We had a railroad! A big crowd had gathered, so each could tell his grandchildren of seeing the first train.

Brakeman Tony Berge was standing on the platform of the end coach as it backed slowly to the end of the line. Suddenly he yelled in great alarm, "Look out! Look out! We're a-goin' to turn around." The crowd unthinkingly scattered wildly.

The track dropped from 5200 feet elevation at the top of Dixie Mountain down to 3539 feet at Prairie City, in a few miles. The last part of the road was built of cheap rails laid on a rough roadbed. It was said that once a conductor, half-asleep when the train hit the smooth part, awoke and yelled, "Jump for your lives, she's off the track!"

There was much talk of pushing the road right down the valley to connect with a spur road from the south. Some of us were strictly opposed to that idea. Later a highway went down the narrow valley, straightening out the curves of the county road. But if we had had both a railroad and a highway, there wouldn't have been much good meadow land left on many ranches.

The trains ran in the county for 23 years, but the railroad was useful to us for about forty years, because we could ship things in and out from Sumpter. Eventually another railroad came into the south end of the county, from Burns to Seneca. This pulled much of the livestock south. About the same time the highways came and it was cheaper to keep a truck rolling west, after it was loaded, than to haul by truck to Prairie City or Bates, load on a narrow gauge to Baker, reload there on the main line, and ship to Portland. Thus, with freight going west by truck and east and south by rail through Burns, the road gradually lost most of its business and in 1933 the tracks retreated to Bates. But in 1947 all the tracks of the Sumpter Valley railroad were pulled up and the line is no more.

The rails and some of the cars were shipped to Alaska where part of the equipment is still in use. It was rumored that Eccles merely rented most of the rails, intending to replace them with the heavier rails needed on a standard gauge line.

But we had our own pet railroad for a long time.

The Olivers shipped from Prairie City the first trainload of sheep to go out of there. We sold a band of breeding ewes to Coffin Bros. of Yakima. Stanley Coffin didn't want to trail them, so he and I went to the SVRR to talk about the deal. I had shipped cattle over the road.

There were no double-deck cars. The rule on the main line is that if there are no double-decks available, the road will furnish two cars for the price of one. The Sumpter Valley road wouldn't go for that. We then tried to get a cheaper rate. The cattle rate was $43 per car for the small cars the road owned. The SVRR finally agreed to furnish cars for sheep for a third off, or $34.50 per car. This rate held as long as the road operated.

The railroad had very few stock cars, not nearly enough for our band of sheep. They had boxcars, but these are not ventilated and not very good for sheep. We got them to furnish flat cars. They were larger than the stock cars, and would take 25 to 35 more sheep. The railroad built a fence around each flat car. They pulled these for the same $34.50 price.

There were 23 carloads in this shipment. There is a switchback on the west side of Dixie Mountain with room on it for only the engine and five cars. As soon as we had five carloads ready, the little engine would haul them to the top of the mountain, then come back for five more. The ten were then pulled to the top of the mountain between Sumpter and Whitney, set out on a siding, and there they waited for the 13 other cars to catch up.

Such an unprecedented operation threw the whole railroad out of gear. The rule was that the livestock owner had to have a representative with all livestock shipments. I went with the last 13 cars.

We rolled down to Bates where they gave me 30 minutes to eat at the Bates Hotel. I was back in plenty of time, but the train had pulled out. I reported the facts to the agent, so he sent word to next station to back the train clear to Bates to pick me up, which was done. I'll probably never again have a train return for me.

The little narrow gauge furnished lots of conversation in our country. It had many local names, the puddle jumper, the teakettle, the galloping goose, the stump dodger, the Prairie City Express—and on and on.

Once a 10-car cattle train was pulling out of Whitney for Baker. The wooden brake beam on the car behind the engine dropped down and derailed the front car. This pulled all the other cars off and tipped them on their sides. As the cars fell, the tops flew off, letting all the uninjured cattle loose. They promptly got away from such goings-on without stopping to ask, and disappeared in the surrounding timber.

The road management hastily recruited some cowboys and offered $5 for each head of cattle returned and run into a corral for re-loading. The cowboys really warmed to this plan. They'd been working all their lives for a dollar a day, and this business of driving back a critter for a fee of $5 seemed downright gorgeous. The offer had to be shut off when a count of the corral showed more cattle than were in the ten cars originally.

There was a deep cut on top of Dixie—15 or 20 feet. It eliminated a steep pull, but in those days of deep snow, it tended to blow into this cut. There was no rotary plow, so the Japanese section crew had to shovel it out. There was a line of Japanese on each level, with the lower level passing the snow to the next, just as the Chinese miners threw the rocks out of the placer cuts in the mining days. I remember one time in a heavy snow storm, when passengers and mail were snowed in all night. The next day more locomotives came and the train was pulled out.

The line owned 15 engines, and it took two or more to huff and puff up the steep hills and high passes. The engineers called the smoke stacks "cabbage heads" because of their shape. These engines all burned slab wood, piled at convenient places along the line. The cars were small, holding 14 to 16 cattle and 80 to 100 sheep.

The conductor, for many years, was David Baird, father of Dean David Baird, of the University of Oregon Medical School. David Baird, Senior, was a striking looking man with black eyes and black hair, ruddy cheeks, and a splendid black moustache. For duty he wore a blue-black uniform with a swallowtail coat and big brass buttons that shone like gold. He treated everyone with great consideration, as though each merited special attention. Each customer was an important person on that train.

When it was necessary to load slab wood on the fuel car behind the engine, there were no troublesome union rules that defined duties. The conductor, brakeman, engineer, and fireman all helped. At such times conductor Baird took off his grand uniform, put on coveralls, and worked just like the others. The job finished, he changed back and became a man of importance again.

Dean Baird often speaks of his father and remembers incidents of his conductor days. He recently told me this story.

"As you remember, it was not unusual in that wild eastern Oregon country for the train to have to stop because of cows, wild horses or sheep on the tracks. It was difficult to stop the train at times, particularly on a downgrade. The steam brakes were not too efficient, even if working, and it was necessary to run from car to car to set the hand brakes which was accomplished by turning a large wheel at the end of the platform on the back end of each car.

"One time I remember this combination of inconveniences could have been disastrous. The passenger train was coming down a slight incline approaching a large wooden trestle that spanned a deep gully. As the train approached this trestle, it frightened some horses close by. The horses scattered, but one large black stallion started to trot straight down the track. When he reached the trestle, he continued at a full trot across the trestle

ahead of the train. You can imagine the fright and excitement as all possible means to slow up the train were put
into effect.   Fortunately the stallion never slowed up,
never missed a step, cleared the trestle and disappeared
into the woods on the other side. My father said many
times that the Lord must have been on the train's side;
at other times he said it must have been on the stallion's
side.   I think he finally decided the Lord was on both
sides because a possible catastrophe was avoided."

The train, of course, was quite slow. It took all day to
run from Baker to Prairie City, about 90 miles. Once
when I was trailing sheep to Baker, the train came along
on Whitney Mountain.   I was horseback and I rode
alongside the engine and talked to the crew for maybe
a mile. My horse walked, or occasionally jog-trotted a
little.

Once when father and I were going to Baker, a lady
got on at Sumpter. The train had two coaches. After a
couple of hours, Conductor Baird suddenly herded all of
the passengers, except the lady, into the front coach. He
then assisted the lady in giving birth to a baby girl. An
ambulance met the train at the edge of Baker, removed
the mother and baby daughter, and took them to the
hospital.

Such incidents, of course, were fodder for all the wits
of the country, who claimed the lady may not have been
pregnant when she got on the slow train.

I remember that when the passenger traffic began to
slow down, there was at last only one coach on the train.
It was partitioned in the middle. Half of it had only
cane seats and had a liberal sprinkling of sawdust on the
floor. This part was for "timber beasts," miners, and such
others as were addicted to "eatin' terbaccer." The other
part had a red carpet down the center aisle with matching
upholstery on the seats. Ladies and dignified gentlemen
rode in that half. The only difficulty was that the refined
set had to walk through the other half before coming to
their more genteel portion. The ladies were careful to
lift their skirts high and display their buttoned shoes as

they daintily stepped around the brown pock marks in the sawdust, made by the terbaccer chawin' males. This made a nice social arbiter out of the conductor. The segregation he had to enforce was built around social rather than racial lines, but it could have resulted in disaster at any time. It speaks well for Mr. Baird that, so far as I know, he never made a mistake and got a Sumpter dancehall girl in with the ladies, nor did he outrage a tobacco hater by surrounding him with it in its worst form. There were some narrow escapes. A professional gambler may be hard to tell from the pastor.

I well remember my first sight of an engine. Father was taking two four-horse loads of wool to Baker. The tracks had gotten as far as McEwen then. He let Frank and me go along, just for the excitement. A four-horse load of wool is an inspiring sight. The huge sacks are piled high on a wagon so that the top is over ten feet high. We stopped at McEwen and all got down on the ground. Father had just gone into the stage office when here came an engine, the biggest, blackest thing Frank and I had ever seen, right out of a bad dream. We looked wildly for father, then scampered frantically up to the top sack of wool.

We proceeded on to Baker where father bought some big shorthorn bulls from George Chandler and Mr. Wisdom. My brother George trailed them back to the ranch at John Day.

Baker, in those days, had a horse-drawn streetcar that ran the length of Main Street. It enabled ladies to get downtown without hitching up a buggy and without getting their long skirts muddy. When it got to the end of the street, the conductor pulled a pin that held the horse, drove him to other end, put the pin in another hole, and he was set for the return trip. This seemed the height of city elegance to Frank and me. The fare from one end to the other was five cents, so we got on and rode and rode, back and forth, as long as father would put up the nickels.

I have mentioned that the Burns road, and later its extension to Seneca, took much of the traffic in livestock. This was due to the fact that Seneca is right in the mountains and was handy to thousands and thousands of sheep summering in the forest, and to more thousands of cattle in the high country for the summer. Also, it was standard gauge, so we could load livestock bound for Chicago and just let them ride, whereas, over the Sumpter Valley line we had to unload at Baker and put them into larger cars.

The road from Seneca southeast to the main line of the Union Pacific at Ontario, has some history. In 1916, following wild rumors about all kinds of railroad development in Oregon, the Union Pacific built a branch line west from Ontario. Unofficial street corner railroad experts all agreed that the road would of course continue on south, either by Lakeview or Klamath Falls, and hook up with the Southern Pacific somewhere along the way. Others, equally loaded with inside information, said it was just a feint, to head off Jim Hill and keep him out of central Oregon. Anyhow, the road stopped at Crane, on the east edge of the Harney Basin, 30 miles east of Burns. Even now, no one knows what Harriman's intentions were.

In 1923 the Forest Service sold to Fred Herrick a big tract of timber north of Burns. Mr. Herrick was to build a mill at Burns, extend the rail line on to Burns, thence up to Seneca and the railroad was to be a common carrier. Contracts were duly signed and a $50,000 performance bond posted.

Herrick was an old-time public-be-damned type of lumberman, an extinct breed now, but common forty years ago. He signed the contract, but bragged that no blankety-blank person would ever haul a log or head of cattle over his railroad, and furthermore, he would never haul a log out of the mountains to a mill. He said everyone knew a mill should be where the logs were, so you wouldn't have to haul all the sawdust, slabs, and waste. In other words, the mill should have been at Seneca, where he originally planned it.

When a listener mentioned his contract, he said that was only a formality, that he had hired two ex-forest service men to look after those little details.

This kind of talk alarmed the ranchers. We had met repeatedly with the Forest Service folks and asked them to insist upon common carrier privileges if and when the big timber holdings were tapped, and they had agreed. The Herrick contract was everything we wanted. We wanted to ship our cattle and sheep by rail from Seneca— if a railroad came!

But Herrick delayed and delayed and delayed. Finally he forfeited his $50,000 bond for non-performance and they gave him a new contract, giving him to December 15, 1926, to lay the rails to Seneca, and March 1, 1927, to build a mill. By December 15, 1926, there was no sign of either rails or mill, so we went to work. We were disturbed by Herrick's big talk and it looked to us as though there might be something in his brag about paying no attention to his contract.

The Grant County Stockmen's Association and others got a Congressional investigation, which proved mostly that Herrick, in fact, had no hold of any kind on the Forest Service, but that they had been lenient with him solely because his bid was $2.80 a thousand, and the only other bid was for $2.00. Even at that low price, when applied to 890,000,000 board feet of timber, the difference was worth considering.

Those prices seem outrageous now, with standing timber selling for $40, or even up to $50 on the stump. But timber has increased in price more than anything else I know of; while land was quadrupling in price, timber was increasing from twenty to thirty times. We have numerous timber millionaires in Oregon, due to that fact.

Herrick's first move, in line with his contract, was to extend the railroad from Crane, on the east of Harney Valley, to Burns, 30 miles to the west. It turned out later that this was financed by the Union Pacific. They took charge of the road in 1924. This was all to the good, so far as Burns was concerned, because the town finally had a railroad. It helped Grant County stockmen too, because it put us 30 miles closer to a railroad. This saved us two days at least in driving cattle or sheep.

The Congressional committee that heard the case against Herrick and the Forest Service recommended:

1. That Herrick give renewed evidence of financial ability to complete his contract.
2. That timber cutting start on or before October 1, 1927.
3. That the sawmill at Burns be operating on or before January 1, 1928.
4. That the railroad from Burns to Seneca be operating by October 1, 1927.

Herrick could do none of those things, or at least didn't, so the Forest Service re-advertised the sale. At this point the Edward Hines Lumber Company became interested. They had no western mills, had never bought Forest Service timber, and were not familiar with cutting marked trees, piling brush, making roads, and other Forest Service requirements.

Their bid:

Pine—$2.86 per thousand board feet
Douglas Fir—$1.10 per thousand board feet
Other species—$ .60 per thousand board feet

Herrick also bid, but his bid was thrown out, due to his previous attitude and failure to prove financial resources.

The contract with Hines was signed June 21, 1928. Hines then paid Herrick $827,000 for work done to date on the Burns-Seneca road and speedily completed it. On January 22, 1930, the mill started in the midst of a full scale celebration in Burns with closed schools, flags flying, speeches by notables.

This contract was for 770,000,000 feet of pine with other timber not specified, and was to cover five years of cutting. Thereafter new contracts were to be written every three years. No one then even faintly guessed at present prices of lumber, but the Forest Service was wise in the provision calling for a new contract every three years.

It looked very shortly as though Hines had bet on the wrong horse. National use of lumber dropped to the lowest point since 1840, 90 years previously. Hines had invested $7,000,000 in the deal, partly raised by bonds. He was obligated to cut and buy so much timber, but he couldn't sell any of it at all. So he defaulted on the bonds and a bondholder's committee ran the company for a while. The Forest Service modified the contract and its methods, and by 1939 Hines had completed all of the original requirements.

The mill has had an unusual career. While strikes have been common in places in the West, the Hines employees have always met, discussed it, and voted not to strike. They have had an unusually smooth operation, at least partly due to the fine personality and ability of A. R. Dewey, manager for many years.

Through the depression years the ability to load at Seneca was a great help to stockmen. Up until 1940 the station shipped yearly around 400 cars of livestock, sheep predominating. Sheepmen could take their ewes and lambs to the mountain feed, then separate the lambs when fat, and load them fairly close to the feeding grounds.

Then most range sheepmen went out of business, the roads and trucks improved, and the railroad is not of so much value to us now. In 1959 it carried seven cars of cattle and no sheep, as compared to 142 cars of cattle and 275 cars of sheep in 1935. Carloads of logs daily go downhill from Seneca to Burns, a drop of over 1000 feet in elevation. The Oliver Brothers shipped the first sheep and the first cattle that went out of Seneca.

This concludes the story of Grant County railroads. We tried to get the rails for years, finally got them, but eventually surrendered them and turned most of our cattle and sheep business over to the trucks.

CHAPTER 16

FROM HORSEBACK TO JET

I have lived in exciting times from afoot or horseback through autos and planes up to the jet age, and maybe the rocket age. Just for curiosity, I hope to be alive when the first visit is made to the man in the moon. It's probably pretty silly, spending all this money and effort on space. My own time has been spent on tangible things—things you could touch, such as soil and horses. I learned to judge the value of those things. I can't seem to find a handle to take hold of space.

I knew many of the Grant County pioneers—the first miners and ranchers who settled here. They were determined and fearless. They believed in themselves and weren't worried by any psychiatry problems. Life was simple. The only question was, "How do I make a living?" If you solved that, you were set, for the time being.

My father liked people and liked to visit. I was often with him as a small boy. He especially liked the pioneers and visited with them at length, while I sat and let this pioneer spirit soak into me. Perhaps some of their dust blew off on me.

In the early days, only three farm products went out of here, sheep, wool, and cattle. The wool was hauled out by six- or eight-horse freight outfits with two and sometimes three wagons hitched together. It was about 200 miles to The Dalles and the round trip took two to three weeks or longer, depending upon the road and the outfit. The location of the night stop was determined by water. Drivers seldom slept in a regular bed, they unrolled their blankets under the wagon.

At first Grant County reached from Umatilla clear to the Nevada line. It was only in 1889 that Harney County split off.

Originally mail and supplies came by pack trains with about 35 or 40 mules or horses, usually mules. Pony express took out letters for a dollar apiece.

Our small streams ran water-power band-saws that were nicknamed "try-weekly". The saw went up one week, tried to come down the next. In 1865 a grist mill opened in John Day, also water-powered.

The grain for the mill was at first harvested with a cradle. This was a frame with long wooden teeth fastened to a scythe operated by some high-octane muscle on a powerful young man. No job for a weakling. The scythe cut the grain. The wooden teeth enabled a skillful harvester to put it down in small sheaves, with heads all pointing the same way.

At first, threshing was done by smoothing and packing a corral, spreading the sheaves out, then chasing horses round and round to trample the kernels loose. Later a flail was used, a stick six feet long with a 14-inch piece of wood at the end fastened with a buckskin string, allowing the end piece to be loose and flexible. This was used as a club to beat the grain from the heads. In either case, whether threshed by flail or horses, the grain was winnowed by tossing it in the air on a windy day. The chaff and straw blew away and the grain fell on a canvas.

Later, when the first crude mowers came, the grain was mown and raked mechanically. The first mower I remember was the Adriance Buckeye, sturdy and heavy.

Seeding was by hand. A good man learned to seed with both hands. Horse-minded ranchers did this on horseback, putting ear stalls on the horse, so the kernels wouldn't go into the animal's ears. Later "whirlwind" or "end gate" seeders were fastened to the rear end of a wagon bed. First run by hand, these were soon powered by a chain drive attached to the wagon wheel. This saved up to 75 cents a day of high-priced labor by doing away with one man.

Next came a self-rake reaper, really a mower with a platform behind the cutter bar, and a big sweep that came down and swept off a sheaf of grain. Of all farm implements, these were the most ungainly. They looked like a combination Dutch windmill and mower. The sweeps were run from an eccentric. They were loose-jointed and seemed about to fall to pieces at every action.

A man followed, gathered the sheaf swiftly into the proper size, then grabbed a handful of straw with the heads all pointing the same way, separated it into two, twisted one around the other below the head, then threw both around the center of the sheaf, twisted the ends to-gether, and tucked the knot under the encircling strand. This was done in less than the time taken to tell it. For each reaper it took five men to tie the bundles and shock them. There was a great difference' in men. Some were slow at this tying, binding and shocking and their bun-dles came loose or their shocks always fell down. Some were fast and sure.

The first threshing machines in the valley were horse powered, needing 8, 10 or 12 horses. The term "10-horse-power" meant something then, aside from a theoretical figure out of a book indicating so many pounds lifted one foot in so much time. The horses traveled in a circle with a shaft and gear in the center that transferred its power through a "tumbling rod" to the separator cyl-inder. The bundles were hand-fed into the machine. They were hauled in and pitched onto a table. The men who fed the bundles in, after cutting the ties, were im-portant. They could clog the machine anytime by care-lessness, could crack the grain by going too slow, or could, by varying the feed, fix the machine so it only got part of the grain out of the straw.

The separator carried the straw away a few feet on a slotted canvas conveyor, dumped it in a pile, and it was up to the "straw buck" to keep the pile from getting too high and stopping the whole operation. The straw was moved by a fence rail rigged with a rope on each end. The ends of these ropes came together about 25 feet out, and fastened to a ring, which in turn was fastened to a long rope that led to a clevis on the doubletree of a team. The straw buck had to ride the rail to keep it down, a sort of a dangerous job, for he could fall and have the rail pulled right over him. He had a rope to hold on to. It was fastened to the same ring mentioned and it passed over the pile of straw. The rail was put behind the pile, the go-ahead jerk given by the "straw buck" and the team would pull the rail forward onto the stack. Stacks were usually 24 feet wide, 50 feet long and maybe 25 feet high, exact size depending upon the crop.

Riding this rail that pulled the straw could be dangerous. I saw one man stick his toes a little too far forward across the rail. His toes dug in, pitching him forward, and the rail hit him on the back of the head, knocking him cold as an icicle.

Another time the man on the rail had some loose clothing that caught in the elevator. He was jerked off his feet and nearly choked to death by a tight neck band he was wearing to keep out the straw. I was jigging sacks, saw him just in time, and cut the neck piece loose. His face was black and his tongue stuck out in a grotesque way, as one might imagine a hanged man would look. Had I not seen him, or not had a knife handy, he would have been a hanged man.

The grain was run into seamless sacks, two bushels in each, and hauled to the granary, where they often had to be lifted high onto a platform and dumped into a bin from above. It took a pretty skookum man to handle these sacks all day. They weighed from 80 to 120 pounds, depending upon the grain.

We and several of our neighbors went in together and bought a threshing machine and it fell to me to run it. I liked to feed the machine and listen to its steady hum when I fed it just right, each bundle with its head under the butt of the forward bundle, so as not to crack the grain.

Later came grain drills that assured better stands. Binders soon came, that automatically tied with a string. The knot tier on these machines was invented by an erratic genius. Every attempt to find a better way failed, though sometimes it would begin to skip and no one on earth could figure why.

Soon big steam engines began to run the threshers. Every small boy on any ranch was bursting with excitement when these big black monsters pulled onto the place, with the accompanying separator, water tank and fuel wagon, with whistle blowing and steam hissing. Modern living holds no such thrill. The big threshing crews were fed at the ranch where they were working. This meant meals for 30 men three times a day. The crews always managed to get in an extra meal or two at those ranches setting the best tables.

Gas engines, less exciting, followed, then combines, horse drawn at first, then pulled by big steam engines, later by gasoline tractors.

The grist mill at John Day, erected by A. R. McCallum and G. I. Hazeltine in 1865, was well patronized. It was the first flour mill east of the Cascades and the machinery was hauled in partly by pack mule. There was a small mill at the Marcus Whitman mission near Walla Walla, but it wasn't commercial and didn't last long. The John Day mill ran for a long time. We took our wheat to the mill and had it ground into flour for $2.00 a barrel; getting back screenings and middlings. Usually we raised some extra wheat to sell to the mill so didn't have to pay out any money at all.

Father said, "Watch a farmer for several trips to town. If he goes to town with an empty wagon time after time, and takes home a load of things, he will fail. But if he always leaves home with a full wagon and returns with it empty, he will succeed."

It was a good rule. He practiced what he preached. He always had things to sell; horses, hogs, cottage cheese (called schmeercase) , sausage, vinegar, wool, corned beef, bacon, potatoes, hay, honey, lard. The folks had something to sell every day in the year.

We surely didn't go hungry. We could, at any time, have withstood a siege for months. The cellar, smoke house, and pantry were full of hundreds and hundreds of pounds of food of all kinds.

There is a story about the northern man who stopped at the place of a negro farmer during the depression years. The negro had told him no one was making any money around there. The northerner looked at the garden, the cow, and the pigs, and said, "Well, you farmers at least ought to get enough to eat." The old negro said, "Yassuh, yassuh. Never did see so many fat niggahs runnin' around naked." That's a good story now, indicating that farmers need other things than food. It didn't apply so well when I can first remember, because we didn't buy much in town.

It's easier to go broke now. We raised our own power then, we buy it now. Taxes were only a token amount then, we pay out from a third to a half of our gross income now. Even if we have no net income, we still pay property taxes, that run pretty high, most of the money going for education. Machinery of all kinds is high in price, but necessary, because hand labor is even higher. The graduated income tax now rules business operations. Formerly we didn't have to figure the effect upon the income tax every time we wanted to sell something. The income tax takes flexibility out of management. A man can scarcely change from selling two-year olds or yearlings to a cow and calf operation if the change concentrates too much income into one year. Because of drought, or shortage of hay or grass, due to weather, a man may want to sell most of his herd and buy stock back later, but the income tax will prevent it. A man liquidating debt has to pay a heavy tax on every dollar of debt he retires.

The income tax may make it almost impossible to sell land. It often forces a man to trade instead of selling. I know of one conspicuous case where a rancher with a sawmill ownership, can't raise his own heifers. If a heifer raised on the ranch happened to die, the loss is not deductible. But if he buys his heifers, say for $200, and one of them dies, he can deduct $200 as an expense.

The income tax adds to the cost of everything we buy. Take the case of an executive of a factory that sells clothes to us regularly. He is wise and forceful and the company wants to keep him. He is married. If they paid him $1000 a week, $52,000 a year, he is taxed $30,130 on his income. He points out to them that the tax is taking over half of his pay, so they raise his salary to $100,-000, whereupon the tax, Federal and state, is $61,850, making a net raise of $16,280 out of a gross raise of $48,000. But the point is that we, as consumers, pay every cent of his $61,850 tax. Every time we buy anything at all, we are paying someone's income tax, because the factory naturally adds it to the cost. Rightly so, because all salaries and wages are part of their cost. The farmer though, can't add his taxes to his selling prices, so taxes are a direct expense to him. In case of a crop failure, he pays his heavy property taxes anyhow, even with no income whatever.

Small farms can't pay for modern machinery. Most every successful cattle ranch is the result of combining a whole group of smaller places. A man with a few cows could formerly raise his own feed, trade work with neighbors, hire no help, raise his own food and get along. Now it takes ten cows or more to pay for each automobile, 25 to pay for a truck and 50 to pay the taxes, even on a rather small place. That is why farms have consolidated.

The power from horses is still the cheapest and probably some people would be better off if they depended upon it more than they do. It doesn't necessarily take a $10,000 tractor to pull out a few bales of hay.

I wouldn't go back, of course. No one could, even if he wanted to. But it was simpler then.

Some years ago, when there were still a few homesteaders just hanging on, I asked one of the hired hands how he supposed some of the little farmers made a living. He said, "Oh, they don't make what you might call a living. They just *resist.*"

There is now only one big advantage in ranching, aside from the fact that as a way of life it beats anything else I know of. Commercially, though, it has one advantage.

Our money has been devalued, our income tax has raised values, we have borrowed into hundreds of billions, so we have inflation. We will have more, because no Congressional candidate dares to run on an anti-inflation program. As a result land values have quadrupled in the last 30 years—a 300 per cent rise. Suppose a young man had bought a place 30 years ago and barely made expenses. Inflation has averaged 10 per cent a year, so he has made 10 per cent yearly on his investment, even if the ranching operation just broke even. That is pretty good if the investment is large. A man can live on inflation if he starts with enough. The person on a salary or wages, or living on a fixed income, such as life insurance, can keep getting leaner and leaner.

Before the railroad came, logs moved, as shown, from forest to mill at the headlong pace of one and a half miles an hour. Now trucks take them down the highway at 50 m.p.h.

PART THREE—PUBLIC SERVICE

CHAPTER 17

THE BANK OF GRANT COUNTY

Neither my father nor my brother Frank really wanted to be in the banking business; and I didn't, either. Force of circumstances drew us in. We were stockmen.

Father owned stock in the Grant County Bank at John Day. He was on the Board of Directors, but had no taste for it. He suggested to the other directors that I go on in his place, so he could retire. When they agreed, he gave me five shares of stock. All the other directors were men of his age, and I felt strictly out of place. But I felt that I did know ranch management—perhaps better than some of the others, and it wasn't long until I saw that the bank's business was to finance ranches and livestock, and it didn't hurt a bit to know things about them. So gradually these older men began to look to me to help with decisions about ranch loans and they elected me vice-president.

After World War I there was a bad farm depression in which one-fourth of American farmers lost their farms. Cattle dropped from 18 cents down to 5 cents, wheat dropped from $2 to 60 cents, sheep went to almost nothing, wool from 70 cents to 10 cents, and prices of manufactured goods stayed high. Taxes went up.

An old Holland farmer, Jake Fischer of Baker County, said, with some heat, "I say to my poys only dis morning. Poys! Ve must lif vitin our means if ve haff to borrow money to do it." Many ranches, previously debt-free, had to be mortgaged in this period and money was hard to come by.

There were two other banks in the county. One at Prairie City and one at Canyon City. In 1923 the president of the Prairie City Bank came to our place about midnight. He said the bank examiner was at Prairie City, and had ordered the bank to close unless there was paid in a 50 per cent assessment on the capital stock of $25,-000. But the stockholders found this either difficult or impossible. The president wanted us to put up this $12,-500 assessment and brought a note, signed by six stockholders, pledging to pay back a 90-day loan in this amount. I certainly didn't want their bank to close its doors, with all the hardships that it would bring, so I reluctantly gave them our check and took the note. But in 90 days the signers could not pay.

In a few months the National Bank examiner came around again and said he'd have to close them up. The examiner, accompanied by Billy Pollman, banker of Baker, came to our place one June day. I was getting our fleet of horse-drawn mowers ready for the haying season and I was covered with black grease.

A well-dressed man approached, tried to shake my black, grimy hand and this conversation occured:

Stranger: "I am a Federal bank examiner. Are you the man who made a loan of $12,500 to the Prairie City Bank?"

I: "Yes."

Stranger: "How would you like to own a bank?"

I: "I wouldn't like it at all. I am a rancher."

Stranger: "Unless new money comes into that bank and a new manager is appointed, the bank can't open tomorrow."

A bank failure, of course, puts a blight on a community, endangers neighboring banks, cuts off credit, and often needlessly wrecks perfectly good businesses. I didn't want any of those things to happen.

So we went to the manager of the Grant County Bank at John Day, E. J. Bayley. He at first refused to have any part in any move to save the bank. He said he was busy enough at John Day.

I argued that the county couldn't afford a closed bank. Too many persons would lose in the compulsory liquidation that would follow. Bayley saw the point. He said that Patsy Daly of Prairie City had recently sold his mercantile business and perhaps we could get him to go in as president and help salvage the bank.

We again had a first-class argument with Daly, who insisted that he wasn't a banker and had no desire whatever to be one. He had sold his business in order to take life easier. To try to save a failing bank was no way to achieve that ambition. At last he agreed to look over the books.

We went to the bank at 3:00 o'clock that afternoon and by 2:00 o'clock in the morning we all agreed that the bank could be kept alive. It was in bad shape. If liquidated then, it could not have paid over 25 to 30 cents on the dollar to the depositors.

Oliver Brothers put in $12,500 and the same amount was raised by Patsy Daly and some friends of his. Billy Pollman put in $1,000 just to show good will. E. J. Bayley, Joe Deardorff, J. J. O'Dair, and Paddy Finlan were the main new stockholders. Wayne and Jane Stewart of Dayville later bought some stock.

The old stockholders turned in their stock and new stock was issued. In that way, they were not assessed the full value of their stock, as they would have been had the bank closed; but the stockholders lost their stock just as we had lost our first $12,500. We reorganized the bank with Patsy Daly the new president, Dave Hughes cashier, and an entirely new board of directors. I was elected vice-president.

The bank opened the next morning and no one in Prairie City seemed to have any idea that anything out of the ordinary had happened. It was business as usual; no newspaper stories, no rumors, no alarm, no withdrawals of accounts.

We ran the bank for ten years before it was a paying business and all the old, worthless or practically worthless paper had been wiped out, including three little sawmills that the bank appeared to own. In 12 years, 1935, it was consolidated with the Grant County Bank and has been run since as a branch. This consolidation will be mentioned again.

The next scene in the financial drama of the county was in 1928 when the National Bank of Canyon City got into trouble. Again stockholder assessments precipitated it. They were assessed until they rebelled and refused to pay any more.

The bank examiner told the bank officers to close its doors. The president and vice-president were able to continue their assessments, but were not too much inclined to do so, with the other stockholders opposed. So they asked me if the Grant County Bank would absorb them.

I put it up to the board and they at first refused, thinking they had enough trouble of their own. They finally agreed to send a committee to examine the books.

The bank wasn't in terribly bad shape, just a difficult position. So, working with the examiners, the Grant County Bank took it over, liabilities and all. Customers and depositors were protected and did not lose.

But clouds were gathering. In the early '30s banks every where, including some of the big ones, began closing. John Thornburg, veteran banker of Forest Grove expressed it, "Business in our town is so still that you can stand in the middle of the street at the busiest time of day, and all you can hear is the sound of the notes, drawing interest."

The Grant County Bank was almost exclusively a livestock bank and livestock prices tumbled to almost nothing.

Sheep hurt us most. We had mortgages on 25,000 sheep, all the way from three dollars up, per head. The life of a sheep is short. If you hold off selling until prices revive, the sheep is too old to sell for any price, or maybe is dead, so the mortgage holder is caught. He doesn't want the sheep, but he must either take them or else advance more money for taxes, bucks, herders, shearing and feed. But, each year the holder of the mortgage puts up money, the ewe is a year older and worth less. So as the debt increases, the value of the mortgaged property decreases. This broke many western banks in the long period from 1930 to 1940. During this 10-year period, lamb prices stayed under 10 cents.

We assessed our stockholders, trying to keep the bank going. This reached a point where the majority of the stockholders forfeited their stock, rather than pay the assessments. Oliver Brothers paid their assessments, took over the forfeited stock, and paid the assessment on that, in order to meet the demand of the bank examiners. Assessments reached 100 per cent.

We classified all the notes and other securities, tried to sort out the ones that were worth something under panic conditions, and tried to borrow money from the Reconstruction Finance Corporation, the Federal Reserve Board, and the U. S. National Bank of Portland, offering these notes as security. We got a little money, but not nearly enough.

At this point, let's explain a little. Suppose you have a country bank, such as ours, with $40,000 in stock and an accumulated surplus of about $75,000. The Federal law says that no bank can lend to any one depositor more than 10 per cent of the combined surplus and capital. Ours was a state bank. When the depression started, state banks could lend to an individual 20 per cent of their capital and surplus. Right in the middle of the bad times the limit was dropped to 10 per cent.

Thus, you see that in 1929, we could legally lend to any one stockman up to $23,000. We had several loans approaching this.

Now, let's see what happened in the period 1931 to 1935, inclusive, remembering all the time the new 10 per cent limit just mentioned:

Year	Losses of Grant County Bank
1931	$ 14,801
1932	33,151
1933	66,676
1934	39,251
1935	53,919
Total	$207,798

These losses, almost entirely on sheep, had a left-handed impact upon all of our larger cattle loans. How could a small bank absorb losses of more than $200,000 when our capital was only $40,000? We did it like this:

Wipe out the surplus account	$ 77,500
100% stock assessment	40,000
Reconstruction Finance Corporation money	20,000
Wipe out 5 years earnings	70,000
	$207,500

These losses totaled over half of the deposits at the time.

But now let's go back again and see the effect upon cattle loans, limited in 1935 to 10 per cent of our capital and surplus. We had very little surplus left. For ease of figuring, let's assume no surplus, although we did have some at all times.

Amount of capital	$40,000
Largest permissible loan	4,000

But, as mentioned, we had numerous loans based upon the old $23,000 limit. Each time the bank was examined, the examiner spotted the discrepancy at once and ordered that these loans be reduced or closed out. But, if we closed them out, as bad loans, that just transferred the amount to losses, rendering our position still worse, because with no surplus, a loss impaired our capital. As soon as assets drop to where capital is impaired, a bank is broke.

What could we do? The cattlemen couldn't pay anything on their loans, they were already living on cracked wheat grown on their own places, and what their gardens produced, plus their own beef.

At this point we had an unusual happening. Ed Way had been examining the bank for years. He was the man who gave us the tough orders to set our house in shape. The health of our old cashier, E. J. Bayley, declined to where we had to get a new cashier. We had several applicants, but weren't sure of them. In 1935 we persuaded Ed Way to come to work for us as manager and cashier. So, after examining our bank and giving us the toughest orders of all, he came in as manager and we told him to go ahead and carry out his own orders, which was a hard assignment.

After the bad years had become history, I said to Ed, "How did you have the courage to quit your job as assistant superintendent with the state banking department and come here to manage our bank?" He replied that he had made the change only on our assurance that Frank and I would stay with the bank and see it through its difficulties, no matter what came. He said he had reported to Superintendent Schraam many times that I had told him if they would just give us a little time we could pull out because the county was essentially sound, and he believed that statement.

The first thing he did as manager was to propose consolidation of Prairie City Bank with the Grant County Bank, thus adding $25,000 to our capital, making it $65,000, and making the legal loan limit $6,500. This alone put a large number of loans within the legal limit again.

Our customers had been courteous and kind and trusting. We had no run, but if any depositor had come in and asked to withdraw $5000, we couldn't have given it to him.

The big banks tried to buy us out, but I couldn't figure where we had anything to sell. They would have taken us over, but our stockholders would have gotten nothing at all.

Our time deposits had for years hovered around the $100,000 figure. As each of these time deposits matured, some of them for as much as $10,000, we had an anxious moment. If the man had said, "I've decided to put this in government bonds," or if he had decided to draw it out and deposit it in Portland, then we were broke. We just didn't have enough money on hand to pay even one of these larger time certificates. As a certificate matured, the manager would call and advise me that Mr. Jones, for example, would be in that day, either to withdraw or renew his certificate. I would hurry to town, stay out in the lobby, and when the customer arrived, I would greet him cordially. I would talk about crops, weather, his family, and maybe tell him some funny incident. We would both laugh, and then, as the manager and I shivered, he would step up to the counter and say, "I guess we'd better keep this on as a time deposit for another year." The manager and I breathed again.

The bank was saved by one thing—the Oliver ranch. Many ranches are saved by a bank. In this case the ranch saved the bank. In 1929 I had an uneasy feeling, so sold most of our sheep, all steers two years and up, all the old cows, and all the horses we didn't need. With the funds from this liquidation, Frank and I bought government bonds, then selling under par. Within a few months everything dropped except the bonds, which rose. We were able to buy the bonds by reducing our herds and flocks drastically. This money came out of the ranch. The income tax would make that hard to do now, if not impossible.

I took those bonds to the U. S. National and borrowed on them. We turned this money over to the bank which assigned to us ranchers' notes, thus reducing the outstanding loans and giving the bank $103,500 in cash for use in additional lending to hard-pressed people. These notes were not acceptable collateral elsewhere.

Then things got worse. Frank and I jointly borrowed $45,000 and I borrowed $50,000. This $95,000 had nothing behind it but our notes. We put it into the bank to increase deposits so they could have money to lend. Between us, Frank and I advanced $198,500 in cash.

The bank was saved, times eventually turned better, and one after another the notes that we held were paid off in full, the entire $103,500. It took years to get the money, but not one of these livestock men lost his ranch, and none ran away from his debts.

Frank and I jeopardized our ranch property for three reasons:

1. We had confidence in the honesty of Grant County ranchers,
2. We had, even in the worst times, great confidence in the future of the livestock business, and
3. We just simply couldn't destroy the confidence that people had in us.

All of this seems old history now, but I decided that we should never, as long as I lived, get into such trouble again. It's too hard on the heart, too nerve-wracking. The policy of the bank's board of directors had been to pile up the earnings, rather than to draw them out as dividends. We increased our capital stock to $170,000 by declaring a 100% dividend, allowing more loan leeway, but as soon as things started getting better, we let the earnings accumulate. Our position now is:

December 31, 1960, Statement

Capital	$170,000.00
Surplus, Profits, and Reserve	633,511.40
Total	$803,511.40

Our total deposits are over $7,000,000 and our loans only $3,496,000. We have plenty of bonds and other securities. Our bank has been rated as one of Oregon's strongest independent banks.

My father told me, "When a man has no money, and he knows that you know he hasn't, there is nothing in the world so bad in its effect as demanding money from him."

So, in keeping with this principle, we never crowded any-one when we knew he couldn't pay. This principle was hard to maintain at times, due to legal provisions.

Some of the sheepmen changed to cattle and even-tually pulled out of debt. During the depression years, the bank lost about $200,000, mostly on sheep, virtually nothing on cattle. The sheep business is vulnerable in a great depression because of the heavy cash expense. Cat-tlemen can put a wide streak of lean in their personal bacon, cut expenses to the bone, and pull through.

The range sheep business of Oregon never recovered in numbers. It is only a small fraction of its past. Grant County formerly had 140,000 sheep. Now it has about 8,000. All of the other range counties have had the same experience. Sheep have increased in western Oregon on small farms where herding is not necessary, hence, the big cash expense is not present. Range sheep numbers have decreased in all Eastern Oregon counties and in every western state.

We can't blame all the reduction in sheep numbers upon the depression and the difficulty of financing. There were other things such as: Occasional heavy losses from predatory animals; sheep are more susceptible to disease than cattle; a tragic mistake by OPA gave cattle a heavy advantage over sheep during the last war; scarcity of really good herders; and a glamour that has surround-ed cattle due to TV, radio, and Western magazines. Actu-ally, most any range will produce more pounds of lamb than it will pounds of calf, partly because with cattle, more of the feed energy is needed to push around a cow than is needed to push around five ewes.

The income from wool is then a bonus, so sheep should return more money than cattle whenever lambs are anywhere near beef in price. For 30 years sheep and cattle averaged about the same in price, but in the past ten years cattle have run consistently higher.

An old range story is that a stranger met a herder and this conversation followed:

Stranger: "Where you from?"
Herder: "Monta-a-a-na."
Stranger: "Where you going?"
Herder: "Ba-a-a-ack."

I don't know whether the range sheep business will ever come back or not, probably not in our time. Really, for the good of the range, the Australian system is the best. Each range there carries both sheep and cattle, simultaneously, in a proportion determined by experience. The sheep keep out the brush and weeds, thus giving more and better usable forage for both cattle and sheep. The income to the acre is considerably higher than with either alone.

Here are some figures supplied by Ervie Williams, president of the Portland Union Livestock Company:

Average Prices at Portland by Years

	Steers	Lambs
1910-1940 per 100 lbs.	$ 8.47	$ 9.60
1941-1958 per 100 lbs.	23.27	19.88

So, for 30 years at the start of this century, 100 pounds of lamb consistently brought the owner a little more than 100 pounds of beef. In the last 20 years, 100 pounds of steer has averaged $3.39 more. That is 17 per cent more. So, as someone expressed it, you now get 17 per cent more for peddling the bull than you can get for passing the buck. No wonder Grant County dropped from 140,-000 down to 8,000. If the old relationship ever comes back, the sheep business probably will, too.

Our livestock success in the early days was due to the fact that we had both sheep and cattle. In some years the sheep paid for cattle losses, others years the cattle supported the sheep. Sheep will make a man prosperous more quickly than any other kind of livestock—or will break him quicker if prices drop below costs. But, from the money angle, either must be a business, not a gamble.

I think the terms "sheepman" and "cattleman" are wrong. We don't say "bankman" or "shipman". We say, "That man is in the ship-building or banking business."

We should say, "This man is in the cattle or sheep business." If it isn't carried on as a business, the owner is soon "walking down the road talking to himself."

In 1932, the hay crop was short and the winter was long. R. G. Johnson, then County Extension Agent, reported to me in the middle of the winter, that many ranchers, especially those off the main river, were experiencing a serious feed shortage. They had put off doing anything, hoping for an early spring, but the snow was still piling up daily.

A quick survey showed this to be true. We had to act quickly, so I phoned Mr. Ballard, "R. G.'s" superior, and asked him to allow R. G. to leave the county for two weeks. I arranged at the bank for them to honor all checks signed "Oliver Brothers by R. G. Johnson." He then made a trip to Vale and other places and bought several hundred tons of hay, paying about $20. (Right after, the price jumped to $40.) He also bought cotton cake and grain.

We assigned this hay and some other feed to the various communities, as Fox Valley, Long Creek, Monument, and Kimberly. We named a man in each community who would be in charge. As each rancher needed hay, grain, or cotton cake, he drew on the community pile, signed for it, and agreed to arrange at the bank for payment at the end of the winter. To the credit of Grant County ranchers, every man came in and paid in full. So Frank and I put up the money, sold the feed at exact cost, plus trucking, and got back every cent. No interest was charged. The ranchers were kept from some serious losses. In addition to the later high prices, additional storms came, blocking country roads; so ranchers couldn't have gotten feed in to their stock under those conditions, even if they could have found it.

In another year of short hay supplies, we had some extra hay. The previous year it sold for $10 a ton. But this year before spring the price jumped to $40, and hay was hard to find at any price. As the winter wore on and showed no sign of relenting, every few days a worried

Oregon State Highway Commission photo
Indian drawings in Picture Gorge, near Dayville.

ll dressed up. Paiute Indians. The horse gave the Indians mobility and changed their way of life just as the auto has changed the lives of all of us.

Horse gear was prominent on every ranch. Wagons, buggies, carts, and hacks were used; there was a blacksmith shop, usually in its own building; a saddle room was usually in the barn; here shown is the harness room. Once common, such a sight as this is now obsolete and will never be seen again.

The rope, or riata, on the saddle is of rawhide; the bridle reins are of calf hide; the rope on the wall is manila; that to the right of the bridle is of horse hair. This is Herman Oliver's riding gear

Pride of the Sumpter Valley Railroad.

The SVRR burned wood and here all hands are loading the fuel car behind the engine. No "feather bedding" here. Conductor, engineer, fireman, and brakeman all helped load.

Snow piled into this cut in the winter and passengers on the SVRR sometimes had to help shovel it out.

Leaving Baker for Sumpter on the narrow gauge. Small building behind the station is the substitute for plumbing. Wood for fuel is piled high behind the engine.

man would come into the bank, asking for money to try
to buy hay. I had instructed the cashier to tell such people that we had surplus hay, so they came, more and
more of them, as calving and lambing time approached.
They didn't bother to argue about price—they had to
have the hay. There were some pretty surprised people
when we billed them for the hay at $10, the previous
year's price, instead of the going price.

I could tell many individual stories of financing certain ranches, but it wouldn't, as the English say, be
cricket. I doubt if there is another livestock bank in the
West that can honestly say, as we can, that in the tough
times, it never foreclosed or that, if it undertook to finance a man, it saw him through, no matter what came,
so long as he played square.

Financing has changed now, what with guaranteed
savings accounts; FHA to take care of people without
bankable assets; absorbtion of little banks by the big
ones; and the production credit association.

Here is a story of Reub Long, a desert rancher in
central Oregon, near Fort Rock. The area had an all-
day meeting on the subject of credit. Every agency that
lends money to ranchers was there to explain and answer
questions about the basis for credit as seen by his agency.

At the conclusion of the meeting, the chairman looked
around and said, "This has been a fine meeting. Everyone here has contributed something except one of our
prominent ranchers, Reub Long. He has sat here all day
and not said one word. Mr. Long, can you say something
on this general subject of credit?" Reub, never at a loss,
said, "I only know two things about financing one of
these desert ranches. The first is that if you borrow from
a branch of one of the big Portland banks, you have to
prove to them first that you don't need the money. The
second thing I know is that if you borrow from the government you have to prove to them first that you can't
ever pay it back."

That statement isn't exactly true, but it has the grain
of truth there that makes it good to chew on.

CHAPTER 18

NEW FINANCING FOR OREGON AGRICULTURE

The story of the banks in Grant County is the story of the banks in every livestock county in every state west of the Mississippi. The skeleton went something like this:

1. Livestock prices dropped suddenly in 1919 and debts increased.
2. From 1919 to 1929 was a long pull for the stockmen trying to get out of debt, and for the banks financing them.
3. The financial crash in 1929 was another blow that caused stockmen to go farther into debt.
4. In the next six years the banks saw their reserves wiped out, their deposits dwindle and many loans were then above the legal limit.
5. These six years happened to coincide with drought years, that alone would have made livestock raising extremely tough. It was either sell the livestock, or buy feed in many entire counties. This made a huge drain on cash reserves because the money paid for feed left the county.
6. Many banks closed.
7. Many ranchers had debts more than the value of the ranches. Some gave up and walked off, some were forced off by foreclosures, some rode it through and won out.

In Grant County these things didn't happen, because people had faith in the bank, which stayed open, and $198,500 in cash from our ranch business enabled the bank to help each rancher a little bit.

Now let's look at the statewide picture, because I was concerned in it, right from the first.

In the Hoover administration, in 1929, the stock market collapsed after the long upward spiral that made so many paper millionaires. The value of many stocks dropped to a small fraction of what their worth had been in the summer of '29. This caused frantic withdrawals of cash and made it impossible for many country banks to finance farm production. This was hard on farmers of all kinds, but particularly hard on livestock producers, because a man who borrows to buy heifer calves doesn't get that money back for two or three years.

In contrast to this need for short term credit, farmers were pretty well off for long term credit, through the Federal Farm Loan Act that had been running for 13 years. This provided money for buying ranches through the operation of farmer-owned associations. Federal credit was used in this way, but *not* Federal money. The associations paid their own way, demonstrating that farmers as a group were trustworthy and knew how to handle money without cost to the government.

When banks in 1929 could no longer supply farm operating money, it was natural that Congress should look at these successful land banks. President Hoover suggested quick temporary action to be followed later by a permanent banking system to furnish short term credit modeled somewhat along the lines of the Federal Farm Loan system.

Accordingly Congress authorized the formation of the Reconstruction Finance Corporation, to furnish money for all kinds of business, which contained provisions for agriculture by setting up 12 Regional Agricultural Credit Corporations. In this region the main office was in Spokane and branch offices were in Portland, Boise, and Helena.

Each of these branch offices had an advisory committee that passed on all loans. The Portland office had, as its original committee:

> E. H. Sensenich—Portland
> Herman Oliver—John Day
> Fred Phillips—Baker

H. L. Corbett—Portland
A. R. Campbell—Klamath Falls
Mac Hoke—Pendleton
Ervie Williams was chosen as manager.

There was no time to fool around with any red tape or bond issues, such as the land banks used. Farmers were losing their farms every day, especially after bank failures, and most any day, if you listened closely, you could hear the metallic "cla-a-ang" of the doors of another bank as it closed.

We were ordered to "get money out as fast as possible." there was no limit to the loans, except that every loan must be "fully and adequately secured." The only other string on a loan was, "It must be made for agricultural production purposes." The manager, Mr. Williams, after the advisory committee had okayed a loan, drew checks directly upon the U. S. Treasury. A person could argue that this opened the way for gigantic frauds, but in this region at least, there was no fraud and losses were nil. Ranches were saved and so were banks.

Naturally, this order for full security ran head-on into arrangements that the borrowers already had with their local banks. Suppose Sandy McTish had given his bank at Lakeview a first mortgage for $10,000 on 5,000 sheep, his bank was unable to finance Sandy's shearing expense and the wages of his herders, so he applied to the RACC for $5000. We reviewed his situation, found it essentially sound, but the $10,000 mortgage interfered with the clause "fully and adequately secured." Nearly every loan was in the same situation. The country banks, in such cases, were usually willing to let us have the first mortgage and to transfer theirs to a second mortgage. If they did not do that, Sandy couldn't operate any longer, and the local bank employees some morning had to push their way through a ba-a-a-ahing mass of sheep, delivered to the bank. No bank wants to be in the sheep business quite so actively. The sheep won't eat greenbacks and the bank doesn't own any other green feed.

In spite of the fact that many of these emergency loans were made up to the full value of the product, they were eventually paid off in full. I do not know of any other large scale government financing effort that was so successful. Contrast it, for example, with the huge losses on the war constructed factories.

It was a pleasure to work with this committee. We had to be tough. A few local bankers sought to look at us as Santa Claus, sent by a generous Uncle Sam to bail them out. It usually fell to Mr. Corbett to explain, "We aren't an eleemosynary institution, and our purpose isn't to help banks. We are here solely to finance agriculture so the fields won't lie vacant and the herds won't have to go to slaughter." We met frequently, and I don't seem to remember that anyone paid us for our time and expenses. Mac Hoke proved brainy and sharply analytical, Orb Campbell had his feet on the ground all the time, Fred Phillips had, and at 90 still has, one of the keenest minds in the livestock business. Of course, Mr. Sensenich and Mr. Corbett knew how to size up every applicant, financially and personally. It was a wonderful board.

We had several field men. Perhaps I am forgetting some of them, especially those who worked in western Oregon, but I remember: Pat Cecil, Lynn Caton, Pat Dunnaway, John Buell, Earl Halleck, and Jim Lawrence. At least one of us knew every loan applicant, and these field men were good character judges. We lent the money fully as much on character as we did on assets.

In 1933 Congress passed a new Farm Credit Act. This set up permanent production credit machinery that replaced the regional.

Congress intended these new production credit organizations to follow the same trail blazed by the Farm Loan Associations with locals at strategic points. Part of the original capital of the local PCA's was furnished by the government and the balance by the borrowers, out of their loans. As the locals grew, they paid off the Federal capital and today all of the stock of every Oregon PCA is owned by the members.

The government sent some capable men out here to supervise and advise in setting up the locals. Meetings were held all over the state to explain the proposed set-up. All associations were to be organized with the same rules.

At the meeting in Portland, a snag developed. The larger range livestock people objected to the idea of having their loans passed on by smaller operators or general farmers who knew little or nothing of the needs of the range men. Out of the argument came the proposal, first advanced by Ervie Williams, that the range livestock people have their own association. The government advisors were instantly opposed to this. I suppose they thought that every little group of producers would want to follow suit and they foresaw demands for production credit associations for bulb growers, cranberry men, rose producers, and so on. Anyhow, they fought the idea vigorously.

We examined the law and we couldn't find anything in it to forbid any such thing. Mac Hoke, Buck Snider of Paisley, Percy Folsum of Pendleton, E. L. (Dad) Potter of OSC, Gene Courtney of The Dalles, Fred Phillips of Baker, and some others, fought with me for the idea. At our own expense we met here and there, beat the drums and pretty soon there was so much pressure for our own association that opposition, Federal and local, was bowled over.

I think Oregon was the first state to set up such a plan. When Idaho and Montana rangemen heard of it, they pushed for and got livestock credit associations, too. Ours was first called the Oregon Livestock PCA, with proposed headquarters at Baker. But compromises had to be made. The Washington rangemen couldn't get organized and petitioned to come in with us; the Klamath and Lake men said it was too far to Baker; the Baker folks said it was too far to Portland.

Out of all this came the Northwest Livestock Production Credit Association. with headquarters at Portland, and with Ervie Williams as manager. The charter was granted December, 1933. Messers Drumheller, McGregor, and Richardson were the men who carried the ball for the state of Washington.

The association operating in Klamath and Lake counties was allowed to make range livestock loans there, and the Baker association could make loans to range operators in Baker county and part of Malheur. Otherwise, all range loans in Oregon and Washington came to the Northwest office at Portland. A range operator was first defined as a man with a band of sheep or 250 cattle. The government men objected to this on the ground that numbers fluctuated too much. They insisted upon a money limit. This was finally set at $10,000.

So, out of all of these dozens of meetings grew the highly successful system now in effect. Lending money for farm operations are local associations in Pendleton, Baker, The Dalles, Redmond, Salem, Klamath Falls, and Medford. The Baker and Klamath Falls locals also handle range livestock loans. There is a similar set-up in the state of Washington. The Northwest association office handles *only* range livestock loans for the balance of Oregon, all of Washington, and for northern Idaho.

The minimum loan limit for NLPCA is now $30,000. There is no maximum. The largest loan right now (1961) is $445,973 and the total for 1961 was $15,060,-000. The largest individual note that the Northwest association ever held was for $1,769,000. This is the largest commitment of any PCA in this region. The requisite now for a man to qualify for a loan from NLPCA is that 50 per cent of his gross income must be from livestock.

After years of service, Mr. Williams resigned to go with the Portland Union Livestock Company. Jerry Herburger, a Grant County boy, is now manager. William Steiwer, capable stockman of Fossil, is President.

Mr. Williams is still on the board of directors. Starting in 1919 with the Portland Cattle Loan Company, he has been continuously connected with the financing of range livestock for 41 years. I do not know of anyone else who has such a long and successful record. In that time he has known personally nearly every livestock man in the Northwest and has gained the trust and respect of all of them.

To complete the record, the list of the charter members of the Northwest Livestock Production Credit Association follows. Their names will bring memories to old timers. All towns listed are in Oregon..

NAME	RESIDENCE
Leo Hahn	Antelope
Robert N. Stanfield	Baker
Fred W. Falconer	Pendleton
W. H. Steiwer	Fossil
F. A. Phillips	Baker
R. J. Williams	Burns
W. N. Elliott	Baker
J. T. Logan	Brogan
R. J. Green	La Grande
Robert L. Lister	Paulina
Wayne C. Stewart	Dayville
Mac Hoke	Pendleton
Walter A. Holt	Pendleton
W. H. Sanderson	Madras
Wayne E. Phillips	Keating
H. L. Priday	Gateway
Bidwell Cram	Gateway
C. M. Kennedy	Gateway
Wm. Hanley	Burns
F. C. Vaughan	Baker
Herman Oliver	John Day
J. R. Williamson	Baker
S. E. Miller	Union
W. H. Vogel	Union
Ernest F. Johnson	Wallowa
Harold A. Cohn	Heppner
John V. Withers	Paisley
C. E. Grelle	Route 1, Portland
J. G. Barratt	Heppner

R. A. Ward ....1205 N.W. Davis,
Portland

W. B. Snider ....Paisley

First members of the board of directors were:

NAME	RESIDENCE
Fred Phillips	Baker
F. C. Vaughan	Baker
Norman Elliott	Baker
Herman Oliver	John Day
W. B. (Buck) Snider............	Paisley
Mac Hoke	Pendleton
Ernest Johnson	Wallowa
J. G. Barratt	Heppner
Robert Lister	Prineville

Before the next meeting, the Washington people came in, so some of these directors resigned to allow the election of Tom Drumheller, J. W. Richardson, and John McGregor, all of the state of Washington. In addition, Norman Elliott resigned and was replaced by Ed Grelle of Portland. I resigned after a few years of service because of my interest in the Grant County Bank. Farm people were greatly concerned lest the new credit associations should come under the control of other banking interests, so the rule was adopted that no director could be classed as a banker. I have been greatly interested in the welfare of the production credit associations, and often confer with the officers. They have been a great stabilizing factor.

This story, necessarily omitting all the arguments, conflicts, and personal opinions involved, shows that progress in a democracy involves many differences of opinions and compromises. It shows, too, the soundness of livestock as a business. Compare it with most any other kind of business and the contrast is startling. The bankrupt records show that about half of the businesses that start, fail. In Grant County there have been practically no failures of cattle ranches. In Oregon, read again the list of successful charter members. I do not believe that restaurants, stores, nor factories, nor any other kind of business can show such a success record. That is one reason why I am proud of my profession—the livestock business.

Head-and-healing branding scene on the Emile Hyde ranch, Izee. Left mounted holding calf by hind legs, Herman Oliver; in front of him is Carlos Parton; vaccinating calf, Joe Officer; holding head, Bonham Keerins; mounted and holding calf by front feet, Sonnie Brown; Bill Elliott with checkered coat; Perry Hyde on distant horse. This method of branding is fast giving way to a calf chute branding table. As the calf enters the chute, both calf and chute are quickly landed on their side by the use of a lever. The calf is held firmly in a squeeze for any calf operation necessary.

CHAPTER 19

YEARS IN PUBLIC SERVICE

Cattlemen's Association

I sort of grew into the county livestock association, taking part more and more in its meetings, working on its problems. In 1928 I was elected president of the state association and served all through the depression period, ten years in all, and was vice-president of the National, but refused to take the presidency, knowing it would take me away from the ranch almost continuously.

As the voice of the Oregon cattle industry, the State Cattle Association had to represent the growers in dealings with all kinds of organizations. Here are just a few of those groups:

U. S. Forest Service
Bureau of Land Management
U. S. Wildlife Service
State Fish and Game Department
Oregon State College
State Tax Commission
Other state associations, such as Oregon Wool Growers and a dozen others
Interstate Commerce Commission
Internal Revenue Bureau
Railroad Rate Council
Tariff Bureau
Oregon Legislature (especially cattle theft, brand laws, tax, and disease problems)

This is only a sample. It would take pages to make it complete. In all of this time, when we were constantly arguing with someone, or trying to change official edicts, or at least trying to make our viewpoint felt, at no time did we, as an organization, get into a bad position with anyone. We differed, of course, but we did it peacefully at a council table, and could go back and talk again. Our Summit talks did not break up in name calling.

We had plenty of members who were in a fighting mood, especially when Federal agencies came out with rules that restricted freedom of movement or choice. It would have been easy to get into a situation with these people so that agreement would have been impossible. We were always able to treat them as personal friends.

From my father I learned young that if you are going to be forced by your business into almost daily contact with someone, you'd better keep relations cordial. The associations in many of the western states did not take this attitude. Many of them found new regulations intolerable, fought the field agents with fists and even guns, were dragged into court, and had a bad time for years and years.

These things hurt your side. They are distorted in the press and also before some of the ultra-conservation groups, who are always ready to believe that a stockman is their natural enemy. Tensions are built up so that the agency doesn't dare to give in, even if it wants to. If it gives in, it is called weak, and some group three thousand miles away, knowing absolutely nothing of the case, howls to heaven that the cattle barons are intimidating the agency and a congressional investigation is demanded.

When, a few years ago, a committee was formed in Congress to investigate the quarrel between livestock men and the Forest Service, the committee's secretary wrote to the cattle association asking where in Oregon hearings should be held to bring out the stockmen's charges. We replied that we had no quarrel with the Forest Service, other than natural differences that always exist between landlord and tenant, and we had nothing to air in a public hearing. The Oregon Wool Growers made the same kind of an answer.

In other states where hearings were held, the resulting publicity, charges and counter-charges, resulted in quarrels going on even now. The Forest Service has a fine group of men, but that doesn't mean that all rules applied nationwide will fit every location. Our organization, nearly every year, has an argument with someone over grazing rules. But we don't fight. We try to be fair and usually you are met by the same attitude you assume. If you are hostile, others will be. Somehow these others are remarkably like looking glasses. The old saying is still true: "If you take a smile to the glass you meet a smile."

In the days when we had sheep, I was active in the Oregon Wool Growers, one of the oldest of the Oregon commodity groups. They also adopted harmony as their watchword.

STATE BOARD OF HIGHER EDUCATION

When Governor Ike Patterson called me up in 1929 and asked me to serve on the newly created State Board of Higher Education, I turned him down. This new board was to govern the state university, Oregon State College, the three normal schools, (now, colleges of education) replacing the several Boards of Regents. I was an eighth grade graduate, pretty lucky to climb that far on the educational ladder. It appeared to me that I had no business getting away from my home corral quite that far.

For years the different schools, but particularly the two largest, had been in a constant legislative fight over appropriations. If one school got a new building, the other hurried to get in a bill for its campus, just so the first school wouldn't get ahead. Feeling was bad, fanned by bitter and active partisans of both. It showed up in athletic contests, in every legislative session, and in the press.

The governor again called me and in the meantime several friends had done so, asking me to reconsider, advancing the plea that since this is an agricultural state, there should be someone on the board to represent agriculture and its needs. Agricultural research and extension were supervised by the board. Finally I took the appointment for one year.

The board was directed to economize and harmonize. Dr. Hall was President of the University and Dr. Kerr President of the State College. They were opposite in personalities. Dr. Kerr had a passion for "facts." "Gentlemen, what are the facts?" was his constant theme. "Be prepared with the facts before presenting your problem." Dr. Hall was given to oratorical statements. Due to their personalities, they differed radically on almost every question.

We were directed to secure a chancellor and a committee of the board scoured the country for a likely candidate. Everywhere the committee went they were told, "You have in Oregon the best University administrator in America, Dr. Kerr, Why not use him?"

Dr. Kerr had done wonders in Utah, first with the State College, then with Brigham Young University. He had, in turn, built Oregon State College to one of the leaders in America. He had a great ability to recognize and entice to Oregon, professional talent of the highest order. Man after man came to Oregon State for a lesser salary than he was getting just to work under Dr. Kerr, and to take part in a school famous for effective research. The board was created to eliminate duplication, effect economies, and develop harmony, particularly between the two largest schools. These major objectives, in the main, have been reached.

The original conception of these two larger schools, the plan at the time the board was formed, has not been entirely achieved. The original plan was to cut out schools of limited scope, such as journalism and mining; to concentrate on science and technology of all kinds at the State College and to make the University primarily a great liberal arts institution. Just for the record, here are the changes from that idea, made since then:

1941—Science, both under-graduate and graduate restored at the University. This, to a great extent, undermined the original division of functions.

1942—Undergraduate work in business restored to State College. A different type of program than the University had.

1947—Landscape Architecture centered at U. of O. and degree granting taken away from OSC.

1950—Undergraduate work in physical education, first given to U. of O., divided between the two schools, with graduate work still at U. of O.

1951—Graduate work in elementary education, given to all three colleges of education. First alignment assigned all graduate work to U. of O. and OSC.

1951—OSC and U. of O. both given elementary education work, heretofore assigned solely to three regional colleges (Monmouth, La Grande and Ashland).

1952—Three regional schools all given secondary education work (high school teacher preparation), which heretofore was available only at OSC and U. of O.

1946—Lower division work given to what was later known as Portland State College.

1953—Four years of work and limited liberal arts degrees awarded at Portland.

1955—Portland State College authorized and courses greatly expanded, to include ten major fields. All of these are duplicated at either U. of O. or OSC or both. (This was due to legislature, not the board).

1959—Original concept of masters' and doctors' degrees only at U. of O. and OSC now scrapped with some masters degree work granted to Portland State.

1959—Oregon State College authorized to give degrees in areas of liberal arts, each with a strong science background.

Thus, the original idea of dropping schools with low attendance has been broken down, except that degrees in mining and veterinary medicine were both taken from OSC.

The idea of having all graduate work (masters' and doctors' degrees) only at U. of O. and OSC has been broken down.

The conception of science at OSC and liberal arts at U. of O. was abandoned early by granting science to U. of O. Just lately OSC was given restricted work in liberal arts.

These adjustments, made either by the board or the legislature, were dictated by changing times. You can't keep anything exactly the same, on a ranch or in a classroom. The original idea of unified administration, under a chancellor responsible to a single board, has proved sound. It has since been copied by many other states.

I served on the board, in all, 23 years, and it was a source of satisfaction to me. It brought me many friends I would never have known otherwise. I have always tried to be constructive, and higher education is surely that. As the schools have grown, most of the unhealthy and bitter rivalry has disappeared, salaries have been raised, and my special interests, research and agricultural extension, have been well handled. I was especially interested in 4-H Club work and Oregon leads the nation in the percentage of eligible youngsters in the work, so I believe that I did the state some good in that field. F. L. Ballard can be credited for uncanny ability to pick the right extension worker for each job.

Henry Cabell and I are the two persons in Oregon who have served on both the State Board of Higher Education and the Highway Commission.

During my time on the Board of Higher Education total enrollment increased like this:

Year	Enrollment
1930	7,709
1957	20,221

The staff increased from 810 to 2,203. Student fees, annual, were increased from $98.75 to $270. Cash value of buildings on all campuses increased from $14,118,000 in 1933 to $85,762,000. About half of this was due to inflation and increased prices.

During my years on the board, I tried to take somewhat the same attitudes I always took with the ranch: Look ahead and do what is best in the long run; if an employee won't work in one position, try him somewhere else; always build, never tear down; time is a great healer.

There were some trying decisions to make, such as how to treat "fellow-travelers," as one or two showed up in the faculties; what to do with a fire-eating, swashbuckling dean; allocation of funds during the depression when no school had enough. But, as indicated, time healed most of the bad situations and the end result has been a system of higher education that we can all feel proud of.

STATE HIGHWAY COMMISSION

I served on the State Highway Commission three years, 1940 to 1943. Those years marked the near completion of the first big, ambitious program of "getting Oregon out of the mud" with money from gasoline taxes. Oregon was the first state in the Union with such a program. Most other states have followed.

The war came on and it was hard to keep our highways up to ordinary standards, due to scarcity of men and materials. We had to make the hard decision of whether to spread the money or concentrate it. We took the latter course, working mostly on our most important East-West route, the Columbia Highway, and our most important North-South route, the Pacific Highway.

Also, the decision was made then to spend some of the money inside the cities, a new policy.

Another hard decision was to change effort from highway construction to traffic speed-up.

All of these things involved where and how to spend money. In many cases I had to vote against the wishes of my own part of Oregon. Again, as in ranching, I tried to help in deciding upon the proper system and the best over-all policies. Once decided, I stuck with them. It is hard to do that when your best friends come before the Commission with logical reasons why some particular road should be improved. Voting their way would have scrapped the larger plan, sometimes.

I made some fine friends on the Commission. One was a truly remarkable man, Sam Boardman. Maybe some day someone will write a book about him. He was in charge of parks. Oregon, at the time I was on the Commission, had more parks than any other state, and they were nearly all due to Sam's work. Few persons are able to make such a lasting contribution. But he was a joy to know. He was enthusiastic, humorous, full of grand boyish nonsense, yet underneath was a life dedicated to getting a good park system for his state. The remarkable thing is that until just lately, every one of the state's hundreds of parks was donated—and Sam is largely responsible for that.

CIVIC ACTIVITIES

These have been, like the jib-job lots at the auction sales, "too numerous to mention." Some activities include work with Chambers of Commerce; the Masonic Lodge, including the Shrine; Kiwanis; the Oddfellows; and I have received quite a handful of awards of various kinds for things that mainly can be grouped under the term "good citizenship". If a man has prospered in a community, the only decent thing for him to do is to use his time, money, and talents for the good of the community. That attitude, followed out, does not need any public recognition or awards, for the man himself knows what he has done as compared to what he might have done. His own heart should tell him whether his deeds have been good or not.

CHAPTER 20

THE NATIONAL FARM PROGRAM

Recently a well-informed editor said to me that in all of his experience he had not seen farmers' public relations so poor; that the average city dweller blamed farmers for every increase in the cost of living; that retailers everywhere pointed to the grower as the profiteer; that the poor suffering farmer was down to his last Cadillac—and so on. He thought almost the entire thing was due to the farm program. Taxpayers, large and small, believe their taxes are high partly due to farm subsidies.

Then what do the farmers think? Every poll that has ever been taken shows that they also are overwhelmingly opposed to the program. Then why do they keep voting for it? The answer is that the way the law is stated, they have no alternatives to vote for. Actually, what the wheat growers vote for is whether they want $1.80 a bushel for wheat, or want the world price, that would be far less. No one can vote in the wheat referendum but wheat growers, no one can vote in the cotton referendum but cotton growers. If all farmers voted, the program would be out the window tomorrow.

The whole subject is so wrapped up in misinformation that maybe someone may welcome an explanation. As an example of how little the consumers know, try this: Hang around the meat counter and ask the housewives what they think of having the government buy beef to keep up the price for cattlemen. Out of 100 beef purchasers, I would be surprised if the entire 100 didn't say something like—"I think it's the greatest outrage in history—taxing us to keep the big cattlemen rich!" But the government has not spent one penny to buy beef— there is no guaranteed price on beef, no loan program, and never has been. When you tell consumers that, they do not believe you. The only exception to this is that in the drought years some cattle were bought to keep them from starving.

Another error with political results was to blame Benson. But Benson was the one man in public life who had the moral courage to stand out against the farm program. He appeared annually before the Congress and pled for authority to ease the government out of the mess. The Congress refused—and then publicly blamed him for spending more money on price supports than any other secretary. He warned these same men years ago, told them exactly what would happen and begged them to change their policy. They would not, and blamed him for their mistakes. Such actions create a bad image of politicians.

Let's go back and see about this whole thing. When Franklin D. Roosevelt was elected, the country chose a man who had never earned a dollar in any kind of business. He seemed to have an inner contempt for business success, and chose for advisers hundreds of similar-minded persons. He combed the colleges for socialistic economists.

These persons had as a doctrine—*whatever is, is bad; any change is good*. So they set out to make a planned economy—modeled somewhat after Russia's numerous "Five Year Plans". As a result, the depression was unmercifully prolonged. It was brought on because after the First World War, America loaned billions of dollars to foreign nations to use in buying American products. That created a false prosperity here. Then when in 1929 we began to ask these nations to start paying us back, and they refused, we stopped lending to them. This suddenly stopped their purchases, so factories closed in America and raw materials of all kinds began to pile up. This was the panic. Depression followed.

But we had had many depressions before, and our vigorous growing nation had snapped out of them quickly. This time, though, we couldn't, because NRA and other restrictions forbade the low-cost operators from going ahead—just as the farm program does now. So the planners had a marvelous time. When some trick legislation didn't work, the planners tried to cure it with amendments to the law, and then needed other amendments indefinitely. Now if a doctor prescribes wrong medicine and makes a man desperately sick, the cure should not be more of the same. The nation found it impossible to recover because everyone with an idea was chained down. In 1937 when a little more of re-employment followed in the wake of a better crop year, President Roosevelt smugly said, "We planned it that way," only to have unemployment increase. He was finally bailed out by war.

The agricultural story is different only because we have kept the New Deal laws on the books, whereas most such laws applying to business were dropped, due to war-time needs.

The original farm law was not so bad. It created a device whereby a tax could be collected from processors and rebated back to farmers. It was so geared that the greater the production, the less the farmers would receive. The theory was that this alone would be a powerful brake upon over-production. This money came out of the pockets of consumers, so it was not a drain on the treasury. During the three years this law was in effect, we had the worst drought in American history. In 1934, '35, and '36 there were many thousands of wheat farmers and cotton farmers who raised nothing at all. They had to sell all their livestock. So the payments they received from the government were regarded somewhat as relief money. Without it, nearly all the farmers in entire states would have lost their land. But in 1936 the Supreme Court ruled this law unconstitutional. It was then that President Roosevelt angrily demanded authority to pack the court with his own "yes" men. It was not granted, but he got it anyway, through deaths and old age.

During this time, the Oregon Wheat League came forth with some principles for a national farm plan that has not been equalled. Here they are:

A farm plan, economically sound and of lasting value, must include these points:

1. It must not pile up storable products.
2. It must not interfere with normal markets for the product, or price it beyond use.
3. A procedure for one product must not hurt or ruin the demand for another.
4. Costs must be borne by the product, not the U. S. Treasury.
5. Drastic acreage cuts should be only temporary, because whenever land is withdrawn from production, such action sets up a chain reaction of unemployment. Thus, the wrong program can, in itself, cause or prolong a depression.

How has the present program, set up in 1937, checked with those five points? Of course, it runs exactly counter to all of them. Wheat, cotton, tobacco, corn, and all the others have piled up in storage; it has priced wheat too high for feed, has priced cotton out of most export markets; it has diverted land to other products, resulting in ruining other markets (example: Oregon's malting barley) ; costs have been 100% out of the Treasury; drastic acreage cuts have been so much a part of the program that a farm's "allotment" has come to be a prime factor in figuring its sales value.

The evil was compounded during the war. At first, the plan was to include only the so-called basic crops— wheat, corn, tobacco, cotton, rice, and peanuts. But, during the war, the Secretary of Agriculture was given authority to set the price in accordance with parity, on any agricultural product. So our government began to buy honey, seeds, turpentine, eggs, milk, pork—almost everything except beef.

The beef men, though sorely pressed at times, steadfastly refused to go along with *any* price control or any production control schemes. The New Deal starry-eyed boys lost patience entirely. Here was a large group, some of them in every state in the Union, and they were so ignorant that they couldn't understand that Uncle Sam knew what was best for them.

The funny outcome of nearly 30 years of continuous price fixing and production control of nearly everything else is that the beef business, on the whole, has been better off than any of the others. Apparently old man "Supply and Demand" has been smarter than any of the young intellectuals who were so busy trying to shove him off the scene.

We cattlemen could just sit back and laugh at the whole thing, except, as mentioned, we share in the general resentment of city consumers, even though we are in no way to blame.

It is popular now to sneer at Congress because they have been so silly and have regarded this whole thing as a way to get themselves re-elected. The entire treatment has been so lacking in patriotism. But lack of knowledge has been just as large a factor as deliberate political finagling. For example:

Congress, after years of trying this and that, began to believe that the basic trouble was too much land. Horses formerly needed about 50,000,000 acres. They need little now. The "agricultural revolution" suddenly made chemicals available and production boomed. So they created the soil bank to retire some of this extra land. Of course, this would have worked if they had retired enough, but they carefully kept this from happening by setting a $5000 limit per farm. Eighty percent of the nation's wheat is grown on large farms. No large farmer can afford to lay out a little field for such a payment. So the soil bank, by this restriction, can't get enough land in it to do any real good at all.

When this is called to the attention of a Congressional committee, some senator stands up, strikes an oratorical pose, and shouts, "Gentlemen! I am for the little man. As long as I have breath in my body, I shall stand for the family farm in the country and the humble American home in the city." (Applause) .

That word "applause" has been misspelled for years in the Congressional record. The right spelling is "applesauce". A researcher wouldn't need to leave Oregon to find a Congressman making such statements.

Of course, all the others hurriedly say "Me too," so the $5000 restriction is on and the law is a waste of money.

To strip this farm plan of all the side issues that have been built up, let's make a fanciful case. Let's pretend that the automobile business got into trouble a few years from now so that Congress created another AAA, "Automobile Adjustment Act." I will not bring anything new into this at all, just apply what has already happened with wheat.

PARITY FOR AUTOMOBILES*

A Fantasy

Congress passed this law in 1970, amidst public rejoicing and we are now looking back on events from 1990. The slogan that won the 1968 election was "Parity for All Automobiles." The President and the new Congress were both committed. It was to usher in a new day and lead the way for "Parity for Everything."

The conservatives succeeded in getting a few things into the law. Senator Circumspect of New Hampshire got a sliding scale in so that if surpluses began to pile up, production must be curtailed. Opponents though, got this curtailment to apply to factory space, not units of production. Moreover, the diverted space could be used for anything except to build cars.

But Senator Circumlocution of Iowa gathered together a coalition from non-auto manufacturing states and forced through a provision that any new manufac-

---

* All names and dates used herein are fictitious. Any resemblance to any person, living or dead, is purely coincidental.

turer *must* be given a quota equal to such factory space as would be economically sound. Furthermore, any manufacturer at all could turn out 15 cars a day, but the price would not be guaranteed. Such production would not qualify for a loan.

By 1975, these developments had occurred:

A. Vast increase in car production.
B. Thousands of new firms making 15 cars a day.
C. Drop-off in exports.
D. Increase in imports.
E. Pile-up of cars in government storage—30,000,000 in 1975.

Then it became necessary to vote on allotments of warehouse space and quotas. One clever President had stalled this off a few years by the device of over-estimating foreign sales. It won the election for him. The vote on allotments carried by 87%. It was not known what was wrong with the heads of the other 13%.

Then these things happened:

A. Thirty-five percent of the factory space was marked off and auto making prohibited there.
B. Production was stepped up wonderfully in the remaining space, so it was as large as before.
C. In the diverted space, the companies made trucks and swamped the market.
D. The 15-car-a-day factories couldn't get loans, so they dropped their prices a few dollars and sold *all* of their cars, forcing Fords and Chevrolets into the government warehouses.
E. Storage charges mounted. The government was soon paying $1,000,000 a day storage. A few storage scandals developed.

When the 1978 Congress met, the government owned 60,000,000 cars. Somehow the theories hadn't worked as intended. Congressmen, knowing their hearts were pure, and knowing they would pass only good bills, blamed the administration. Never a day passed that someone did not bitterly condemn the cabinet officer in charge, though he had pleaded, almost on his knees, not to pass the bill. He had told them what would happen. Squads of Congressmen beseeched the President to fire the cabinet member, so they could report back to their angry constituents that the cause of the trouble had been erased.

In this session, 1978, public clamor grew for these actions:

A. Give a car to each underprivileged person. By a curious coincidence the number of such persons was figured as exactly the same as the number of cars in storage.

B. Give one to each school child.

C. Give all the cars to the Iron Curtain countries.

D. Destroy all the cars and start over.

E. Give all the cars to backward nations.

Congress couldn't unite on any of these, so compromised and extended the parity principle to trucks. This resulted in a steady stream of trucks into storage also.

They also passed a "car bank" bill to reward any factory owner who would quit making cars. This didn't work well, because Senator Bleeding-Heart was for the little man and he tacked on a provision that it should apply only to small factories. Of course, the big factories made 80% of the cars.

The move to give the cars away abroad made some headway. The nations that needed them worst wouldn't take them, because they didn't want to ruin their own car makers. Germany took five million and sold us five million more Volkswagens. Further sales to Germany were blocked.

Other nations did not take them because of the clause in the law making it necessary to send the cars in U. S. ships. They didn't have the money to pay the freight. They offered to take millions if they could only use their own ships. This was turned down. It was an affront to American labor.

The 1980 Congress was confronted by 75,000,000 cars in storage and plenty of trucks. Idle ships, caves, abandoned mines and schoolhouses had to be used for storage space. Fury against the cabinet member who had to buy them was now a steady roar. It was his program. He should be punished. Lacking storage for more, Congress passed millions to lend to each factory to build storage for cars they were about to make to sell to the government. Storage charges were raised so the factories would be encouraged to do that.

Now a strange psychology seized the nation. Confronted by 75,000,000 cars in storage, the populace decided that sooner or later the government would have to give them away, so everyone quit buying cars. This built up the storage still more.

Both parties by now were demanding the resignation of the Cabinet Secretary in charge of car buying; some insisted he had planned this mess. Senator Redundant said his presence in the cabinet was an intolerable insult to American labor. Senator Hrrumph of Minnesota said the Secretary's mismanagement was the greatest disgrace ever to afflict the nation. Both owned foreign cars.

Senator Oracle of Oregon was most critical. He blamed the President mostly, but also the Secretary, newspapers, Chamber of Commerce, all members of the opposition, and all members of his own party, except one. He called for the adoption of the Oracle Plan. By this plan, all profits from car-making were to be turned over to the Teamsters Union to compensate them for losses when cars replaced their teams.

His impassioned speech brought thunderous applause from the packed galleries. The speech made every front page.

At this point the Secretary made the worst of his many political errors. He pointed to the original law and suggested that loans on cars be reduced gradually to 60% of parity, as written in the law but annually postponed by Congress. This was met by stunned silence, then outraged cries from all sides. Congress members, one by one, washed their hands of such an absurd idea and the Unionists raised huge sums to defeat the party in power.

There were many side programs—Conservation of Factories, with government technicians to search out termites and rust; Factory and Home Adjustment loans, and many others. By now it was evident there were far too many factories, but these loans provided money for building more and kept present factories up to high efficiency.

There were dozens of plans. Solutions that might have worked were frowned upon because such solutions would take cars out of politics. Some of the Unions worked for a scheme they called "Compensatory Payment Plan." All quotas were to be discarded, cars sold for what they would bring, and the difference between selling price and parity paid out of the treasury. This was to be gradually extended to everything, including bobbypins and straw hats. The huge increased income taxes would finance the whole thing, they said. It gained wide support.

In the hearings on these various plans, the economists from Harvard and Yale took opposite sides. The big labor organizations had different plans. Things were getting confused.

Congress again compromised and passed a bill to make everything hunky-dory by "modernizing parity," as they called it.

Finally, in 1985, the whole thing was thrown out, due to war. Planes and helicopters pretty well displaced cars. As this is written, 1990, sentiment is building up for a parity price law on helicopters.

———————

Now all of that sounds like utter nonsense, but everything mentioned, and many many more, has taken place with wheat between 1933 and 1960.

As soon as the asininity of a portion of the law becomes evident, Congress tries to fix it by an amendment. It has become like an old Model-T, never replaced, just cobbled up, when a complete scrapping job is needed.

In all of the ideas presented, the original framework offered by the Oregon Wheat League seems the best place to start.

I realize that in the 30 years of tinkering, the price supports have been transferred into real estate values, business and bank values—all sorts of things. The young men now operating many farms would surely lose their equities if the present law were scrapped with no replacement. But that does not make it right, and nothing can ever make it right to try to legislate supply and demand out the back door. One law will constantly make another necessary, and in the end, such thinking can only lead to socialism in some form. It doesn't make much difference whether it is in the form of dictatorship, communism, or what is called "benevolent socialism." None of these works except by dictator powers. Most wheat growers now active have never seen a free market for wheat.

It looks as though we have a bear by the tail, and, like some of our other big national issues, such as race, we aren't likely to see it cured in our day. Eventually our rapid population growth will cure the farm problem, as it has been cured with most products in other nations. It sounds callous to say it, but some day hunger may solve it.

This entire farm program is actually only a symptom of a disease. There are other symptoms: Federal aid for education; mounting social security; unwillingness of Congress to pass effective labor control bills; inflation; rising cost of living; drive for Federal medical insurance. There are many more, all indicating the same thing—irresponsible Congressmen elected by people they have fooled.

Let's take just one issue to show this. I could take any of them, but will take the Federal power issue because it has elected two senators from Oregon and several representatives.

The federal power arguments, boiled down, are:
1. It is cheaper.
2. Cheap power will bring industry to Oregon.
3. The water that makes the power is God's gift to all the people and it is immoral for anyone to profit from it.

All other arguments are merely off-shoots of these three.

Argument No. 1—*"Federal Power Is Cheaper"*

There is no doubt about the truth of the statement, but let's carry it to its logical conclusion. If we should have Federal power because it is cheaper, then the argument is equally valid for gasoline. If the government took over all the oil wells, refineries, pipe lines, trucks, storage tanks, and filling stations, gasoline could be sold to everyone for something like seven cents a gallon. Wouldn't that be wonderful!

So let's go on. If the government owned all farms, food processing plants, railroads, truck lines, and grocery stores, meat should cost not over ten cents, and a loaf of bread maybe three cents. Marvelous!

What else do we spend money for? Automobiles. All right, let's have the government take over all of the iron mines, steel works, auto factories, railroads, garages. We could easily then buy a Ford car for $500, maybe $300.

What's wrong with all this?

Merely that there would be no one left to pay all of the local and national taxes. As soon as we begin to tax all of these employees to pay for schools, police, and national needs, the cost would be about twice what it is now. For example, in Russia where these things are all done by government, it takes a worker's entire wages for two months to buy a suit of clothes. Here it takes not over a week, or one-eighth.

So Federal ownership is *not* cheaper. Logically extended, it is several times more costly. To be sure, we can take one article, whether it's power, automobiles, claw hammers or bobbypins and the government can make it cheaper, because all of the other, privately owned concerns help finance it through taxes.

Argument No. 2—"Cheap Power Will Bring Industries to Oregon"

Same as above. If only one place in America has it, that place has an advantage. Natural gas is even cheaper than water power. Suppose the demand arises for government to take over all the gas wells and sell at cost? You'd see every aluminum factory in the Pacific Northwest hightail it for the gas producing states overnight.

Argument No. 3—"Water Power Is God's Gift, Etc."

Here are America's natural resources:
1. Land
2. Mines, including petroleum and gas
3. Water
4. Timber
5. Fish and game

One can add a few other things, such as people, scenery, air, but these aren't controllable. Of all the arguments for Federal power, this one has produced the most oratory and it appeals most to herd thinking. Politicians love it, because they know that a speech is most effective if ended by emotion. It doesn't need a smart person to make an emotional appeal about the big power mogul stealing part of God's gracious gifts to mankind and converting them to his own greed. It's sure-fire, as shown by the elections.

But if a person really and honestly believes that, then how can he escape from the belief that all land should be Federally owned? For land is one fundamental resource, water another. Belief in Federal ownership is herd thinking. I don't know how to cure it. You can't punish a sheep for wanting to follow the herd, even though it is headed for a cliff and destruction.

Of course, it is all right for the Federal government to build a dam when there is not enough private capital, but I think it is not all right to go ahead and sell the power forever. If that same policy were pursued with other things, we would have the Forest Service owning all the sawmills, all the logging railroads, and even the retail lumber yards. They would also own all livestock that graze the forests and all fish and game.

The value of the water power is a mere speck as compared to the value of the land itself. The value of our great mass of land is thousands of times greater than the value of the water power, but if it is immoral somehow for private industry to convert a natural resource into some profit, then it is a thousand times more immoral for a farmer to own land or a city dweller to own a home.

The power should be handled exactly as a Reclamation project is handled. Let the government build, but sell to the users as fast as they can buy. As soon as this sale occurs, get the government out of the picture. Our farm credit is handled exactly that way and experience shows it is far better than to suffer forever under the dead hand of government control.

I referred earlier to the farm program, Federal aid to education, and Federal power ownership as all symptoms of the same disease. That disease is a constant, maybe irresistible movement toward socialism. If we let it win, the Russians will have the last laugh. Karl Marx preached that it *must* win, and the Russians believe that. Under socialism all workers, whether they work with head or hand, work for the government.

Here in this country, we now spend 35 per cent of our time working for the government, and, at the present rate of increase, that will be 50 per cent by 1970. How much of that can private industry afford? From its nature, private ownership is a risk, so there are losses. Hail takes a crop; disease kills the livestock; a new invention ruins a good business. But if government takes the profit, while business takes the loss, it is only a ques-

Dave Baird, conductor on the SVRR (page 196) was tall, dark, and handsome. He enforced social segregation by separating dance-hall girls from ladies, professional gamblers from gentlemen. In the seat beside the open window, he helped in the birth of a baby girl. He is the father of Dean Baird, U. of O. medical school, brother of Judge Baird of Baker County.

"That looks like my cow, but sure's Hell it's not my brand." Here is one of Homer's favorites.

tion of time until all businesses fail. Inflation kills a business, too, because each year this erodes away some of the value. Say a factory costs $100,000. The owner can have a depreciation allowance, but only up to the cost. So, if, when it needs replacing, the cost of an identical factory is $400,000, the owner will either have to quit, or else he may lose his business to a money lender.

Fundamentally, I am opposed to socialism in all of its forms. It has nothing to offer mankind except unmeaning words, drivel really. Why any worker would follow its call, leading to slave labor, is beyond me. Chinese workers neither strike nor leave their jobs.

Contrast its failures with the dramatic, exciting, always moving, always changing, inspiring record of private incentive. Socialism kills everything worth while in life: Art, music, literature, science, proud self-reliance, initiative, self-confidence, reverence, and those things that, together, we call the soul.

Yet, in our political life you can count on the fingers of one hand the persons who have resisted the call of socialism. They don't call it that. They don't even call it inflation, because nearly everyone is opposed to both words. I suspect if Russia could work, directly, for a program for America, they would be plugging these things:

1. More Federal, less state power.
2. Federal aid to farmers, veterans, schools, aged, workers, roads.
3. Inflation, including deficit spending.
4. More and more power for labor unions.
5. Public ownership of electricity, and, as fast as possible, other natural resources. They would favor gradual acquisition of more land for Forest Service, Bureau of Land Management, Army, Soil Conservation Service, Department of Agriculture.
6. Gradual supplanting of state agencies by Federal agencies.

My only suggestion is to check every man or woman who runs for Congress and see which candidates are in favor of those six things. All of them would react with outrage to a suggestion that they favor Russia over the United States, yet they go out and pledge themselves to work for a program that is assuredly more Russian than American.

Picture taken in the 1890's on OO Ranch, Harney County, then owned by Riley and Hardin. Cattle are low grade, mixed breeds, including dairy. High taxes now, and all-around high overhead, that total $60 or more per cow, make it impossible to operate without the best cattle available.

Front row, left to right: Buck Spencer, father of Mrs. Chester Mace, who lives in Burns; Andrew Greeley; Bob Settlemeir, cook; Sam Glaspie, on horseback, holding steer by hind legs; Charles Cramer, holding steer; Ray Jackson, holding iron; Julius Chandler, on horseback, holding steer by head; Chappo, extreme right on horse (Mexican).
Others unknown.

CHAPTER 21

THE NATION NEEDS THE LIVESTOCK

When the little boy in town, fresh from a rootin' tootin' TV program, says eagerly, "Mama! How can I get into the cowboy business?" he is only putting into little-boy words the thoughts of millions. When eight out of ten of the leading TV programs are Westerns, that must give some sort of a lead to the national mind. Both little kids and grown persons try to look like cowboys. Why don't they ever try to look like bankers, sheepherders, or loggers?

I have noticed that in this state, just as soon as a lumberman has converted some depression-bought trees into some 70-dollar boards, and finds that his cup runneth over, he wastes no time in finding a cattle ranch he can buy. The doctor who finds that it pays better to be a dermatologist than a skin doctor and accumulates half a million dollars to prove it, can't wait until that money is invested in a good ranch with some good deer hunting on it.

The number of farmers is shrinking, but the number of persons in the whole farm business picture is increasing all the time. So it is wrong to say agriculture is less important than it was. About half of the population in the United States works directly or indirectly with farm products. Let's see some of the chinks in our economy that are filled by livestock.

1. Of course, livestock are important as food. As a nation prospers, its per capita meat consumption goes up. A poor man in India or Burma seldom sees meat of any kind. It is used in such countries only for flavoring. In this country, the recent high wages have put beef on every table. Also, modern diet accents meat, par-

ticularly lean meat. Dan Fulton of Montana said at a cattlemen's meeting, "Every American woman is interested in fat; she is either putting it on, or taking it off, or shoving it around."

2. Labor needs for livestock fan out in all directions. There is first, the labor on the ranch; then the labor to make the thousand things used on the ranch; then transportation of goods and livestock; labor around feed lots, stockyards, packing plants, wholesale and retail groceries, butcher shops, and super-markets. A laborer in a steel mill in Pennsylvania may think he has nothing to do with agriculture—many mills would not be running without the farm demands for steel. The farms of America use more steel than our automobile factories, yet it is auto output that people watch.

3. Materials and articles are bought for the ranch such as autos, gasoline, trucks, fences, fertilizer, sprays, salt and lumber.

4. The ranch requires services of veterinarians, carpenters, cement workers, electricians, doctors, truckers, railroads. All of these people have homes that need, in turn, hundreds of services that are paid for indirectly by the ranch.

5. The ranch, good years or bad, supplies tax dollars for schools, roads, police, and county and state services of all kinds. If income is good, a big chunk goes to the Federal government for foreign aid, defense, and the expanding services demanded by our people, who can't seem to understand that it is cheaper to raise and spend our money at home, rather than to send it to Washington and then only get part of it back.

6. Financing the ranch takes a hoard of people, running through local banks, mortgage companies, big city banks, production credit associations, Federal Land Banks, and individual money lenders, such as neighbors who sell hay and agree to take the pay when the steers are sold. These agencies have inspectors, bookkeepers, stenographers, field men.

7. In the West are 700,000,000 acres of rangeland of no real value except for grazing. This land cannot be plowed—it is too dry, rocky, thin, rough, alkaline, or too inaccessible. In addition, about half the plowed land of the nation is in pasture, hay or silage—crops of no value except for livestock. Part of our huge yearly grain crop goes to livestock, including nearly all the corn, barley, grain sorghum, and oats. Livestock also use by-products of many factories, such as sugar, canning, distilling, brewing, and cereal packaging.

Livestock farming is essentially conservation farming, in contrast to the cultivated crops that lead to erosion and land destruction in so many cases. The man who advised the county agent scornfully, "You can't tell me anything about farming, I've already worn out three farms" was *not* a livestock man.

8. The nation's livestock furnishes hundreds of by-products. Fertilizer, hormones, vitamins, glue, leather for countless uses, hair, surgical thread—these are only a few. Of course, wool is, and probably always will be, our best fabric for clothing, some kinds of upholstering, and many household uses, such as draperies and carpets.

The cattle industry is proud and independent. In the New Deal days when cradle-to-the-grave security was advocated, the cattle owners steadfastly refused to take any help in the way of price support or production control. Lyman Brewster, cattleman of Montana, said, "The President has listed the Four Freedoms. He forgot the most important one, 'Freedom to go Broke'. I hope we never lose it. In it is wrapped up the whole theory of private enterprise."

Supply and demand still rule the cattle industry. It is a tough rule, made for the strong and far-sighted. The rules are rigged against the in-and-outers, the faint-hearted, the starry-eyed, and the cry-babies. But aren't the rules of any game that way? The fullback who gives up when a big man opposes him doesn't win any ball games. Much of our trouble in the nation is due to our attempts to legislate this rule out of existence.

I think that American agriculture would be far better off now, if the government had never stepped in. I'll trust to the rule of supply and demand every time, as compared to the rule of some government bureaucrat who makes a rule without foreseeing the consequences. One rule begets another, and that rule another, in an unending stream. No man is smart enough to govern the huge livestock business and I hope we can keep anyone from ever getting the chance. I am not against bureaucrats. I am just against any system that turns over part of our business to them.

The Brannan plan to let each product sell for what it will, and then pay farmers the difference between the price they received and the parity price, sounds like the song of the siren to some farmers, but they forget the core of that pretty apple. The inside of the plan is to keep it from bankrupting the nation by assigning only so much production to each farm, even down to cabbage, chickens and pansy seed. That would be bureaucracy run wild, with an inspector for each setting hen. Secretary Brannan confessed before a Congressional committee it would probably take an inspector for each 50 farms.

During the last war, the sheepmen were in trouble. They were issued coupons for gas, groceries and supplies on the same basis as other persons. It was scientifically figured that 40 per cent of the groceries were fresh things, such as lettuce, fresh milk and the like, but sheep herders move every day and they are far out in the mountains where there isn't any grocery store. So the Oregon Wool Growers sent Mac Hoke, sheepman of Pendleton, to Washington to try to wangle more coupons for canned goods and bacon for the herders.

Mac, now dead, was one of the smartest men in the business, well equipped to deal with lawyers or anyone else. In Washington he was only one of thousands of persons trying to get special treatment and he was given the well-known run-around from committee to bureau to special agent to committee. But finally he got a special committee to deal with his problem. These were eight or ten New York lawyers sitting around a table in a council room.

They listened closely to Mac's able presentation of the sheepherder's plight, confined largely to rationed foods and unable to get 40 per cent of his diet from un-rationed fresh garden produce. At the end, the committee looked around at each other and one of the spokesman said, "Vell, Mr. Hoke, if as you say, your herders do not have enough food to sustain dem, and if as you say dey do not have access to fresh wegetables, for vy den do dey not grow wictory gardens?"

This left Mac speechless, but it indicates as well as anything the hopelessness of trying to run a ranch from Washington or make decisions far from the scene. That is fundamentally why Russia is constantly behind in planned food production. A raging flood or untimely frost can make a livestock man change his plans instantly, maybe in the middle of the night or on a holiday, but if he had to go to some government agent to get authority for the change, the livestock might die before the proper committee could act.

The nation not only needs the livestock, but it determines our livestock business. When housewives began to demand smaller cuts of beef, every cattle owner in America and every cattle feeder had to change his operations. On our ranch we changed from selling three and four year olds to selling two year olds, then long yearlings, and most ranches now sell the current crop of calves.

Housewives have recently demanded less fat. That has set in motion a whole train of events: chemists in dozens of laboratories are studying how to tenderize lean meat; breeders are frantically trying to breed tenderness into the meat; chefs and domestic science experimenters in a thousand kitchens are trying to work out ways of cooking that will make lean meat tender; feeders are trying to make animals tender with new kinds of feed—all because madame housewife complained that she wanted the beef tender, but had no use for the fat.

Sooner or later she will get her steaks lean, but tender. For generations "the best color for a beef animal is fat" has been the rule. The small layers of fat, intermingled with the layers of lean, has distinguished the beef animal from the dairy critter, which puts its fat all around the outside and leaves the steaks lean, but often tough. A big national magazine for women says, "Never underestimate the power of a woman." We livestockmen surely don't. Her whim is one of iron, so far as we are concerned. We don't like to change our business all around just to suit her, but she rules the ranges and corrals, just as she does the meat counter, so lean tender meat will be the next big change in our industry. I don't know how to do it, nor does anyone, but she says that's what she wants, and she'll get it somehow.

Right now, though, her demand for "no fat" results in the butcher cutting off the fat and adding it to the cost. That's why we have $1.25 steak at retail, where the farmer gets maybe 25 cents.

Consumers and farmers were once close together. The housewife bought her potatoes and radishes right from the ground, from the farmer who grew them—as they bought things from father. She saw what she bought and selected with great care. Now she sees only a pretty picture on a can. The can is only one out of 7000 different items in a super-market. Such places now sell 80 per cent of our food supply. The butcher shop selling nothing but meat has all but vanished.

This change, like all changes, has both good and bad results. It has removed farmers from the acquaintance of city folks. Now farmers in the minds of city consumers, are only strange, unseen, mythical folk, like creatures from Mars. The wife of the city lawyer thinks farmers are responsible for high food prices.

Only advertising, constantly carried out, can combat this. It must be of a grade and quality to compete with advertising of autos, liquor, cigarettes, and cosmetics. The rancher provides feed for his cattle, works with them in wind and storm and intolerable heat and cold. Then one day he sells them to a feeder, turns his back on them and walks off. No one else does that now. The insurance man comes back to you time after time to talk over your policy with you and explain away harmful ideas. The chemical company has a nationwide corps of field workers who spend their entire time visiting users, locating troubles, asking for ways in which they can serve you better. These men aren't bums picked up down by the tracks. They are carefully chosen college graduates, the best of the crop, young fellows who are pleasing, plausible and persuasive.

If any of these folks locate permanent dissatisfaction with the product, the factories withdraw it from the market instantly and supply something more to the liking of the consumers.

But we cattlemen pay little attention. A few carry the load of advertising, and it is so small as to be almost apologetic. Every attempt to organize a campaign is defeated. Someone said, "The only place where cattlemen really get together is in the cemetery."

We must help the retailer. He can't possibly be a specialist in 7000 different things, so he sells beef only to the people who insist on buying it. He does little persuading.

I have wondered and thought a great deal about advertising, such as we see and hear on TV and read in magazines. Of course, its primary purpose is to sell things, but the consumer pays for all of it, so his living costs are jacked up to that extent. The reason advanced for advertising is that it is educational. A new mouse trap comes along, superior to all other mouse traps, and no one would know about it, were it not for advertising. This reasoning then leads to the conclusion that our American way of life is founded upon advertising, because all of us constantly demand the new superior products, and this demand builds new factories, employs more men, and rewards initiative and bold imagination. This is our contribution to the world, it is said—constant change, constant improvement, a high standard of living.

If this is true, then we seem to be advertising the wrong things. You can't listen to TV longer than ten minutes without hearing that X brand of cigarettes is the real Peruvian doughnuts, and within five minutes you are told that Y brand is far more Peruvian. When you are thoroughly sold on that, along comes Z brand and you are utterly crazy if you don't dump X and Y and buy Z.

If the claims made for advertising are to hold up, it seems to me that American people will have to demand that it tell the truth and that it be constructive. Why not tell the public about beef? It furnishes, in its most palatable form, the protein we need so badly. I doubt if one consumer in 10,000 knows as much about protein as the least intelligent cattle feeder. If the story of protein were pounded into us like the cigarette story is, we would be a healthier nation overnight.

The cigarette story is mainly a scramble to tell people that X brand has *less* tars and nicotine, therefore it isn't so unhealthful. Suppose you would read or hear an ad to the effect that this new cake mix was not nearly so likely to cause cancer as all the others on the market? Wouldn't you feel that an advertising agency was completely nutty to put out such stuff? That's exactly what we are hearing every day, with cigarettes.

The wives of our cattlemen have an organization called the Cowbelles. They are advertising beef in a highly effective way and the nation's beef consumption is going up spectacularly. But even with this, most of the city women don't know too much about the protein of beef.

A butcher told me that a town woman came into his place with half of a large beef to be cut up for her locker. He asked her how she wanted it cut, and she said, "Our family seems to like T-bones about the best, so you'd better cut it all up as T-bones." This seems to be another place for advertising—the roasts and stews have just as much food value as the small percentage of the animal that can go into steaks. Only 6 per cent of the carcass weight can go into the high priced steaks, yet every bit of meat in the other 94 per cent is just as valuable, just as nutritious, and if cooked right, just as palatable as the 6 per cent in steaks.

It can be argued that educational advertising isn't interesting — people don't want education, they want amusement. If this is so, what's so amusing about a product not so likely to give you cancer? Or if you are a woman, to have someone insinuate that unless you have his product slathered all over you, your odor would drive a dog out of a tanyard? Or to see by a diagram of your skull how little hammers knock your brains out? Or how one product can't find its way out of all that mess on the inside of your stomach, whereas our pills go right on down into those nasty intestines?

With beef we have a product the nation needs, but a housewife buys it only through instinct. She takes her basket-on-wheels down the super-market aisles and mentally plans her meal. So she buys beef as the meal's foundation, then fills in with other things, apparently guided by what TV has told her. But maybe on that day her dollar would have gone farther had she bought some other cut. She knows little about that. TV is silent on the all-important point of real values in foods.

I think that TV advertising will have to head down the track of truth or else it will run out of gullible customers. They may demand and get TV for pay, with no commercials at all. I think, too, that if livestock men would hire the right people, truly educational ads could be made as attractive, surely, as some kind of soap that is hard as nails on hard surfaces, but soft as feathers on soft surfaces, such as hands.

We, in beef, have a truly great story to tell, but we haven't told it. Why are American tourists so amazed at the small size of Asiatics, most Europeans and some of the South Americans? It isn't the whole story, but the size of a nation's people is almost in exact ratio to the amount of meat consumed per capita. The life expectancy is somewhat in the same ratio. Isn't it of interest to know that in India the per capita consumption of meat is two pounds a year, the average height is about four feet and life expectancy is 27 years; whereas in Australia the per capita meat consumption is 246 pounds, average height six feet, and life expectancy 70 years?

Such things as that, dinged constantly into people's ears, surely would do them more good than to learn that even with buffering added, aspirin is pretty old fashioned, as compared to what *we* offer. *Our* product doesn't upset the stomach of the suffering lady in the picture, either. Well, it upsets mine, whereas beef doesn't.

From a public relations angle, it seems to me that we could also tell people, over and over, that the old bogy, HCL, can be beaten by any housewife who wants to beat it. I can tell any housewife in any city how to cut her grocery bill to a third of what it is. Just buy in quantity and buy by the pound, cutting out foods that are triple wrapped in tinsel. The cost of groceries is almost entirely due to wrapping, packaging, and service. Anyone can learn to buy the things where such items don't enter in. With many items, the retail costs would scarcely change if the farmer gave the food away.

It is also poor public relations to my mind, to hear the big stories about selling a prize bull for $50,000 or $100,000. These sales are often just a publicity stunt of an oilman who owns a cattle ranch. They remind me of the little boy who traded off his $100,000 dog for two $50,000 cats, thereby getting his asking price. But the consumers read these stories and it seems to them that here are some rich cattlemen, throwing their money around. They say, "No wonder steaks cost a dollar a pound."

PART FOUR — RECOGNITIONS OF
PUBLIC SERVICE

CHAPTER 22

GIFTS, AWARDS, AND REWARDS

HONORARY DEGREE

Of all of the public recognitions, I suppose I am proudest of these two: the title given me by the Oregon Cattleman's Association, "Dean of Oregon Cattlemen," and the honorary degree of Doctor of Science conferred upon me by Oregon State College. Here is the citation read by President A. L. Strand when he conferred the degree.

Citation—Read To
H E R M A N   O L I V E R
When Presented with the
Honorary Degree of Doctor of Science
June 1957

In recognition of your unique place among western ranchers as "guide, philosopher, and friend" for an entire industry; because you have always stayed on any trail you laid out, despite criticism, storms, destruction of signs, or failure of landmarks; because truth has been more important to you than expediency; because your steadfast course has, in some degree, been of help to every other stockman; because your wise counsel has been loaned so generously to all citizens in the state; because your manifest pride in your chosen calling has lent dignity to it in the minds of others; and because you personify those things dear to the West: self-reliance, humor, hospitality, quick sympathy, a high sense of personal responsibility, and action rather than words;

I have the honor to confer upon you by virtue of the authority vested in me by the State Board of Higher Education by law and on the recommendation of the faculty of Oregon State College, the Honorary Degree of Doctor of Science.

August LeRoy Strand,
President.

S. F. SWIFT CENTENNIAL FOUNDERS AWARD

In 1955 Swift and Company celebrated their Centennial year. As a feature they presented awards to certain persons who had contributed to the livestock industry. I was the first to receive one of these awards.

OTHER AWARDS

In 1956 the Grant County Educational Association gave me a plaque for outstanding citizenship in the field of education. Also, the Oregon Farm Bureau Federation named me for distinguished service to Oregon agriculture.

The Oregon State Employees Association chose me as "Citizen of the Year" in 1959.

I have been called upon to judge many regional and local livestock exhibitions, rodeos, and horsemanship contests. Once, while judging the riding events at the Pendleton Roundup, I was sitting on my horse waiting for the next event, while the Indian women, in their finery, happened to be lined up in front of me. They were back to me and another judge was appraising them and their costumes for the title of "Indian Queen". An old Indian saw me, noticed the "judge" sign, hurried up and told me confidentially but emphatically, "You no judge squaw's behind! You judge 'em in front."

I now serve on the Board of Trustees of the Pacific International Livestock Exposition, on the Board of Trustees of the 4-H Foundation, and on the Board of Directors of the First National Bank of Oregon.

GIFTS

Eliza and I have felt that we owe much to the Grant County friends who always helped when we needed it. We have tried to share that feeling by community gifts.

We gave to the county a brick library with enough space to take care of reasonable growth. Since the county's population is scattered, we provided a bookmobile, a portable library. It travels on regular trips around the county, dispensing and picking up books. It is used by hundreds of adults, but we are especially warmed by the heavy use made of both library and bookmobile by students. We know that the well read student is usually the one that succeeds in college and later in business or farming. The reading student isn't listed among the trouble makers.

The schools of today seem to think more of sports events than of cultural activities. It seems easy to send athletic teams 100 miles or more to compete, and relatively easy to get chambers of commerce or civic clubs to buy athletic equipment when needed. It is not so easy to send our high school band to a music festival or to buy needed musical instruments. We felt that music benefits a person for life, so presented some horns to the band and helped to send our school band to the regional music festival. We think that even a little musical training is never wasted. We aren't opposed to sports, but think the good effect of music is more lasting.

Charley Brown, born in a mining camp in Idaho, and lifelong resident here, had an amazing collection of antiques, including not only articles, but pictures, newspapers, circulars, and materials reaching into every phase of the past life of the county. His collection, for example, of side saddles and high buttoned shoes, is probably unequalled in the state. So we built a museum, purchased the collection and presented the whole thing to Canyon City and John Day, jointly. Charley reigns supreme in this building and it is visited by hundreds every year. They are entranced by his stories of the early days and by the many historical things in the museum.

We have a special niche in our hearts for 4-H Club work. A busy girl or boy is never a problem child. The idle young people, with nothing profitable to do, are the groups that furnish the juvenile delinquents. I had always been close to the grand old citizen of Oregon, O. M. Plummer, who was also wrapped up in 4-H work, and to Dick Richards, with a similar interest. Plummer for years and years headed the Pacific International Livestock Exposition and right now, 1961, Dick Richards has charge of it. When Dick came to Grant County as county extension agent in 1925, he went to work at once with the boys and girls.

R. G. Johnson followed Richards, then Ralph Brooke, then M. E. Knickerbocker, and now Bill Farrell. With six children of his own, and a natural understanding of them, Bill has devoted nights, Sundays and holidays to 4-H. Eliza and I put up $500 a year and authorized Bill to divide it where it would do county-wide 4-H the most good. It is distributed each year among different project winners.

Grant County boys and girls have been winning state and national awards of all kinds; many local folks have willingly served as leaders; and 4-H is a vital force in the county. The junior rodeo at John Day has been written up in national magazines, is often on TV, and has been copied all over the West. Our riding clubs and range clubs have been widely copied, too.

Anna and her husband, Sam Keerins, became equally interested in this youth work. The 4-H building at the county fair grounds was named Keerin's Hall as a memorial to Sam, who had been active in getting it built. It serves as a meeting place, not only for 4-H, but also for all sorts of civic and county committees. A dormitory and good kitchen are attached.

We think the 4-H work has paid off in helping to develop alert, busy, successful young people in the county. They are going out from here to lead fine lives, or they stay here as successful ranchers or businessmen. Not one 4-H boy or girl from here has turned out wrong. I am Vice-president of the statewide 4-H Foundation, an organization to receive gifts, endowments, and the like for 4-H.

The Canyon City cemetery, where my father and mother are buried, had no water and due to its location, high on a dry hill, had no way to get any. Eliza and I provided the money for a deep well, with electric pump and sprinkling system. Now it is a green oasis, young trees are growing and perennial flowers and shrubs are appearing. This was done as a memorial to father and mother and to other members of our family who are buried there. The water system was then presented to the Canyon City Cemetery District.

REWARDS

I grew up young, and in looking back over my 60 years of mature life, conscious of my many mistakes and failures, still some things have brought satisfaction. Some of these are:

1. I am extremely grateful to Eliza, my wife for 55 years. We have carried on together a full and interesting life. That part wouldn't be changed any if I could live my life over again.

2. I am grateful to my parents for my inheritance of a sound body, and some qualities of mind, but I am most grateful to them for their philosophy of good will and for their firm determination in carrying out plans.

3. I am glad that the family and I saw fit to carry on with the foundation laid by my parents. I do not know what lies beyond, but I cannot escape the feeling that they may have watched with satisfaction as we took the inheritance they left and built upon and strengthened it, using their principles in so doing.

4. It was a great satisfaction to remain with my parents as long as they lived, and for Eliza and me to care for and comfort them in their declining years.

5. With only one living child of our own, Eliza and I took two boys to raise. They were about to be sent to an orphan's home. They grew up to be good citizens, and we have been proud of them. That has been a satisfaction.

6. With all of the transactions we have had in land, cattle, sheep, hay, pasture, lending money, lending labor and machinery, I have never sued anyone and no one ever sued me. There were disagreements of course, because in complicated deals, often by word of mouth, there can be honest misunderstandings and differences in memory. But these things have all been settled by reason and by an honest attempt to see the other man's viewpoint. I am glad that my life has not been clouded by law suits and long drawnout neighborhood or family feuds of any kind.

7. In Cleveland's administration, lambs brought 50 cents each; wool five cents a pound; a cow and calf by her side $12; and three-year old steers $14 a head. I was 10 years old. I have seen other hard times since. In each case the future was dark and there seemed no hope. Many gave up. I am glad that I have been able to remain in the same business all my life in the same place. It has brought to me a satisfactory feeling of stability. I do not believe that those who drift to this and that new business can possibly have that satisfaction, even if successful.

8. I am grateful to my many friends, both in town and country. They stood by me when it counted, and were there to rejoice in small and large successes. A man's calibre can be judged by his friends and I am proud of mine. This book ends by including letters from some of them, but many were not letter writers, they were

cowboys or sheep herders who were more likely to express friendship by a handclasp and some such remark as "you old — — — —, I'll bet you are as ornery as ever."

9. I am grateful to the many faithful men, young and old, who have worked with and for us on the ranch, many of them most of their mature lives. They were loyal and always talked of "our sheep," "our steers," "our hay." I cannot see how a ranch can succeed without this kind of help.

10. I am now (1961) 76 years old. If asked for a single sentence of advice to anyone starting a ranch or any other business, I'd say, "Be constructive." Time spent in fighting neighbors, fighting the business people, fighting other organizations, is wasted. We improved the meadow, improved the breed, made our association stronger, built harmonious relations, made friends everywhere. The policy has made our lives smoother and has made it fun to live.

E. R. Jackman, editor of this book, is well known to Pacific Northwest readers through dozens of articles in local and national magazines. His writing is characterized by unusual clarity and humor. Now retired, he was formerly Crops and Range Specialist at Oregon State University.

CHAPTER 23

LETTERS

About This Chapter
By E. R. JACKMAN

When Herman, Eliza, and I began to plan this book, we reviewed the material available: old pictures, ranch records, newspaper clippings. Then we listed 21 topics, such as "education," "horses," "freighting," and classified the material under those heads. But we kept running across letters from old friends and new. Herman valued these letters highly, because they came from friends whose opinions counted. There were hundreds of them.

In a book about the Oliver family, it seemed important to use some of them. They contain things not easy to put into the narrative, and, together, they furnish an inspirational quality that no description or story can hope to equal. So I searched the files, taking out all of the letters that dealt directly with the subject of this book. I sorted them time after time. Many of the best had to be omitted. Some were too intimate; some too long; other had comments about affairs of only passing importance; many contained confidential statements.

So out of this prolonged shuffling came this chapter. The letters are heart warming, sincere, and most of us would be gratified if we could marshal a similar list.

LETTERS FROM SCHOOL CHILDREN

In explanation, the Portland papers carried a picture of a large herd of Oliver cattle passing through the town of John Day, very similar to the photograph in this book. With the picture was a story about the man who owned the steers. A Portland teacher with imagination and genius, Marie Patton, uses such things in her teaching in an attempt to relate classroom work to the exciting life around us. So she asked those who wished to do so to write to Mr. Oliver and asked them to draw a picture of a cowboy. The letters follow.

E. R. Jackman

Dear Mr. Oliver:

In my third grade class there are more thrills a minute than in a "Big Top." They can create more breathless magic than Barnum and Bailey could imagine.

It's a show that's sprinkled with star dust and run by a man named "Herman Oliver"! with fabulous ranches and steers. It's the stuff their dreams are made of.

Enclosed, their letters to you and "Pictures" of "how you look!"

Kind thoughts,
Marie Patton
Room 19

Dear Mr. Oliver,

I like cattle. Where do you get water.

Your friend
George Chinakas

Dear Mr. Oliver,

I never saw any cattle. Our class has been talking about your steers. How big is a steer?

Love,
Janet McIvor

Dear Mr. Oliver,

I like cattle. Just how many steers are in 1000? How do you count them?

Love,
Bruce Fraser

Dear Mr. Oliver,

I like cattle. Our class has been talking about your horses. Does it snow very much? How many steers do you have? Where do you keep your cattle at night? Are your cattle all the same colors?

Your friend,
Kathy

Dear Mr. Oliver,

I like cattle. Our class has been talking about you. How many barns do you have? Do you have a shed for the cattles food?

Love,
Judy Everidge

Dear Mr. Oliver,

I like horses. Our class has been talking about you. Why did you sell your ranch?

Love,
Curtis McCullough

Dear Mr. Oliver,

I read about you in the newspaper that is how I know about you.

Love,
Sheila Miller

Dear Mr. Oliver,

I like cattle. Our class has been talking about you. I would like to know, how do you get the cattle to bed? How old is he when you sell him? How many cattle do you have? How many barns do you have?

Love,
Martha Chapman

Dear Mr. Oliver,

Do you have cowboys? Could I be a cowboy?

Your friend,
Mark Myer

Dear Mr. Oliver,

I like cattle. Do you brand steers? When do you do this?

Love,
Patty Farley

Dear Mr. Oliver,

I like cattle. Are cattle courteous?

Your friend,
Robert Moss

Dear Mr. Oliver,

I like cattle. Our class has been talking about you. We would like to know you!

Your friend,
Philip Gorg

Dear Mr. Oliver,

Do you keep all the steers together in one place? Who watches them?

Your friend,
Carol Roswall

Dear Mr. Oliver,

Our class has been talking about you. We would like to know:
1. Are steers wild animals?
2. Why did you sell your ranch?
3. Do you have any snow in eastern Oregon?
4. How long do you keep them before they are sold?
5. How many miles do you have?
6. Where do you keep them?
7. How long did you live on the ranch?
8. What do they eat and drink?

We would like to meet you and thank you very much for letting me ask you questions.

With love,
Suzanne Culver

DR. STRAND REMEMBERS THE OLD STUDEBAKER WAGON

Dear Herman:

Not having seen you around the Imperial lately, I decided to write you. I've been in a sort of reminiscent mood and you may understand. A few days ago I read an article in The New Yorker magazine that got me started this way. It was by a U. S. Navy captain who was born in Texas about the same time I was and not far from my birthplace. The author's father kept him and his family wandering around west Texas in a Studebaker wagon for years, always hunting for "new country," which is the title of the article. Well, this recalled many things to my mind. If there was anything I knew better than a Studebaker wagon in my boyhood days, I can't think what it would be. My acquaintance with that sturdy mode of transportation continued after my family moved to Montana in 1901 for *my* father was looking for "new country" too. And like the father of the Navy captain, he never found it either. We finally settled in Helena where I did the rest of my growing up in Last Chance Gulch. It wasn't as bad as that may sound for we lived on a street that had wooden sidewalks. I remember delivering milk in the south end of Helena, which was still pretty lurid in that part of town. The Capital Music Hall was going strong. I don't know what use it had for milk, but I always took some there and got out as quick as I could. During summer vacations I worked on ranches in the Dearborn country; I was big for my age. This went on until I was sent off to the agricultural college. Somehow my Mother had heard something about scientific agriculture and thought it ought to be a good thing.

The early life of the Navy man was so tied up with the Studebaker wagon I got to thinking that people partake of some of the characteristics of the vehicles with which they have been associated. Now you, Herman, are the Studebaker wagon type. You may not like that, but it is as good a compliment as I could pay anyone. The Model T is supposed to have brought enlightenment to farmers and ranchers, but it never was so important as the Studebaker wagon. The Model T enlarged the rancher's mobility, but it was the SW that got him where he wanted to be in the first place. The hired hands could ride their broncs to town on Saturday nights, but what they brought back with them wasn't groceries, repairs, or a lot of other things from the general store. Trips to the "super market" then were made with the old faithful SW and it might take all day or longer. And the

Studebaker was convertible long before the name was associated with rubber tires. Just think of all the uses for which they were valuable. They were indispensable and universal.

I don't know how Eastern Oregon could have gotten along without the vehicle with the red (or yellow) running gear and the green wagon box with the fancy scroll work painted on it, that is, until age and the weather took off the makeup. I don't recall seeing one that was repainted. Kidding the public with a new model every year wasn't invented by the Studebaker people until they began making automobiles. The original model was so good it didn't need to be changed. On second thought this may be boring to you. These wagons, loaded with plows, lumber, bedding, often a baby carriage and all the families' goods and gods, traversing the landscape in the homestead days, were the forerunners of barbed wire. So maybe you have some reservations about them. But I can't believe that you didn't admire them, too. As my friend Bob Fletcher used to say, you can't stop civilization whether you like it or not.

This is a long introduction to say that the generation that knew the Studebaker wagon, and partook a whole lot of its characteristics, is rapidly giving way to the generations that know only jeeps, jets, and jaguars. They travel faster now but I wonder if they know where they're going, and someone else seems to tell them what to think. It was men like yourself who gave stability and direction to the development of the West. You built the roads, some being pretty rocky and tortuous, that have now been shoved around and paved. You established the institutions that are now taken for granted. You kept your head in good times and lived through panics without resorting to cheap dollars. You took part in the long, hard constructive period of Oregon's history. Most of all, you thought your own thoughts and stood by them. You had the old Studebaker's strength and value. I'm glad I knew you.

Sincerely,

A. L. Strand, President
Oregon State College

Oregon's Best Known Statesman and
Former Governor says the Compass
often Pointed to John Day

My dear Herman:

Recently I heard — you know how news travels — that Jackman of OSC was setting about to do a book on your career. I want to commend the enterprise. You are a proper subject for a biography and Jackman certainly is well qualified to do the job.

You have been so modest in your endeavors that your friends have to take a hand to see that "justice is done" for the remarkable success you have had in private life and in public service.

Leadership has just gravitated in your direction. Without a "reaching out" on your part responsibilities have been thrown on your shoulders and you have carried them well. This is true in the important livestock industry of Oregon and in local affairs.

And when we have looked for a man of stature from Central Oregon for statewide duty the "compass" always seemed to turn in your direction. Your service on the State Board of Higher Education and on the State Highway Commission was of a high order of merit. You not only contributed out of your rich experience and your practical judgment, your name gave to the public a high degree of confidence in the work of these important bodies.

So I have been one to applaud you for your public service and to hail you as a friend. I wish for you many

more years of active living, interesting to you and fruit-
ful for the community.

    With warm personal regards I am

               Sincerely yours,
               Charles A. Sprague

AN OREGONIAN EDITOR GIVES A BOOK FORMULA

Dear Herman:

    The out-back telegraph has been sputtering. I hear
you are writing a book. Well, that does it! Now you
have tried everything, and I am glad.

    Let me tell you the best formula for a book about
your life and times. Just tell it in your own way, with
that wonderful sense of responsible citizenship leavened
by an even more wonderful warmth and humor. It's a
formula you have applied to all your successful under-
takings, from growing stock to helping give Oregon a
fine system of higher education. It can't fail.

    I cherish the times we have visited together and the
unimpeachable honesty of your reactions to events
around us. I know that anything you write will be in
the same vein and will give pleasure and help to your
readers. Good luck!

               Sincerely,
               Herbert Lundy

A FORMER P. I. MANAGER LIKES A GOOD USIN' CITIZEN

Dear Herman:

    The finest possession of a range cowman is a "good
usin' horse." To a commonwealth there is nothing that
outranks a good usin' citizen. You have been just that
to Oregon. Superior as a long-time leader of the state's
great livestock industry, as a member of the Highway
Commission and the Board of Higher Education. They
will have to dig deeply into Oregon history to surpass

such a record as the facts of the chronicals of your life will be made available to the long list of your friends throughout Oregon and the West.

Most sincerely,
Walter A. Holt

Manager of the Big Pacific International Exposition Says This Book Will Rope a Bunch of Facts

Dear Herman:

So a cowman is writing a book — if you had bought three or four more ranches or 1000 good cows, that would have been no surprise, but for you to be writing a book — well, that is a new venture. But, I will guarantee you will rope a lot of facts about Grant County and tie them into a bundle of real good reading.

You developed the outstanding herd of range cattle in the Northwest — good enough to always sell for the top dollar. Your bands of sheep were big outstanding ewes that produced record pounds of wool and from which you sold 140% average lamb crop of market-topping lambs. Your bunchgrass was the best in Grant County.

Your ranch had a wonderful set of good useful well-kept buildings and with the help of your wonderful wife, Eliza, your home was a place where western hospitality was at its best.

You always rode a good horse with a good outfit, so I will guarantee you will write a good book that will tell a real romantic story of the development and progress of Grant County.

Sincerely yours,
D. E. Richards

Kindly Words from an Old Neighbor

Dear Herman:

As we look back over the wonderful years spent in Grant County, I often wonder about the great changes that have taken place during my lifetime and also think of the changes that took place in the earlier days before my time.

As I think of all these things, the name of Oliver seems to be prominent all along the way and I often wonder if the people of Grant County realize how much the Oliver's have done to make Grant County and Eastern Oregon what it is today.

The present rush of life seems to have done away with one of the truly great aspects of our pioneers' way of life and that is the neighborly feeling that existed between all the pioneer families, the time we always had to visit with our neighbors and to aid them in their misfortunes.

At the beginning of this letter I had in mind the idea of trying to pay to you some of the honor that is justly your due, but I seem to be at a loss for adequate words to say the things that should be said. What can one say to a man who out of the goodness of his heart donates a magnificent library to the people of Grant County; what can one say to a man that builds a building, purchases a collection of relics, then gives all this to the cities of Canyon and John Day; what can one say to a man who drills a well and puts in pump and pipe to irrigate our cemetery and make it a show place rather than a dry arid spot as it has been from its inception; what can one say to a man who on so many occasions has come to the rescue of projects small and large and helped to make them successful.

Your recent gift of the beautiful chairs for our lodge rooms was a wonderful gesture and should not go unrewarded.

The record of your achievements is long and distinguished, and as you continue in your active career as Mayor of John Day and as Grant County's number one booster, I know that you will receive great satisfaction in seeing people enjoy the many fine projects that could not have been made possible except for your generosity.

I know that you did not do these things alone as your
good wife Eliza shared with you in many of your fine
contributions.

May the years ahead bring you both much good
health and much happiness.

Very sincerely yours,
Whit Finlayson

THIS CAME CLEAR FROM IRAN

Dear Herman:

Time for just a short visit and to let you know that
I am now in charge of the ICA program as acting director
in Iran. Director Brenn left for his home leave and con-
ference in Washington, D. C., about 10 days ago. I
thought I would have to pinch myself to realize that a
county agent cowpuncher would ever have to head up a
program such as this! However, grim reality of two teams
of investigators—one from our organization and one from
our General Accounting Office—takes the place of the
pinching! One often longs for the good old days of dealing with friendly county courts while being backstopped
by understanding cattle and sheep growers!

Herman, the years from 1928 to 1935 when I was
in Grant County come to mind so very frequently.
Whether you know it or not, you are one of those rare
individuals who can see and plan far ahead. You have
long since spread the benefit from this God-given endow-
ment to where it has benefited the whole State. I always
knew these things—but had to go a long way in time,
miles, and responsibility to be able to fully appreciate
the good fortune I had to be in Grant County with you
in the 30's. Instances to show what I mean:

1. In the fall of 1929 you sold a trainload of steers
for about $100,000 and put the entire check into gov-
ernment bonds. This far sighted move saved the banks
of Grant County. Those bonds were the only things in
America that went up.

2. When range was still cheap, you were among the first to start range improvement in a big way.

3. From 1928 to 1934 each fall you quietly made a feed survey. If it showed the county might be short of hay, you bought some from an outside source and several times this prevented liquidation of livestock. In many cases it saved thousands of dollars for other stockmen. You always sold this at cost.

4. In the late 30's you spotted the fact that many of the livestock leaders were getting old. You began pushing young men into important committee chairmanships, giving them training. These men are now our leaders.

5. In the fall of 1928 you said, "Sheep made the money for the Oliver ranch in the early days, but I'll be out of sheep when I'm 55." About ten years later, one day at Burns, you told me, "I am 55 today and yesterday I sold our last sheep." Cattle have outsold sheep every year since.

While I am in a reminiscing mood, I must comment upon how fortunate some of us are in having wives who inspire us when we become complacent; support us when we become depressed or discouraged; and daily carry the everyday backstopping a man must have. You have been most fortunate—Eliza has been a "tower of strength." Eliza has always been an understanding human being.

Helen and I are very busy—too much so for our own good, I fear. This job is like a hay feeding job on a long winter in a depression—no let up, no days off and shorthanded.

Sincerely,

Ray G. Johnson
USOM Iran
APO 205—P. M.
New York, N. Y.

A FELLOW BANKER SPEAKS

Dear Herman:

Word has come to me that you have sold the last of your ranch and are now out of the cattle business for the first time in your life. I feel rather sad about that happening for in my mind you have always been one of the stalwarts of the livestock business in the state.

You certainly have lived through an exciting period —the Oliver ranches have extended through from the pioneer horseback days of Grant County right up to the present jet age. The Olivers have been through both boom times and panics, and have always come through with flying colors.

I want you to know how very much I appreciate the fine contributions you have made to the three segments of our state life with which I have had some acquaintance, and they are, first, the livestock business, both sheep and cattle; second, your banking experience, you having been a very constructive force in banking in eastern Oregon and setting a fine example, especially to your own extensive community; and, third—from my own personal knowledge and association with you—your great contribution toward the growth, stability and service of higher education in Oregon.

Herman, I don't want this to sound like a farewell letter in any respect, because I am sure you have many years of effective service for the state and the nation ahead of you, but I do want you to know how greatly I have valued the associations I have had with you, both in higher education and in the field of banking.

Your severing yourself from the active cattle business, in a way, is somewhat like the closing of one chapter of the state's history. It has been a fascinating chapter, and one, I hope, that you can some day put down on paper for historians to know and understand.

In my book you have definitely been one of Oregon's most worthy and valuable citizens. Before anything happens to either one of us, I want to express myself here and now as a sincere admirer of yours, and to wish you many years of happiness and of usefulness to your family and to your community.

> Very sincerely yours,
> E. C. Sammons
> The United States National
> Bank of Portland

AS ONE REAL GOOD COWMAN TO ANOTHER

Dear Herman:

I have just learned, thru a mutual friend, that you are going to write a Book of Remembrances. With your life filled with so many activities since your *retirement* (and I use that word loosely) I can't see here how you are going to be able to "shade up" long enough to get the job done. I hope you do though, and this letter is to lend encouragement.

The story of the many and varied contributions you have made to the cattle industry of the state would, in itself, be sufficient to fill a good sized book. Your activities thru the years have touched many lives and though you will always be "Herman Oliver the cattleman" to those of us who have known you intimately, your circle of influence has extended far beyond into almost every activity where a greater and more influential Oregon Commonwealth has been the ultimate goal.

To have known you these many years as a cowman with interest extending into the field of education—highway planning—finance, etc., and to have known you as an apostle of industry good will have all been rewarding indeed but greater than all this has been to have known you as a friend.

> Sincerely,
> Harry Stearns
> Stearns Cattle Co.
> Prineville, Oregon

A Pure-Bred Cattle Breeder Pays Tribute to a Range Operator

Dear Herman:

It has come to my attention that you have sold the last of your ranch and are now out of the cattle business for the first time in your business life.

This would be very sad news to all the cattle industry of the Northwest were it not for the fact that your recent association with The First National Bank of Oregon will give the chance to, through this great institution, continue the wonderful help and advice you have always given to the cattlemen of this area.

I know you are aware that I have for many years held you as my best example of my idea of the very tops in a citizen and successful cattleman. I have also been flattered that as far back as the late twenties you have seen fit to use some of our Beau Donald bulls to assist you in developing one of the outstanding commercial herds of cattle I have known.

I would like to add that in my 47 years with this herd of cattle I have never had a cowman come to my place that knew better what he wanted and how to select for these things. I wish to thank you for the knowledge I believe I gained in watching you make your selections in my herd and later to watch your grading of the bulls at the Red Bluff Sale.

The cattle industry will suffer from not having the example of your operations before them; but I am sure we will benefit even more from your advice and guidance through your future years. We are looking forward to this and hope you will also get a lot of pleasure and happiness out of giving us the benefit of your wonderful experience and knowledge.

Sincerely
Curtice H. Martin
CURTICE HEREFORDS
Stevensville, Montana

Integrity and Wisdom Are the Words for Fred Phillips

Dear Herman:

I learned that you are planning on writing a story on the history of the Oliver family. I am sure such a manuscript will be well received by present-day citizens as well as future generations. As I know from my long association with you over the years, your book will enfold much valuable information on the growing, and marketing of livestock, of which you have a good knowledge, and what brought changes about, and the effect the changes have had on the economy of our country.

In working with you on many committees and various problems, you always thought things out thoroughly, and came up with a sound opinion. I will never forget your valuable council in setting up the R. A. C. C. during the dark days of the depression. Your knowledge of livestock and people and your experience in financing made your opinion most valuable.

Again I want to say I am sure your book will be a valuable asset to present and future stockmen in helping them round out their program.

Yours respectfully,
Fred A. Phillips, Sr.
Baker, Oregon

For a Colorful Country Editor with Words and Ideas, Know Giles French

Dear Herman,

Unless a man come to some untimely end there comes a day when he sits under his own vine and fig tree and thinks back over the road he has taken, the friends he has met, the changes he has seen. And if he be of philosophical bent he thinks of what it all means, if anything.

In your case you have seen a lot, done a lot and now I am sure, think a lot about it. There is a time when if a man be realistic, he knows it is time to finish a life by putting down what experiences have taught and what thinking has evolved. Lucky is he who has the opportunity to do it and lucky are the friends and acquaintances who can read and thereby profit from it. Maybe, after all, the best we can get out of life is to serve as an example.

The old timers who developed this land in spite of Indians, drouth, lack of transportation, lack of financing, are rapidly passing away. They will not long be here in the flesh; may enough of them write their lives so they can remain with us in the spirit, for the spirit of the pioneers is our most stimulating heritage.

Therefore, Herman, I hope you complete the job of living by recounting your story and add to that by saying what you have thought of it all.

My Very Best Regards
Giles French
Sherman County Journal

Ernie Fatland Has One of the Best Heads in Oregon

Dear Herman:

One of the most cheering news items to come to me recently, is that you intend to write your recollections of the progress of eastern Oregon, and particularly Grant County during your lifetime.

I know you have personally seen the transition from pioneer to modern times as very few other living men have seen it. More than that, you have the memory and the understanding to relate these changes so they will make factual and interesting information.

The story of your life should be an inspiration to others as it has been to me. More than any other person I know, you have blended a successful private life with a most outstanding and unselfish public career.

I do not think this influence is finished. I think it is just starting and am anxiously awaiting the publication of your book.

Kindest regards
E. R. Fatland
Condon, Oregon

Bob Lister Knows What to Say and How to Say It

My Dear Herman:

I have learned that you are setting down for your friends and others in book form some of the things which have made your life so interesting and worthwhile. Few people have had such a wealth of experience and accomplishments to document.

You, having started as a ranch boy without the opportunity of extensive formal education, have attained eminence and authority in agricultural, industrial, financial and educational fields. You are at home whether you are planning and developing a fine ranch spread; presiding as president at a bank meeting; serving as a member of the State Highway Commission; as a member of the Board of Higher Education; as Mayor of your city of John Day, or as heading the many other civic or association committees which you have so ably and willingly done. You have had many honors justly bestowed upon you which is proof that the value of your contribution to your fellowman has been acknowledged and appreciated. I recall the citation accompanying the Honorary Degree conferred upon you by Dr. August LeRoy Strand, president of the Oregon State College, which succinctly sums up your history as Distinguished Oregon Citizen in the words "guide, philosopher, friend".

It is amazing that you have had time to do so many things. For many years, along with your business activities, you have served so freely as the leader of the livestock and fraternal organizations to which you have belonged. You have always had time to visit with your friends, and in the case of sickness or trouble, you have discussed and helped work out with them a solution to their problems. The many things you have done for your friends and the community in which you live have made and will continue to make living much nicer for us and for those who are to follow.

It has been my privilege to associate rather closely with you for which I am thankful. From these experiences, I know you have fully enjoyed your time of living as well as making those around you happy. You and your fine wife are wonderful hosts; you thoroughly appreciate your many friends; you are a fine story teller (with a store of appropriate yarns). You have received great satisfaction in building up your ranches and planning the proper facilities to do an excellent job of handling your livestock. You take great joy in seeing a fine mother cow with her calf along side and you also enjoy seeing some of our beautiful Cow Belles and the calves they have with them. The experiences you have had will make most interesting reading and I am looking forward to getting a copy of your book, which I hope you will autograph for me.

I wish you every success in your writing and publishing experience.

Your sincere friend,
Robert Lister
Prineville, Oregon

"R. L." KNOWS OREGON'S STOCKMEN BETTER THAN ANY OTHER PERSON

Dear Herman:

Bob and Prosser tell me that you have now divested yourself of all the cattle and ranches with which you were invested and that you have now realized your life-long ambition to serve your community, your state and the livestock industry generally without any equivocation, mental reservation or self evasion whatsoever.

I have thought many times as I rode through the valleys of Grant County of the great contrast between the operations of those who despoiled the rich terrain of those valleys in search for gold leaving so much of the area forever unproductive and unattractive, whereas all of the efforts of Herman Oliver have been directed toward preservation, conservation and improvement of every natural resource to the end that it be forever beautiful and productive.

For more than forty years we have done a lot of things together and it has been wonderful, and it is a great thrill right now to contemplate an association with you for many long years to come.

As a citizen of this state, I am honestly glad to have been around, and I covet for you and Mrs. Oliver all the fun there is in just doing the things you want to do.

Most sincerely,
R. L. Clark
Portland, Oregon

ERVIE WILLIAMS HAS SPENT HIS LIFE IN FINANCING LIVESTOCK

Dear Herman:

I understand that you plan to write a story of your life. I sincerely hope that you will go ahead with this project, as your life story will make interesting reading and will be an authentic account of the livestock business, not only in Grant County but in the entire state of Oregon.

All of us who have been engaged in any phase of the livestock business are very familiar with the Oliver name. Going back for a period of 40 years, I have watched your leadership in the affairs of the Oregon Cattlemens Association and the Oregon Woolgrowers Association. Your advice on the best methods to follow in order to get maximum returns from livestock was eagerly sought and I was always impressed by the fact that when you spoke of your own operations, you used the word "we" rather than "I".

While you led an active life in personally directing your own livestock operations, you had time to provide leadership in other fields. The bank which you direct in Grant County is small compared to large city banks, but it has played an important part in financing not only the livestock men but the business men of Grant County. Only you yourself and the people whom you assisted will know how many times you helped the local people through tough spots, and you made advances from your personal funds when the needs would not meet the requirements of a bank loan.

In 1932 I was appointed manager of the Regional Agricultural Credit Corporation. I was more than pleased when I learned that you were to be a member of our original advisory committee. With your intimate knowledge of the needs of livestock men and farmers in the state of Oregon, you were able to give us sound advice on the type of loans we should make. You gave freely of your time to that organization with no thought of remuneration for your services and you played an important part in the favorable record made by the Regional. When it was decided to liquidate the Regional and provide permanent credit for agriculture through Production Credit Associations, you were again called upon and you served on the first Board of Directors of the Northwest Livestock Production Credit Association.

Although you have disposed of your livestock and ranch holdings in recent years, you have continued to take an active interest in the problems confronting livestock men. In 1959 when it was decided to celebrate Oregon's 100th Anniversary by holding a Centennial Exposition, you were among the first to suggest that the livestock story be forcibly brought to the attention of the visitors. You gave freely of time and effort in promoting a non-profit organization, known as Beef, Inc. As I was treasurer of that organization, I know that your early cash contribution of a substantial amount and your leadership of the finance and display committees resulted in a very attractive exhibit at the Centennial. Everyone who visited the exposition agreed that Beef Inc. exhibit was the most outstanding one in the agricultural division and ranked favorably with any in the entire show.

The First National Bank of Portland recognized your leadership when they elected you to be a member of their Board of Directors and every livestock man doing business with that bank knows in you they have a strong friend who speaks their language and understands their problems.

While you have already lived a very full life, I know that you will continue to serve your community and your state for many, many years to come.

Sincerely,
Ervie Williams, President
Portland Union Stock Yards
North Portland, Oregon

PAT IS A NEIGHBOR, A CATTLEMAN AND A FRIEND

Dear Herman:

I have just been thinking about you and all the things you have done for the livestock industry in your county and state. One of your outstanding contributions to the good of the industry has been your sponsorship of the Cattleman of the Year contest. The primary purpose of this program is to stimulate leadership, not only in ranch and cattle operations, but in all-over industry leadership.

The honor of being the outstanding Cattleman of Oregon has been bestowed on several of our producers and it has just occurred to me that I would like to nominate you as Oregon Cattleman for the past twenty-five years.

I marvel how you have found time to operate one of the best cattle ranches in Oregon, one of the most perfectly managed and at the same time contributed so much to county, state and national affairs. The cattle industry owes you a deep debt of gratitude for your services. Of course, your real reward stems from the satisfaction of knowing that you have contributed immeasurably to the advancement of the industry that has been your life work.

Sincerely yours,
J. C. (Pat) Cecil
Burns, Oregon

HE SITS ACROSS THE TABLE FROM HERMAN

Dear Herman:

The action of the Board last week, electing a new President and naming me Chairman, was of course a milestone in my career. I fell to thinking about it afterward, indulging myself in a few moments of relaxed anticipation toward the time when I will turn over to someone else many of the vexing problems that seem to require the president's attention almost daily. Being a bank president yourself, I am sure you have had your fair share of perplexing situations with which to deal, so I will not extend my remarks any further in that direction. I do want to record, however, some further thoughts that came to me in my reflections.

Even though we see each other quite often, there are things I do not get around to saying. One of them is to tell you how pleasant it is to have you seated at the table at our regular monthly board meetings. You are a distinguished citizen of our state, serving your beloved John Day, Grant County, and the State of Oregon in countless ways. I feel grateful that you are willing to spend time and energy to help run this important institution. It is not only your presence at board meetings, but your willingness to share your wealth of knowledge, not only with other board members, but those of us in management, that I value.

You are a grand guy, Herman, and I hope that I am as "young" as you are ten years hence.

Sincerely yours,
C. B. Stephenson, President
The First National Bank of
Oregon, Portland, Oregon

BUD'S OPINIONS COMMAND RESPECT, TOO

Dear Herman:

It's good to hear that you are writing a book. You have a responsibility to do it, it seems to me. You have been closely identified with so much of significance that has occurred in eastern Oregon in this century.

I don't know how much you are going to tell us about your activities in banking, agriculture, education, transportation, highways, etc. I do hope you will express your opinions of all you have seen in the many facets of Oregon life in which you have participated. There are few men in Oregon whose opinions command so much respect.

I am awaiting your book with keen anticipation. Kindest personal regards.

Sincerely,
J. W. Forrester, Jr.
East Oregonian
Pendleton, Oregon

A FINE NEIGHBOR AND A GOOD JUDGE OF CATTLE IS DON

Dear Herman,

We just returned from a trip to the Hawaiian Islands where we went on the Western Livestock Journal tour. We visited a number of the larger commercial cattle outfits where we saw quite a lot of their operations.

It became very apparent that these ranchers are all working on a herd improvement program. I thought this might be of special interest to you, as your own livestock program always worked for improved herds. You were never satisfied to coast along but were always looking for better sires, larger and more uniform calf crops, better fleshing ability, early maturity, uniformity in size and markings in the cattle you had for sale and everything that goes to make a better and more profitable operation.

These same things seemed to predominate in the operations of the ranches we visited. Their methods of trying to reach these objectives differed with different ranching conditions and different managers. Most all were fertilizing their grasses because, with their higher rainfall, warm climate and year around growing season, their grasses didn't have the strength that most of our grasses have here. Some were trying to breed up their herds from the stock they had by the use of better sires, cross breeding and artificial insemination.

At the Kahua ranch on the Island of Hawaii, they had imported some breeding heifers from the mainland. This is where your long improved breeding program came into the limelight. We saw two hundred Hereford heifers that had just been shipped in from John Day, Oregon, and were purchased from Mr. Hayworth, the present owner of what was originally part of your ranch and cow herd.

In discussing the heifers with the manager, Monty Richards, Jr., he told me that when he came to the mainland looking for replacement heifers, the Herman Oliver cattle had been recommended to him before he left the Islands. He also told me that when he purchased these heifers, he insisted that they be calves off of the original Oliver cows. The heifers had only been there a short time and it was raining that day when we saw them, but they were still cattle to be proud of. In mentioning these cattle over the loud speaker system, I couldn't help but notice that they were referred to as the Herman Oliver cattle. There were about 272 people on this tour. We also saw some Angus heifers from the Phillips herd at Baker, Oregon.

> Best regards,
> O. D. (Don) Hotchkiss
> Burns, Oregon

CLEAR FROM COOS BAY

Dear Herman:

I apologize for not responding to your very nice letter dated April 1, as it was the first of three I received.

You, like I, have given years of unselfish service to our communities and state, and our only hope being that we could do a good service without publicity, good or bad. You have done a greater service than I have and that makes me feel very happy, that you took time out to express your feelings.

Friendships like yours are the best reward I could have for my feeble efforts to get better highways and parks for Oregon.

I do appreciate your friendsip and will be in the Great John Day Valley before too many moons and will look forward to a visit with you.

> My kindest regards,
> Very sincerely yours,
> Ben R. Chandler
> Coos Bay, Oregon

JIM SHORT RECOGNIZES A TOP HAND

Dear Herman:

I was so pleased to be present when the honorary Doctor of Science degree was conferred upon you at the Oregon State College commencement program.

I do not know of a better top hand to receive such an honor and I want to extend my sincere congratulations to you.

Best personal regards.

> Sincerely,
> James F. Short
> Republican State Central
> Committee of Oregon
> Salem, Oregon

HOWARD BELTON RECOGNIZES GOOD ADVICE

Dear Herman:

May I congratulate you on your election to the board of the First National Bank of Oregon. I was happy to read of your being so honored and I am sure you will have much to contribute to that organization.

Since talking with you January 7th I have had time to give a good deal of thought to the subject we discussed and as a result have modified my thinking a good deal. I feel that I owe you a vote of thanks for expressing yourself as you did. I am now endeavoring to activate our membership as voters, as citizens, and as taxpayers to inform themselves and participate in local school problems. Most of us do a lot of complaining at tax paying time but very few participate in the preparation of the budgets or in determining the subject matter taught.

I served for 15 years on a school board where some two to three thousand were qualified to vote but on only one occasion were there more than 22 out to pass on the budget and elect a director. Most of those who vote are beneficiaries of the taxes levied. We learn as we go along and I appreciate the council of men who have had experience such as yours.

Fraternally,
Howard C. Belton
Canby, Oregon

SAYS EASTERN OREGON IS RECOGNIZED

Dear Herman:

You bring more recognition to eastern Oregon with your election as Director of First National Bank of Oregon.

My congratulations to you for this well earned reward.

Sincerely,
R. K. Evans, Vice-President
California-Pacific
Utilities Co.
Baker, Oregon

A PROFESSIONAL WRITER IS GRATEFUL AND PLEASED

Dear Herman:

I have been thinking for several days what I'd write you congratulating you on whatever the honor was that you received at the cattlemen's convention, but we have been "whirling" so fast for a week that there just hasn't been a moment.

I remember thinking at the time, when reading of it in the Oregonian, that there wasn't a man anywhere who better deserved honors of any kind anyone felt like bestowing, or whom I personally honored more in my thoughts, than Herman Oliver. From the very first of our acquaintance I admired you immensely; and naturally to have my friend singled out for national honors gratified me.

> Cordially yours,
> George N. Angell
> Oswego, Oregon

THIS WAS 1955—MARK WASN'T GOVERNOR THEN

Dear Mr. Oliver:

Congratulations upon your receipt of the Swift award as dean of Oregon cattlemen.

We have so many mutual friends who have so often spoken fondly of you that I wish it were possible to visit sometime. As one who serves in the legislature and teaches college courses I am aware of my inadequate knowledge of livestock, ranch and farm problems. The people at Oregon State College have been very helpful but I would like the opportunity to go over some matters with you one of these days.

All good wishes for the summer season.

> Sincerely,
> Mark O. Hatfield
> Dean of Students
> Willamette University
> Salem, Oregon

EVERYONE LIKES EDGAR SMITH

Dear Herman:

Have just returned from the East and find the news--paper story of the Dean of Oregon Cattlemen who was awarded Swift's plaque presented for outstanding contributions made to the beef cattle industry of Oregon.

Heartiest congratulations! Certainly there never was any person better qualified and more deserving of this distinctive honor. More power to you!

Sincerely,
Edgar W. Smith
Portland, Oregon

A FINE COWMAN FROM HARNEY COUNTY SPEAKS UP

Dear Herman:

A little time has now passed since the meeting at Prineville, and I would like to take this means of thanking you again most sincerely for your wonderful support of the Cattleman of the Year contest.

I believe most heartily that the contest which you sponsor through the Oliver Trophy is very significant in the progress of the livestock industry. I know that it has given me added enthusiasm and I looked over my unit in a little different light after talking to all of the judges and fully understanding the contest. I think that the contest which you sponsor does contribute a great deal to Oregon and the cattle industry throughout the state.

Very truly yours,
Lloyd H. Hill
Crane, Oregon

JUST A FRIENDLY NOTE

Dear Herman:

One week from today you will celebrate another birthday. Good wishes for continued good health and much happiness will come from literally thousands of friends.

You give so much of yourself in the many things in which you are interested, and perhaps that is what is a contributing factor to your drive and energy that a younger man would envy.

I want you to know how much I value your friendship. May the good Lord steer your course away from ills that plague mortal man — we need men like you around a long, long time.

Happy Birthday!

Sincerely,
John I. Sell
The First National Bank
of Oregon
Portland, Oregon

A NATIONAL PUBLICATION REPRINTED HERMAN'S BULLETIN

Dear Mr. Oliver:

Our reprint of your Oregon circular on "Range Cattle Management" made a fine feature presentation of great practical interest and application in our Herd Bull Edition. I am sure that every western cattleman who is trying steadily to do a better job will read and study your ideas and conclusions.

We are grateful for having had the opportunity to use your piece which reflects great credit upon the good work you have been doing in the ranching business for many years.

Sincerely,
Don R. Ornduff
Editor
Hereford Journal
Kansas City 5, Missouri

CONCLUSION

A Word from Herman Oliver

It has been a pleasure for me to work with the writer in supplying material and information. It has given me a chance to look at my experiences as a whole, instead of piecemeal, as one lives them. It has revived old, half-forgotten events for me, and reminded me of many old time friends. It was almost like visiting with all of them. I have enjoyed seeing a book emerge from these dozens of little memories.

I hope that you, the reader, have had some pleasure from the reminiscences of this old timer.

Sincerely,
Herman Oliver

E. R. Jackman's Part

I have thoroughly enjoyed writing this book. To start it, I lived with Herman and Eliza for ten days. We spent all of every day on the book. First we talked it over for a day or two and decided upon the needed chapters and what to put in each. Then Herman either dictated the chapter to me, or wrote it out for me to edit.

In addition, I went through his numerous files and through the old ranch records. After I had written a chapter, Herman, Eliza, and I went over it, corrected it for errors, or for wording that might be misconstrued, and decided upon additions or deletions. Thus, the exact wording is mine, but the contents were supplied by Herman and Eliza.

The book was outlined and partially written in those ten days. We talked book through all the meals and from early morning until late at night. Afterward we had to redistribute some material and in the process we added two more chapters.

Growth of the ranch from nothing to one of the large properties of eastern Oregon; saving of the three banks of the county; life in an isolated county in the previous century; gold and the stories around it; the little country school; freighting before the days of good roads; the coming of the railroad—all of these things have been intensely interesting to me, particularly because I went through many of the same experiences in Montana. When I left our little valley to go to college at Bozeman, I traveled part way on a six-horse stage. I went to the same kind of school as Herman did. I have hauled grain and other goods over crude roads with four and six horses and high-wheeled Moline wagons. So, in living Herman's experiences, I relived part of my own.

But in the case of this book, all of the experiences were colored by the philosophy of Herman's father, old Joe, and by Herman himself, and the events have a vitality that I could not have given them.

E. R. Jackman

INDEX

A

Adobe, 72
Adriance Buckeye mower, 204
Advertising, 263, 264, 265
Ah Shee, 27
Aldred, William C., 17, 20, 24
Aldrich, 47
Aldrich, Mt., 173, 174
Alforjus, 85
Amity, Oregon, 54
Angell, George N., 300, 301
Antelope, Oregon, 18
Antone, Oregon, 18, 27
Aparejo, 85
Arabia, 149
Arlington, Oregon, 17, 51, 177
Armstrong Creek, 54
Ashford, Dr. J. W., 163
Astor, John Jacob, 176
Astoria, Oregon, 18, 176
Auburn, Oregon, 19
Austin, Oregon, 27, 54, 192
Austin House, 191
Austin, Ma, 191
Azores Islands, 1

B

Baird, David, 196, 197
Baird, David (Dean), 196
Baker County, 33
Baker, Oregon, 19, 25, 124, 156, 169, 189, 198, 229
Ballard, F. L., 222, 238
Bannock War 36, 46, 141
Barkdoll, Lloyd, 50
Barratt, J. G., 230
Barry, George, 30
Basic crops, 244
Basque sheepherders, 144
Bates, Oregon, 192, 193, 195
Battle Creek, 55
Bayley, E. J., 166, 213
Bear Valley, Oregon, 66, 69, 156, 192
Beech Creek, 54, 144
Beef, incorporated, 294
Begg, Arthur, 41
Begg, Dr. Roderick, 64
Bell, Hal, 136
Belshaw, Charles, 45
Belton, Howard, 299, 300
Bend, Oregon, 189
Berge, Tony, 193

Big dogs (Indian name for horses), 126
Bingham, Cy, 111
Black Dan, 162
Black Horse Creek, 142
Black Rock Tom, 142
Bluebucket Creek, 54
Blue Bucket Mine, 31
Blue Mountains, 31, 186
Blue Mountain Eagle, 164, 165
Boardman, Sam, 240
Boer War, 144
Boise, Idaho, 169, 225
Boots, 138
Boswell, Bill, 112
Boyce, Ira, 156
Brannon plan, 260
Brewster, Lyman, 259
Bridles, 137
Brigham Young University, 236
Bright, J. M., 49
British Columbia, 84
Brooke, Ralph, 270
Brown, Bill, 133, 142
Brown, Charlie, 41, 47, 269
Brucellosis, 123
Buccaroo, 132
Buccaro Jim, 49
Buckaroo Sam, 159
Buell, John, 227
Burgess, Charlie, 61
Burma, 257
Burns, Oregon, 35, 189, 199, 200, 201
Burnt Ranch, Oregon, 18, 23, 86
Burnt River, 185
Bushman, Patrick, 50

C

Caballada, 132
Caballo, 152
Cabell, Henry, 238
California, 141
Cal Kern, 46
Campbell, A. R., 226
Cant, Jimmie, 41, 183
Canyon City, Oregon, 2, 7, 20, 27, 35, 46, 47, 48, 83 179, 214
Canyon Creek, 18, 20, 35, 83
Canyon Mountain, 20, 83
Carson, George, 41
Cascade Mountains, 40, 132
Caton, Lynn, 227

Caverhill, Oregon, 54
Cavvy, 132
Cecil, Pat, 227, 295
Celilo, Oregon, 47
Chambers, Martha, 105
Chandler, Ben R., 298, 299
Chandler, George, 198
Chandler, Herb, 99
Chaps, 134
Chicken Hill, 54
Chickenhouse Gulch, 54
Chief Joseph's War, 141
China Ranch, 3
Chinese, 158
Chinks, 134
Chrome Ridge, 54
Cimarron, 142
Clark, Bill, 4
Clark, R. L., 292, 293
Cleveland, Grover, 9, 272
Coffin, Stanley, 194
Cohn, Harold, 59, 230
Coles, Ed, 118
Colorado, 136
Columbia River, 126, 186
Conchas, 138
Conforth, 102
Congress, 245
Conservation, 115
Copperfield, Oregon, 27
Corbett, H. L., 226, 227
Cornucopia, Oregon, 27
Corral Basin, 142
Courtney, Gene, 228
Cow identification, 112, 113, 114
Cozad, Rod, 171
Cozad, V. G., 163
Cozart, J. J., 41, 46, 84, 85
Craddock, Chet, 111, 172, 183, 184
Craddock, Jack, 41, 44
Cram, Bidwell, 230
Crane, Oregon, 199, 200
Crook County, 37, 133, 142
Crooked River, 32, 33, 185
Crowley, Bob, 185
Crum, Chester, 50
Cullen, J. P., 136
Cummings Creek, 54
Cuprum, Idaho, 27

D

Daly, Patsy, 213
Dalton, Bill, 182
Daly family, 41
Damon, Robert, 40
Davis, Bruce and wife, 173
Day, John, 177

Dayville, Oregon, 173
Deadhorse Ridge, 142
Deardorff, Joe, 213
Dean Creek, 25
Deer, numbers, 62
Deschutes County, 142
Devine, John, 142
Dewey, A. R., 202
Ditch, Eldorado, 28
Dixie Creek, 22, 158, 166
Dixie Mountain, 95, 189, 194
Doghouse Gulch, 54
Drumheller, Tom, 229
Dunlap family, 41
Dunnaway, Pat, 227
Dyer, Minnie Myrtle, 42

E

Eccles, David, 189
Einstein, 79
Eisenhower, 79
Eldorado Ditch, 28
Elkhorn Hotel, 34, 106
Elliott, W. N., 230
Enchanted Prairie, Oregon, 54
Eugene, Oregon, 42
Evans, R. K., 300

F

Fairview, Oregon, 54
Falconer, Fred, 230
Fatland, E. R., 290
Farm Credit Act, 227
Farm program, 241 to 251
Farra, Harley, 136
Farrell, Bill, 270
Fate, Doctor, 69
Federal Farm Loan Act, 225
Federal power ownership, 251, 252, 253
Federal Reserve Board, 215
Fell, Dr. J. H., 163
Fern Hill, Oregon, 54
Fields Creek, 54
Fields, Harvey, 159
Finlan, Paddy, 41, 213
Finlayson, Whit, 283, 284
Finlayson family, 41
First National Bank, 268
Fischer, Jake, 211
Flagtail Mountain, 55
Flail, 204
Fletcher, Bob, 279
Florence, Idaho, 17, 18, 20, 27
Flour sacks, 12
Folsom, Percy, 228
Foot rags, 12

Forrester, J. W., 297
Fort Klamath, 139
Fort Rock, Oregon, 223
Fossils, 175, 176
Fossil, Oregon, 176
Foundation, 4-H, 268
Four freedoms, 259
4-H Club work, 270
Fox, Oregon, 55
Fox Valley, Oregon, 55, 222
Freedom, 54
Freezout Saddle, 142
Freighters, 87, 88, 89, 90, 91, 92, 93
French, Giles, 289, 290
French, John, 183
French Pete, 143
Fresno, California, 173
Fulton, Dan, 258

G

Galena, Oregon, 51, 54
Gay, Arlene, 101
Geese, 14
George family, 137
Gilliam County, 186
G. I. Ranch, 32
Glad Tidings, 54
Gold, 9
  price, 28, 29
  weight, 38
Grande Ronde River, 17, 143
Grangeville, Idaho, 27
Granite, 54
Grant County, 25, 30, 33, 52, 129, 133, 140, 175, 180, 224
Grant County Bank, 106, 168, 211, 214
Grant County Educational Association, 268
Grant County Stockmen's Association, 200
Grant County Museum, 47
Grant, Linnie, 53
Grass, 168
Gray and Son, 99
Great Plains, 135
Green, R. J., 230
Greenhorn Peak, 54
Gregg, August, 3
Gregg, Henry, 10
Gregg, Lizzie, 10
Gregg, Mrs. August, 3
Gregg, William, 10
Grelle, Ed, 230
Grist mill, 204, 207
Grub Creek, 144
Guker, Ike, 27
Gutteridge family, 41

H

Hackamore, 137
Hahn, Leo, 230
Haight, Clint, 31
Haines, Oregon, 118
Halfway, Oregon, 102
Hall brothers, 41
Hall, Dr. Arnold Bennett, 236
Halleck, Earl, 227
Hamley, 136
Hankins, Gerald, 103
Hankins, Kathie, 103
Hankins, Pleas, 164
Hanley, Bill, 40, 230
Hare, Ike, 48
Harney County, 33, 45, 53, 133, 142, 143, 203
Harriman, 189
Harrisburg, Oregon, 40
Harrison family, 40
Harvey houses, 192
Hat, cowboys', 138
Hatfield, Governor Mark O., 301
Hawaiian Islands, 175
Hazletine, G. I., 41, 207
Healy, Pat, 59
Heim, Mrs. S. E., 55
Helena, Montana, 49, 225, 278
Hells Canyon, 186
Hemlock, poisonous, 4
Henning, May Jeanette, 102, 103
Herburger family, 41
Herberger, Jerry, 229
Herrick, Fred, 199
Herron, Daniel, 34
Hey, Doctor, 26, 159
High Lake, 57
Hill, James, 189, 199
Hill, Lloyd H., 302
Himes, George, 42, 43
Hines Lumber Co., 35, 192, 201
Hoke, Mac, 226, 228, 230, 260
Holliday, Ben, 132
Holt, Walter A., 230, 281, 282
Homestead laws, 97
Honda, 135
Hoover Administration, 225
Horse, Appaloosa, 141
Horse Creek, 142
Horse Heaven, 143
Horse Ridge, 142
Horses, 133
Horses, numbers, 133
Horses, wild, 44, 144
Hoverson, Oscar, 50
Hotchkiss, Don, 297, 298
Howell, Jack, 35
Hudson's Bay Co., 176

Hughes, Dave, 213
Humboldt, Mine, 25
Hunting rights, 187
Huntington, Oregon, 17
Hunt, Wilson Price 126, 176
Hupprich, Antone, 12, 66
Hupprich, Dutch, 25
Hyde family, 40

I

Idaho, 84, 144
Imperial Hotel, 164
Income tax, 121, 208
India, 257, 266
Indians, 36, 47, 126, 127, 139, 141, 149, 180
Indians, Cayuse, 141
Indian Creek, 24
Indians, Nez Perce, 141, 177
Indians, Palouse, 141
Indians, Snake, 141
Inflation, 119, 121, 210
Inventory, ranch, 120
Investment, cow, 122
Isthmus of Panama, 2
Izee, Oregon, 35, 40, 54

J

Jackman, E. R., 274, 280, 304, 305
Jerkline, 83, 90
"Joaquin, et al.," 43
John Clay Commission Co., 44
John Day, Oregon, 4, 7, 28, 52, 83, 124, 144, 156
John Day River, 5, 8, 17, 18, 20, 28, 158, 185, 188
Johnny Kirk Spring, 54
Johnson, Audrey, 103
Johnson, Ernest, 230
Johnson, Felix, 166
Johnson, R. G., 181, 222, 270, 284, 285

K

Kane, William, 48
Kansas City, 132
Keerins, Barbara, 103
Keerins, David, 103
Keerins, Herman Oliver, 102
Keerins, Mary, 103
Keerins, Ray, 103
Keerins, Sam, 69, 101, 102, 270
Keller, Frank, 136
Kennedy, C. M., 230
Kerr, Dr. William Jasper, 236
Kiester, Colonel, 129
Kilby, Quincy, 178

Kimberly, Oregon, 51, 188, 222
Kirk, Johnny, 41
Klamath County, 126, 139
Klamath Falls, 173, 229
Knickerbocker, M. E., 270
Kuhl family, 41

L

Labor, ranch, 116, 273
Lake County, 133, 142, 143
LaFollett, Daniel, 162
Lakeview, Oregon, 189
Lariat, 136
Lasso, 136
Laurance, Eliza, 10, 105
Lawrence, Jim, 227
Laycock, J. A., 36
Leon (Chinese), 159
Lewis and Clark, 126, 141
Lewiston, Idaho, 10
Lister, Robert, 230, 291, 292
Little Slide Lake, 57
Liver flukes, 123
Lockwood, Robert, 50
Logan, J. T., 230
Long Creek, 51, 167, 188
Long, John, 24, 35
Long, R. A. (Reub), 151, 183, 185, 223
Lucas family, 41
Lundy, Herbert, 281

Mc

McCallum, A. R., 207
McCarty, 136
McClellan family, 41
McCorkle, Charlie, 34
McEwen, Oregon, 189, 198
McGill family, 40
McGinnis, Patrick, 49
McGregar, John, 229
McKrola, Charlie, 34

M

Macrae, Kenneth, 41
Mail carrying, 94
Magone Lake, 55
Magone, Major, 55
Malheur County, 33, 142
Malheur River, 32, 57, 185
Mallory Hotel, 164
Maple, Joan, 103
Maple, John, 103
Maple, James, 103
Maple, Mary, 103
Maple, Thomas, 103

Marketing, 116, 117
Marron Creek, 132
Marshall, Bob, 166, 167
Martin, Campbell, 41
Martin, Curtis H., 288
Marysville, Oregon, 7, 18, 24, 76
Masson family, 41
Mazama Club, 118
Medford, Oregon, 41, 229
Meek, Joe, 31
Meek, Steve, 31
Metschan, Frank, 171
Metschan, Phil, 7, 41, 106, 164
Mexico, 134, 149
Middle Fork (of John Day River),
     166
Milk, price of, 5
   deliveries of, 6
Miller, Billy, 45
Miller, Henry, 109
Miller, Juanita, 43
Miller, Joaquin (Cincinnatus Heine),
     41, 42, 43
Miller and Lux, 109, 180
Miller Mountain, 34, 35, 36
Miller, S. E., 230
Miners, Chinese, 22, 25, 26, 167
Mining, claims, 20, 21, 22
Mining, dredge, 28
Mining, placer, 28
Mint, The Dalles, 23
Mitchell, Oregon, 18, 86
Monfort, 112
Montana, 84, 132, 278
Monument, Oregon, 222
Mormon crickets, 157
Mount Vernon, Oregon, 45
Mule, Oregon, 143
Mules, pack, 84, 85
Muleshoe Mountain, 143
Munroe, Tommy, 41
Murderer's Creek, 46, 55
Murietta, Joaquin, 43
Murray family, 41

N

Nealan, Johnnie, 41
Nevada, 144, 203
New Deal, 29, 243, 244, 259
New York, 169
Norman, Mr., 161
Norman, Mrs., 160
North Fork of John Day, 129
North Powder, Oregon, 124
Northwest Livestock Production
     Credit Association, 228, 230
Noti, Oregon, 142
NRA—National Recovery Act, 242

O

O'Dair, J. J., 41, 213
Ochoco National Forest, 37
Officer, James, 40
Officer, Joe, 46
Oklahoma, 136
Oliver, Anna, 100
Oliver, Arlene, 101
Oliver Brothers, 100, 202
Oliver, Claire, 103
Oliver, Eliza, 102, 119, 269, 270, 271,
     272
Oliver, Frank, 10, 69, 100, 101, 198, 219
Oliver, Gay, 101
Oliver, Herman, 225, 230, 267 304
Oliver J. C., 1, 4, 101
Oliver, Joe, 69, 101, 103, 134
Oliver, Joseph Cayton, 101
Oliver, Kay, 101
Oliver, Margaret, 100
Oliver Ranch, 20, 59, 218
Ontario, Oregon, 44, 94, 148, 199
Oregon Cattlemen's Association, 233,
     267
Oregon Cowbelles, 264
Oregon Farm Bureau Federation, 268
Oregon Legislature, 233
Oregon Lumber Co., 189
Oregon State College, 79, 233, 235,
     236, 237, 267
Oregon State Educational Association,
     268
Oregon State Employees Association,
     268
Oregon State Fish & Game Depart-
     ment, 233
Oregon State Highway Commission,
     69, 238, 239, 280
Oregon State System of Higher Edu-
     cation, 235, 280
Oregon State Tax Commission, 233
Oregon Trail, 32
Oregon Wheat League, 244
Oregon Wool Growers, 233, 234, 235,
     260
Ornduff, Don R., 303
Oro Fino, Idaho, 48
Owyhee River, 143
O'Shea, Dan, 35
Overgrazing, 114

P

Pacific International Livestock Ex-
     position, 14, 268
Pacific Livestock Co., 171

Parada, 152, 153
Parity for automobiles, 246, 247, 248, 249, 250
Parman, 60
Patterson, Ike, Governor, 235
Patton, Marie, 275
Pendleton, Oregon, 17, 170, 173, 229, 268
Penstock, 28
Phillips, Fred, 225, 228, 230, 289
Phillips, Wayne, 230
Pine Creek, 24, 166
Pitt River, 27
Plummer, O. M., 270
Pollman, Billy, 212, 213
Pony Butte, 142
Pony Express, 85
Porter, Allen, 41, 185
Porter, John, 167
Portland Cattle Loan Co., 229
Portland, Oregon, 2, 3, 11, 18, 20, 51, 118, 169, 225
Portland State College, 237
Portugal, 1
Potter, E. L. (Dad), 228
Prairie City, Oregon, 27, 52, 105, 125, 156, 192, 213
Prairie Diggins, 19, 20
Priday, H. L., 230
Prineville, Oregon, 37, 189
Production Credit Associations, 227, 228, 229
Pullen, Tom, 136

R

Rabbit driving, 154
Rader, George, 185
Ranch wife, 107, 108
Range, acreage, 259
Range, Oregon, 55
Ray, Morris, 166
Reconstruction Finance Corporation, 215, 225
Redboy, 54
Redmond, Oregon, 229
Regional Agricultural Credit Corporation, 225
Reno, Nevada, 49
Rhinehart, D. B., 45
Riata, 136
Richards, Dick, 270, 282
Richardson, J. W., 229
Riggins, Idaho, 27
Rinehart, George, 136
Ringsmeier family, 41
Robertson, Gus, 173
Romal, 138
Roosevelt, Franklin D., 242, 243

Roosevelt Hotel, 164
Russia, 242, 255, 256, 261

S

Sacks, flour, 12
Saddle Butte, 143
Saddle Creek, 142
Saddles, 135
Safeway, 112
Sailor Jack, 163
Salem, Oregon, 229
Sammons, E. C., 287
Sanderson, W. H., 230
San Francisco, 2, 3, 11, 47, 182
Sante Fe Railroad, 192
Schmidt, John, 41
School teachers, 75
Sels family, 41
Sels, F. C., 165
Sell, John I., 302, 303
Seneca, Oregon, 58, 193, 199, 200
Sensenich, E. H., 225
Shaniko, Oregon, 46, 94
Sheep, financing, 215, 216, 220
Sheepherder sneak, 152
Sheep killing, 60
Sheep owners, 58
Sheep Rock, 55
Sherar's Bridge, 86
Short, James F., 299
Short, Lum, 139
Silvers, John, 2
Silvies River, 186
Silvies Valley, 164
Slicker, 139
Slide Lake, 57
Small, Jim, 41, 47
Smith brothers, 41
Smith, Gus, 165, 166
Smith, Edgar, 301, 302
Snake River, 27, 132, 149
Snider, W. B. (Buck), 228, 231
Socrates, 123
Soil conservation, 8
Southern Pacific Railway, 189, 199
Southworth, Ed, 111
Spain, 149
Spanish, 132, 141
Spokane, Washington, 173
Sprague, Chas. A., 279, 280
Sproul, Ira, 25
Sproul, Pres. of Univ. of California, 182
Spurs, 138
Squaw Butte, 53
Squaw Tit Butte, 53
Stages, 85
  driving, 5, 86, 95

Stanfield, Robert, 230
Steens Mountain, 143
Stearns, Harry, 287
Steiwer, W. H., 229, 230
Stephenson, C. B., 296
Stewart, Billy, 47
Stewart, Jane, 213
Stewart, Wayne, 47, 213, 230
Strand, August LeRoy, 267, 277, 278, 279
Strawberry Lake, 56
Strawberry Mountain, 186
Straw-buck, 205, 206
Studebaker wagon, 277
Swift & Company, 268
Sumpter, Oregon, 27, 189, 190, 193, 197
Sumpter Valley Railroad, 94, 189
Supreme Court, 243

T

Tapaderos, 67, 135
Taylor Grazing Act, 134
Tebo, 143
Texas, 4, 136
The Dalles, Oregon, 2, 20, 23, 32, 38, 46, 47, 83, 125, 179, 203
Thompson, Bob, 59
Thornburg, John, 214
Thurman, 68
Tiger Town, 83
Tipton, Oregon, 191
Trout Creek, 171
Trowbridge family, 45
Trowbridge, B. C., 45, 46
Trowbridge, Mrs. B. G., 41
Tureman family, 41, 105
TV, 263, 264, 265
TV, westerns, 257
Tygh Ridge, 86

U

Umatilla County, 203
Union Paific Railroad, 199, 200
U. S. Army, 129, 133, 140, 255
U. S. Bureau of Internal Revenue, 233
U. S. Bureau of Land Management, 61, 233, 255
U. S. Forest Service, 37, 61, 199, 200, 233, 234, 255
U. S. Interstate Commerce Commission, 233
U. S. National Bank, 215, 218
U. S. Tariff Bureau, 233
U. S. Wildlife Service, 233
University of California, 176, 182
University of Oregon, 79, 235, 237

V

Vale, Oregon, 222
Van der Vlugt, Dr., 69
Vaughan, F. C., 230
Vaughan, Jack, 40
Vaquero, 132
Vinegar gut, 5
Vogel, W. H., 230

W

Wagons, Bain, Moline, Studebaker, 90, 91, 92, 93
Wah, Bob, 159
Wah, Dr. Eddie, 159
Walla Walla, 207
Wallowa County, 127, 186
Ward, R. A., 230
Warm Springs, Oregon, 47
Wasco County, 86
Waterspout Gulch, 54
Way, Ed, 217
Weather, importance, 177
Weatherford, Tom, 175
Wells Fargo, 22, 25
West, Joseph A., 189
Wey, Barry, 47, 48
Weyerheuser, 189
Wheeler County, 59, 176
Wheeler, H. H., 22, 86
Whiskey Diggins, 24
Whiskey Gulch, 38, 54, 83
White, Dr. Elijah, 31
Whitehorse Creek, 142
Whitehorse, Oregon, 142
Whitehorse Ranch, 142
White River, 86
Whitman, Marcus, 207
Whitman, Massacre, 100
Whitman, Oregon, 27
Whitney, Oregon, 195
Widow's Creek, 55
Wildhorse Creek, 142
Willamette Valley, 2, 33, 40
Williams, Ervie, 226, 228, 293, 294, 295
Williams, Frederick Allen, 169
Williamson, J. R., 230
Williams, R. J., 230
Wisdom, Mr., 198
Wiseman, Anna, 102
Withers, John V., 230
Wolfinger, John, 165
Wyoming, 132, 136

Y

Yeoville, Oregon, 55

Jerold Herburger	C.H.Herburger	J.G.& Robt. Hiatt	Lloyd Hudspeth	Ell & D.C.Hopper	Rhys
Mike W. Johnson	Oliver Keerins	Elmer Kilby	Roy Kilpatrick	Ira Kimball	Loui
Fred Legler	Warren C. Constant	Clifton MacKay	George MacKay	John Masson	Ray
Jack Blackwell	TJ Bryant	L.J. Baucum	Earl&Vera Bankofier	Orville M.Campbell	Wallac
Waldo C. Engle	Dean Enright	Darrel Farrens	Fred Fedler	Edward Feldhauser	Eva F
A. C. Heise	Clyde P.Helmick	Harlan Hansen	George R.Harper	Derrol McKern	Jay
Leslie & Robt. Holland	Ezra A. Nash	Charlie L.Page	Clarence Porter	Una Pope	Phillips
Fred Roach	Melvin G Shaw	Earl Shields	Gilman Shaw	Ervan Simmons	Gera
C. A.Phillips	Merle & L.Swaggart	Hillery Stout	Wynton & E. Gerald Shaw	A.J.Tanler	C.E.